The Tragedy of

Hamlet

Prince of Denmark

By

WILLIAM SHAKESPEARE

EDIT

SIMON & SCHUSTER PAPERBACKS

NEW YORK LONDON TORONTO SYDNEY NEW DELHI

Simon & Schuster Paperbacks
A Division of Simon & Schuster, Inc.
1230 Avenue of the Americas
New York, NY 10020

Copyright © 1992, 2012 by The Folger Shakespeare Library

This Simon & Schuster paperback edition July 2012

SIMON & SCHUSTER PAPERBACKS and colophon are registered
trademarks of Simon & Schuster, Inc.

For information about special discounts for bulk purchases,
please contact Simon & Schuster Special Sales at 1-866-506-1949
or business@simonandschuster.com

The Simon & Schuster Speakers Bureau can bring authors
to your live event. For more information or to book an
event contact the Simon & Schuster Speakers Bureau at
1-866-248-3049 or visit our website at www.simonspeakers.com.

Manufactured in the United States of America

40   39   38   37   36

ISBN 978-0-7434-7712-3
ISBN 978-1-4391-1702-6 (ebook)

act 3
- to be or nah
- madness in gr8
ones must be watched

act 4
my thoughts
be bloody

act 1 scene ii
" Frailty, thy
name is
woman "

act 5
- skull
- apologizing to
Horatio talking
abt how he
wasn't true
to himsel

Contents

Editors' Preface

In recent years, ways of dealing with Shakespeare's texts and with the interpretation of his plays have been undergoing significant change. This edition, while retaining many of the features that have always made the Folger Shakespeare so attractive to the general reader, at the same time reflects these current ways of thinking about Shakespeare. For example, modern readers, actors, and teachers have become interested in the differences between, on the one hand, the early forms in which Shakespeare's plays were first published and, on the other hand, the forms in which editors through the centuries have presented them. In response to this interest, we have based our edition on what we consider the best early printed version of a particular play (explaining our rationale in a section called "An Introduction to This Text") and have marked our changes in the text—unobtrusively, we hope, but in such a way that the curious reader can be aware that a change has been made and can consult the "Textual Notes" to discover what appeared in the early printed version.

Current ways of looking at the plays are reflected in our brief introductions, in many of the commentary notes, in the annotated lists of "Further Reading," and especially in each play's "Modern Perspective," an essay written by an outstanding scholar who brings to the reader his or her fresh assessment of the play in the light of today's interests and concerns.

As in the Folger Library General Reader's Shakespeare, which this edition replaces, we include explanatory notes designed to help make Shakespeare's language clearer to a modern reader, and we place the notes on the page facing the text that they explain. We also follow the earlier edition in including illustrations—of objects, of clothing, of mythological figures—from books and manuscripts in the Folger Shakespeare Library collection. We provide fresh accounts of the life of Shakespeare, of the publishing of his plays, and of the theaters in which his plays were performed, as well as an introduction to the text itself. We also include a section called "Reading Shakespeare's Language," in which we try to help readers learn to "break the code" of Elizabethan poetic language.

For each section of each volume, we are indebted to a host of generous experts and fellow scholars. The "Reading Shakespeare's Language" sections, for example, could not have been written had not Arthur King, of Brigham Young University, and Randal Robinson, author of *Unlocking Shakespeare's Language*, led the way in untangling Shakespearean language puzzles and shared their insights and methodologies generously with us. "Shakespeare's Life" profited by the careful reading given it by S. Schoenbaum; "Shakespeare's Theater" was read and strengthened by Andrew Gurr, John Astington, and William Ingram; and "The Publication of Shakespeare's Plays" is indebted to the comments of Peter W. M. Blayney. We, as editors, take sole responsibility for any errors in our editions.

We are grateful to the authors of the "Modern Perspectives"; to Leeds Barroll and David Bevington for their generous encouragement; to the Huntington and Newberry Libraries for fellowship support; to King's University College for the grants it has provided to Paul Werstine; to the Social Sciences and Humanities Research Council of Canada, which has provided him with Research Time Stipends; to R. J. Shroyer of the University of Western Ontario for essential computer support; and to the Folger Institute's Center for Shakespeare Studies for its fortuitous sponsorship of a workshop on "Shakespeare's Texts for Students and Teachers" (funded by the National Endowment for the Humanities and led by Richard Knowles of the University of Wisconsin), a workshop from which we learned an enormous amount about what is wanted by college and high-school teachers of Shakespeare today.

In preparing this preface for the publication of *Hamlet* in 1992, we wrote: Our biggest debt is to the Folger Shakespeare Library: to Werner Gundersheimer, Director of the Library, who has made possible our edition; to Jean Miller, the Library's Art Curator, who combed the Library holdings for illustrations, and to Julie Ainsworth, Head of the Photography Department, who carefully photographed them; to Peggy O'Brien, Director of Education, who gave us expert advice about the needs being expressed by Shakespeare teachers and students (and to Martha Christian and other "master teachers" who used our texts in manuscript in their classrooms); to the staff of the Academic Programs Division, especially Paul Menzer (who drafted "Further Reading" material), Mary Tonkinson, Lena Cowen Orlin, Molly Haws, and Jessica Hymowitz; and, finally, to the staff of the Library Reading Room, whose patience and support have been invaluable.

As we revise the play for publication in 2012, we add to the above our gratitude to Gail Kern Paster, Director of the Library from 2002 until July 2011, whose interest and support have been unfailing and whose scholarly expertise has been an invaluable resource; to Stephen Llano, our production editor at Simon & Schuster, whose expertise, attention to detail, and wisdom are essential to this project; to Deborah Curren-Aquino, who provides extensive editorial and production support; to Alice Falk for her expert copy-editing; to Mary Bloodworth and Michael Poston for their unfailing computer support; and to the staff of the Library's Research Division, especially Christina Certo (whose help is crucial), David Schalkwyk (Director of Research), Mimi Godfrey, Kathleen Lynch, Carol Brobeck, Owen Williams, Sarah Werner, and Adrienne Schevchuk. Finally, we once again express our thanks to Jean Miller, who continues to unearth wonderful images, and to the ever-supportive staff of the Library Reading Room.

Barbara A. Mowat and Paul Werstine
2012

Shakespeare's *Hamlet*

Hamlet is the most popular of Shakespeare's plays for readers and theater audiences, and it is also one of the most puzzling. Many questions about the play continue to fascinate readers and playgoers, making *Hamlet* not only a revenge tragedy but also very much a mystery. What is this Ghost that appears to Hamlet? Is it Hamlet's murdered father returned from the everlasting fire to demand justice upon his murderer? Is it a "goblin damned"—that is, a demon bent on claiming Hamlet's soul by tempting him to assassinate his king? Or is the Ghost "a spirit of health," an angelic messenger revealing to Hamlet that the young man's mission in life is to cleanse the kingdom of Denmark of its corrupt king?

And what happens to Hamlet after the Ghost commands that the throne of Denmark be cleansed? Does Hamlet actually go mad, becoming unhinged by the accusation that his uncle murdered his father or by the ugly picture the Ghost paints of Hamlet's lustful mother? Or does Hamlet merely pretend to be mad, pretend so well that he makes us wonder if we can tell the difference between sanity and madness? Why is he so hostile to women, both to his mother and to the woman whom he once courted and whom he claims to have loved dearly? Why does he wait so long to confirm the guilt of the king after the Ghost has accused the king of murder? And once he is convinced that the king is a murderer, why does Hamlet not act immediately?

And what about Gertrude? Was she unfaithful to her husband during his lifetime? Was she complicit in his murder? What does she come to believe about Hamlet's madness? And about her new husband?

Beyond such questions about the play and its characters lie deeper issues about the rightness of revenge, about how to achieve an ethical life, and about how to live in a world where tears of sorrow, loving smiles, and friendly words are all suspect because all are "actions that a man might *play*." Hamlet's world is bleak and cold because almost no one and nothing can be trusted. But his world, and Hamlet himself, continue to draw us to them, speaking to every generation of its own problems and its own yearnings. It is a play that seems particularly pertinent today—just as it has seemed particularly pertinent to any number of generations before us.

For "A Modern Perspective" on *Hamlet*, we invite you, after you have read the play, to read the essay by Professor Michael Neill of the University of Auckland, printed at the back of this book.

Reading Shakespeare's Language: *Hamlet*

For many people today, reading Shakespeare's language can be a problem—but it is a problem that can be solved. Those who have studied Latin (or even French or German or Spanish) and those who are used to reading poetry will have little difficulty understanding the language of poetic drama. Others, though, need to develop the skills of untangling unusual sentence structures and of recognizing and understanding poetic compressions, omissions, and wordplay. And even those skilled in reading unusual sentence structures may have occasional trouble with Shakespeare's words. Four hundred years of "static" intervene between his speaking and our hearing. Most of his vocabulary is still in use, but a few of his words are no longer used, and many now have meanings quite different from those they had in the sixteenth and seventeenth centuries. In the theater, most of these difficulties are solved for us by actors who study the language and articulate it for us so that the essential meaning is heard—or, when combined with stage action, is at least *felt*. When we are reading on our own, we must do what each actor does: go over the lines (often with a dictionary close at hand) until the puzzles are solved and the lines yield up their poetry and the characters speak in words and phrases that are, suddenly, rewarding and wonderfully memorable.

Shakespeare's Words

As you begin to read the opening scenes of a Shakespeare play, you may notice occasional unfamiliar words. Some are unfamiliar simply because we no longer use them. In the opening scenes of *Hamlet*, for example, we find such words as *parle* (i.e., discussion, meeting), *soft* (an exclamation meaning "hold" or "enough" or "wait a minute"), and *marry* (an oath "by the Virgin Mary," which had by Shakespeare's time become a mere interjection, like "indeed"). Words of this kind are explained in notes to the text and will become familiar as you continue to read Shakespeare's language.

In *Hamlet*, as in all of Shakespeare's writing, the most problematic are the words that are still in use but now have different meanings. In the first scene of *Hamlet* (1.1.14), the word *rivals* is used where we would use "companions." At 1.1.44 we find the word *his* where we would use "its" and at 1.1.134 the word *still* used (as it most often is in Shakespeare) to mean "always." At 1.1.67, *sensible* means "attested to by the senses"; at 1.1.169, *extravagant* means "wandering"; and at 1.2.66, *cousin* is used (as it is generally in Shakespeare) to mean simply "kinsman." And at 1.2.278, where Hamlet says, "I doubt some foul play," we would say, "I suspect some treacherous action." Again, such words are explained in the notes to the text, but they, too, will become increasingly familiar as you get further into the play.

Some words are strange not because of the "static" introduced by changes in language over the past centuries but because they are used by Shakespeare to build a dramatic world that has its own geography and history and story. *Hamlet*, for example, builds, in its opening scenes, a location, a past history, and a background mythology through references to "the Dane," to "buried Denmark," to Elsinore, to partisans and jointresses, to Hyperion and Niobe and Hercules. These "local" words and references (each of which is explained in notes to this text) build the world of Denmark that Hamlet, Gertrude, and Claudius inhabit; they soon become recognizable features of Shakespeare's Elsinore.

Shakespeare's Sentences

In an English sentence, meaning is quite dependent on the place given each word. "The dog bit the boy" and "The boy bit the dog" mean very different things, even though the individual words are the same. Because English places such importance on the positions of words in sentences, on the way words are arranged, unusual arrangements can puzzle a reader. Shakespeare frequently shifts his sentences away from "normal" English arrangements—often to create the rhythm he seeks, sometimes to use a line's poetic rhythm to emphasize a particular word, sometimes to give a character his or her own speech patterns or to allow the character to speak in a special way. When we attend a good performance of the play, the actors will have worked out the sentence structures and will articulate the sentences so that the meaning is clear. In reading the play, we need to do as the actor does: that is, when puzzled by a character's speech, we check to see if the words are being presented in an unusual sequence.

Look first for the placement of subject and verb. Shakespeare often places the verb before the subject (e.g., instead of "He goes," we find "Goes he"). In the opening scene of *Hamlet*, when, at line 73, Horatio says "So frowned he once," he is using such a construction, as he is at line 91, when he says "That can

I." Such inversions rarely cause much confusion. More problematic is Shakespeare's frequent placing of the object before the subject and verb (e.g., instead of "I hit him," we might find "Him I hit"). When Horatio says, at 1.2.216–17, "This to me . . . impart they did," he is using such an inverted construction (the normal order would be "They did impart this to me"). Polonius uses another such inversion at 1.3.126–29 when he says, "These blazes, daughter, / . . . You must not take for fire." Ordinarily one would say "Daughter, you must not take these blazes for fire."

In some plays Shakespeare makes systematic use of inversions (*Julius Caesar* is one such play). In *Hamlet*, he more often uses sentence structures that depend instead on the separation of words that would normally appear together. (This is usually done to create a particular rhythm or to stress a particular word.) Claudius's "which have freely gone / With this affair along" (1.2.15–16) interrupts the phrase "gone along"; Horatio's "When he the ambitious Norway combated" (1.1.72) separates the subject and verb ("he combated"), interjecting between them the object of the verb ("the ambitious Norway"). To create for yourself sentences that seem more like the English of everyday speech, you may wish to rearrange the words, putting together the word clusters and placing the remaining words in their more familiar order. You will usually find that the sentences will gain in clarity but will lose their rhythm or shift their emphases. You can then see for yourself why Shakespeare chose his unusual arrangement.

Locating and rearranging words that belong together is especially necessary in passages that separate subjects from verbs and verbs from objects by long delaying or expanding interruptions—a structure that is used frequently in *Hamlet*. For example, when Horatio, at 1.1.92–110, tells the story of how King Hamlet won the Norwegian lands and how the prince of Norway seeks to regain them, he uses a series of such interrupted constructions:

> 　　　　　　　　　　　　　*our last king,*
> Whose image even but now appeared to us,
> *Was,* as you know, by Fortinbras of Norway,
> Thereto pricked on by a most emulate pride,
> *Dared to the combat; in which* our valiant *Hamlet*
> (For so this side of our known world esteemed him)
> *Did slay this Fortinbras, who* by a sealed compact, . . .
> *Did forfeit,* with his life, *all those his lands.* . . .
> 　　　　　　　　　　Now, sir, young *Fortinbras,*
> Of unimprovèd mettle hot and full,
> *Hath* in the skirts of Norway here and there
> *Sharked up a list of lawless resolutes.* . . .

Here the interruptions provide details that catch the audience up in Horatio's story. The separation of the basic sentence elements ("our last king was dared to the combat") forces the audience to attend to supporting details while waiting for the basic sentence elements to come together. In the second scene of *Hamlet* (at 1.2.8–14), Claudius uses the same kind of interrupted construction in his opening speech,

> Therefore *our sometime sister,* now our queen,
> Th' imperial jointress to this warlike state,
> *Have we* (as 'twere with a defeated joy,
> With an auspicious and a dropping eye,
> With mirth in funeral and with dirge in marriage,
> In equal scale weighing delight and dole)
> *Taken to wife* . . . ,

where the basic elements of the sentence are simply "we [i.e., I] have taken to wife our sometime sister [i.e., my former sister-in-law]." Claudius's speech, like Horatio's, is a narrative of past events, but the interrupted sentence structure here seems designed to add formality to the speech and, perhaps, to cover over the bald statement carried in the stripped-down sentence.

Occasionally, rather than separating basic sentence elements, Shakespeare simply holds them back, delaying them until much subordinate material has already been given. Marcellus uses this kind of delaying structure when he says, at 1.1.76–77, "Thus twice before, and jump [i.e., exactly] at this dead hour, / With martial stalk hath he gone by our watch" (where a "normally" constructed English sentence would have begun with the basic sentence elements: "He hath gone by our watch"); Barnardo's sentence that precedes the entrance of the Ghost at line 46 uses this same delayed construction, though the Ghost's entrance breaks off Barnardo's words before the subject of the sentence ("Marcellus and myself") finds a verb. Hamlet, in his first soliloquy (1.2.133–64), uses a delayed construction when he says (lines 158–61) "Within a month, / Ere yet the salt of most unrighteous tears / Had left the flushing in her gallèd eyes, / She married."

Shakespeare's sentences are sometimes complicated not because of unusual structures or interruptions or delays but because he omits words and parts of words that English sentences normally require. (In conversation, we, too, often omit words. We say "Heard from him yet?" and our hearer supplies the missing "Have you." Frequent reading of Shakespeare—and of other poets—trains us to supply such missing words.) In plays written five or ten years after *Hamlet*, Shakespeare uses omissions both of verbs and of nouns to great dramatic effect. In *Hamlet* omissions are less interesting and seem to be used primarily for compressed expression. At 1.1.31–32, for instance, Marcellus says "Therefore

I have entreated him along / With us," omitting the words "to come" or "to go" before "along"; a few lines later, Barnardo omits the word "with" in the construction "let us once again assail your ears [with] . . . what we have . . . seen" (lines 37–39).

Shakespearean Wordplay

Shakespeare plays with language so often and so variously that books are written on the topic. Here we will mention only two kinds of wordplay, puns and metaphors. A pun is a play on words that sound the same but have different meanings (or a single word that has more than one meaning). When, in the second scene of *Hamlet*, Claudius calls Hamlet his "son" and asks him why his mood is so cloudy, Hamlet replies that he is, rather, "too much in the sun" (punning on son/sun). In the exchange between Gertrude and Hamlet,

QUEEN
   Thou know'st 'tis common; all that lives must die,
   Passing through nature to eternity.
HAMLET
   Ay, madam, it is common.
QUEEN   If it be,
   Why seems it so particular with thee?
HAMLET
   "Seems," madam? Nay, it is. I know not "seems[,]"
                          (1.2.74–79)

Hamlet's reply is a pun on "seems"; for Gertrude, the question was "Why are you acting as if this death were something particularly awful," but Hamlet responds as if she had asked "Why are you putting on this show of grief." In Polonius's conversation with Ophelia in the third scene of the play, much of his dialogue is based on puns: the word *tenders*, for example, introduced by Ophelia to mean "offers," is picked up by Polonius and used, first, to mean "coins" ("legal tender"), then shifted to its verb form "to tender" and used to mean "to regard," and then, in the phrase "tender me a fool," to mean, simultaneously, "present me," "make me look like," and "show yourself to me." In many of Shakespeare's plays, one may not be aware that a character is punning, and the dialogue can seem simply silly or unintelligible; one must thus stay alert to the sounds of words and to the possibility of double meanings. In *Hamlet*, puns carry a heavier burden (Hamlet packs much of his feeling about Claudius into his single-line "aside," "A little more than kin and less than kind," where "kind" has the double meaning of "kindred" and "kindhearted"; and many of Polonius's speeches are unintelligible until one untangles the puns and related plays on words).

A metaphor is a play on words in which one object or idea is expressed as if it were something else, something with which, the metaphor suggests, it shares common features. For instance, when Horatio refers to the appearance of the Ghost as "a mote . . . to trouble the mind's eye," he is using metaphoric language: the mind is irritated by a question as the eye is irritated by a speck of dust. Hamlet's description of the world as "an unweeded garden that grows to seed" uses metaphor to paint for us his bleak vision; behind his description of Gertrude and Claudius's hasty marriage ("O, most wicked speed, to post / With such dexterity to incestuous sheets") is the metaphor of post-horses running skillfully and swiftly. Metaphors are often used when the idea being conveyed is hard to express or, for Hamlet, simply beyond normal expression; through metaphor, the speaker is thus given language that helps to carry the idea or the feeling to his or her onstage listener—and to the audience.

Implied Stage Action

Finally, in reading Shakespeare's plays we should always remember that what we are reading is a performance script. The dialogue is written to be spoken by actors who, at the same time, are moving, gesturing, picking up objects, weeping, shaking their fists. Some stage action is described in what are called "stage directions"; some is signaled within the dialogue itself. We must learn to be alert to such signals as we stage the play in our imaginations. When, in the first scene of *Hamlet*, Barnardo says "Last night of all, / When yond same star that's westward from the pole / Had made his course t' illume that part of heaven / Where now it burns," it is clear that, on the word "yond," he points toward the imagined star. When Barnardo says of the Ghost "See, it stalks away," the stage action is obvious. It is less obvious, later in the scene, exactly what is to take place when Horatio says "I'll cross it though it blast me" (line 139). The director and the actor (and the reader, in imagination) must decide whether Horatio makes a cross of his body by spreading his arms, or whether he simply stands in the Ghost's path; as the Ghost once again exits, the lines "Shall I strike it with my partisan?" "Do, if it will not stand," clearly involve some violent action. Marcellus describes their gestures as a "show of violence" and mentions their "vain blows," but the question of who strikes at the Ghost and with how much vigor will be answered variously from production to production. Learning to read the language of stage action repays one many times over when one reaches a crucial scene like that of the play within the play (3.2) or that of the final duel (5.2), in both of which scenes implied stage action vitally affects our response to the play.

It is immensely rewarding to work carefully with Shakespeare's language—the words, the sentences, the wordplay, and the implied stage actions—as readers for the past four centuries have discovered. It may be more pleasurable to attend a good performance of a play—though not everyone has thought so. But the joy of being able to stage a Shakespeare play in our imaginations, to return to passages that continue to yield further meanings (or further questions) the more we read them—these are pleasures that, for many, rival (or at least augment) those of the performed text, and certainly make it worth considerable effort to "break the code" of Elizabethan poetic drama and let free the remarkable language that makes up a Shakespeare text.

Shakespeare's Life

Surviving documents that give us glimpses into the life of William Shakespeare show us a playwright, poet, and actor who grew up in the market town of Stratford-upon-Avon, spent his professional life in London, and returned to Stratford a wealthy landowner. He was born in April 1564, died in April 1616, and is buried inside the chancel of Holy Trinity Church in Stratford.

We wish we could know more about the life of the world's greatest dramatist. His plays and poems are testaments to his wide reading—especially to his knowledge of Virgil, Ovid, Plutarch, Holinshed's *Chronicles*, and the Bible—and to his mastery of the English language, but we can only speculate about his education. We know that the King's New School in Stratford-upon-Avon was considered excellent. The school was one of the English "grammar schools" established to educate young men, primarily in Latin grammar and literature. As in other schools of the time, students began their studies at the age of four or five in the attached "petty school," and there learned to read and write in English, studying primarily the catechism from the Book of Common Prayer. After two years in the petty school, students entered the lower form (grade) of the grammar school, where they began the serious study of Latin grammar and Latin texts that would occupy most of the remainder of their school days. (Several Latin texts that Shakespeare used repeatedly in writing his plays and poems were texts that schoolboys memorized and recited.) Latin comedies were introduced early in the lower form; in the upper form, which the boys entered at age ten or eleven, students wrote their own Latin orations and declamations, studied Latin

Title page of a 1573 Latin and Greek catechism for children.
From Alexander Nowell, *Catechismus paruus pueris
primum Latine . . .* (1573).

historians and rhetoricians, and began the study of Greek using the Greek New Testament.

Since the records of the Stratford "grammar school" do not survive, we cannot prove that William Shakespeare attended the school; however, every indication (his father's position as an alderman and bailiff of Stratford, the playwright's own knowledge of the Latin classics, scenes in the plays that recall grammar-school experiences—for example, *The Merry Wives of Windsor*, 4.1) suggests that he did. We also lack generally accepted documentation about Shakespeare's life after his schooling ended and his professional life in London began. His marriage in 1582 (at age eighteen) to Anne Hathaway and the subsequent births of his daughter Susanna (1583) and the twins Judith and Hamnet (1585) are recorded, but how he supported himself and where he lived are not known. Nor do we know when and why he left Stratford for the London theatrical world, nor how he rose to be the important figure in that world that he had become by the early 1590s.

We do know that by 1592 he had achieved some prominence in London as both an actor and a playwright. In that year was published a book by the playwright Robert Greene attacking an actor who had the audacity to write blank-verse drama and who was "in his own conceit [i.e., opinion] the only Shake-scene in a country." Since Greene's attack includes a parody of a line from one of Shakespeare's early plays, there is little doubt that it is Shakespeare to whom he refers, a "Shake-scene" who had aroused Greene's fury by successfully competing with university-educated dramatists like Greene himself. It was in 1593 that Shakespeare became a published poet. In that year he published his long narrative poem *Venus and Adonis*; in 1594, he followed it with *The Rape of Lucrece*. Both poems were dedicated to the young earl of Southampton (Henry Wriothesley), who may have become Shakespeare's patron.

It seems no coincidence that Shakespeare wrote these narrative poems at a time when the theaters were closed because of the plague, a contagious epidemic disease that devastated the population of London. When the theaters reopened in 1594, Shakespeare apparently resumed his double career of actor and playwright and began his long (and seemingly profitable) service as an acting-company shareholder. Records for December of 1594 show him to be a leading member of the Lord Chamberlain's Men. It was this company of actors, later named the King's Men, for whom he would be a principal actor, dramatist, and shareholder for the rest of his career.

So far as we can tell, that career spanned about twenty years. In the 1590s, he wrote his plays on English history as well as several comedies and at least two tragedies (*Titus Andronicus* and *Romeo and Juliet*). These histories, comedies, and tragedies are the plays credited to him in 1598 in a work, *Palladis Tamia*, that in one chapter compares English writers with "Greek, Latin, and Italian Poets." There the author, Francis Meres, claims that Shakespeare is comparable to the Latin dramatists Seneca for tragedy and Plautus for comedy, and calls him "the most excellent in both kinds for the stage." He also names him "Mellifluous and honey-tongued Shakespeare": "I say," writes Meres, "that the Muses would speak with Shakespeare's fine filed phrase, if they would speak English." Since Meres also mentions Shakespeare's "sugared sonnets among his private friends," it is assumed that many of Shakespeare's sonnets (not published until 1609) were also written in the 1590s.

In 1599, Shakespeare's company built a theater for themselves across the river from London, naming it the Globe. The plays that are considered by many to be Shakespeare's major tragedies (*Hamlet, Othello, King Lear,* and *Macbeth*) were written while the company was resident in this theater, as were such comedies as *Twelfth Night* and *Measure for Measure.* Many of Shakespeare's plays were performed at court (both for Queen Elizabeth I and, after her death in 1603, for King James I), some were presented at the Inns of Court (the residences of London's legal societies), and some were doubtless performed in other towns, at the universities, and at great houses when the King's Men went on tour; otherwise, his plays from 1599 to 1608 were, so far as we know, performed only at the Globe. Between 1608 and 1612, Shakespeare wrote several plays—among them *The Winter's Tale* and *The Tempest*—presumably for the company's new indoor Blackfriars theater, though the plays seem to have been performed also at the Globe and at court. Surviving documents describe a performance of *The Winter's Tale* in 1611 at the Globe, for example, and performances of *The Tempest* in 1611 and 1613 at the royal palace of Whitehall.

Shakespeare wrote very little after 1612, the year in which he probably wrote *King Henry VIII.* (It was at a performance of *Henry VIII* in 1613 that the Globe caught fire and burned to the ground.) Sometime between 1610 and 1613 he seems to have returned to live in Stratford-upon-Avon, where he owned a large house and considerable property, and where his wife and his two daughters and their husbands lived. (His son Hamnet had died in 1596.) During his professional years in London, Shakespeare had presumably derived income from the acting company's profits as well as from his own career as an actor, from the sale of his play manuscripts to the acting company, and, after 1599, from his shares as an owner of the Globe. It was presumably that income, carefully invested in land

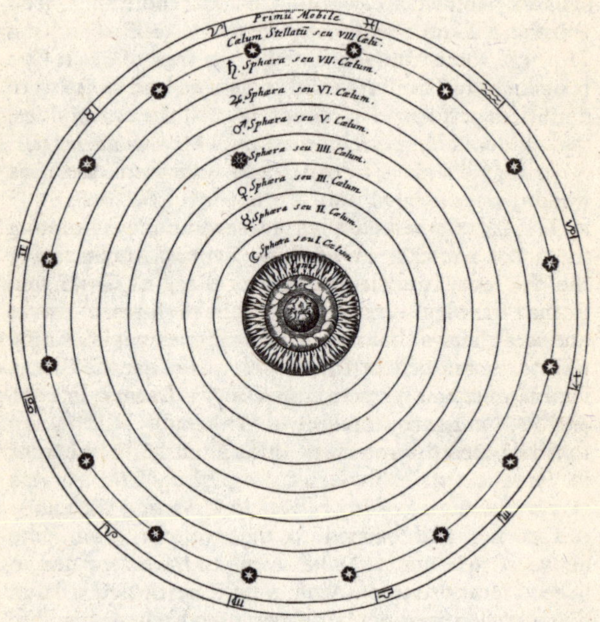

Ptolemaic universe.
From Marcus Manilius, *The sphere of . . .* (1675).

and other property, that made him the wealthy man that surviving documents show him to have become. It is also assumed that William Shakespeare's growing wealth and reputation played some part in inclining the Crown, in 1596, to grant John Shakespeare, William's father, the coat of arms that he had so long sought. William Shakespeare died in Stratford on April 23, 1616 (according to the epitaph carved under his bust in Holy Trinity Church) and was buried on April 25. Seven years after his death, his collected plays were published as *Mr. William Shakespeares Comedies, Histories, & Tragedies* (the work now known as the First Folio).

The years in which Shakespeare wrote were among the most exciting in English history. Intellectually, the discovery, translation, and printing of Greek and Roman classics were making available a set of works and worldviews that interacted complexly with Christian texts and beliefs. The result was a questioning, a vital intellectual ferment, that provided energy for the period's amazing dramatic and literary output and that fed directly into Shakespeare's plays. The Ghost in *Hamlet*, for example, is wonderfully complicated in part because he is a figure from Roman tragedy— the spirit of the dead returning to seek revenge—who at the same time inhabits a Christian hell (or purgatory); Hamlet's description of humankind reflects at one moment the Neoplatonic wonderment at mankind ("What a piece of work is a man!") and, at the next, the Christian disparagement of human sinners ("And yet, to me, what is this quintessence of dust?").

As intellectual horizons expanded, so also did geographical and cosmological horizons. New worlds— both North and South America—were explored, and in them were found human beings who lived and worshiped in ways radically different from those of Renaissance Europeans and Englishmen. The universe during these years also seemed to shift and expand. Copernicus had earlier theorized that the earth was not the center of the cosmos but revolved as a planet around the sun. Galileo's telescope, created in 1609, allowed scientists to see that Copernicus had been correct: the universe was not organized with the earth at the center, nor was it so nicely circumscribed as people had, until that time, thought. In terms of expanding horizons, the impact of these discoveries on people's beliefs— religious, scientific, and philosophical—cannot be overstated.

London, too, rapidly expanded and changed during the years (from the early 1590s to around 1610) that Shakespeare lived there. London—the center of England's government, its economy, its royal court, its overseas trade—was, during these years, becoming an exciting metropolis, drawing to it thousands of new citizens every year. Troubled by overcrowding, by poverty, by recurring epidemics of the plague, London was also a mecca for the wealthy and the aristocratic, and for those who sought advancement at court, or power in government or finance or trade. One hears in Shakespeare's plays the voices of London—the struggles for power, the fear of venereal disease, the language of buying and selling. One hears as well the voices of Stratford-upon-Avon—references to the nearby Forest of Arden, to sheepherding, to small-town gossip, to village fairs and markets. Part of the richness of Shakespeare's work is the influence felt there of the various worlds in which he lived: the world of metropolitan London, the world of small-town and rural England, the world of the theater, and the worlds of craftsmen and shepherds.

That Shakespeare inhabited such worlds we know from surviving London and Stratford documents, as well as from the evidence of the plays and poems themselves. From such records we can sketch the dramatist's life. We know from his works that he was a voracious reader. We know from legal and business documents that he was a multifaceted theater man who became a wealthy landowner. We know a bit about his family life and a fair amount about his legal and financial dealings. Most scholars today depend upon such evidence as they draw their picture of the world's greatest playwright. Such, however, has not always been the case. Until the late eighteenth century, the William Shakespeare who lived in most biographies was the creation of legend and tradition. This was the Shakespeare who was supposedly caught poaching deer at Charlecote, the estate of Sir Thomas Lucy close by Stratford; this was the Shakespeare who fled from Sir Thomas's vengeance and made his way in London by taking care of horses outside a playhouse; this was the Shakespeare who reportedly could barely read, but whose natural gifts were extraordinary, whose father was a butcher who allowed his gifted son sometimes to help in the butcher shop, where William supposedly killed calves "in a high style," making a speech for the occasion. It was this legendary William Shakespeare whose Falstaff (in *1* and *2 Henry IV*) so pleased Queen Elizabeth that she demanded a play about Falstaff in love, and demanded that it be written in fourteen days (hence the existence of *The Merry Wives of Windsor*). It was this legendary Shakespeare who reached the top of his acting career in the roles of the Ghost in *Hamlet* and old Adam in *As You Like It*—and who died of a fever contracted by drinking too hard at "a merry meeting" with the poets Michael Drayton and Ben Jonson. This legendary Shakespeare is a rambunctious, undisciplined man, as attractively "wild" as his plays were seen by earlier generations to be. Unfortunately, there is no trace of evidence to support these wonderful stories.

Perhaps in response to the disreputable Shakespeare of legend—or perhaps in response to the fragmentary and, for some, all-too-ordinary Shakespeare documented by surviving records—some people since the mid-nineteenth century have argued that William Shakespeare could not have written the plays that bear his name. These persons have put forward some dozen names as more likely authors, among them Queen Elizabeth, Sir Francis Bacon, Edward de Vere (earl of Oxford), and Christopher Marlowe. Such attempts to find what for these people is a more believable author of the plays is a tribute to the regard in which the plays are held. Unfortunately for their claims, the documents that exist that provide evidence for the facts of Shakespeare's life tie him inextricably to the body of plays and poems that bear his name. Unlikely as it seems to those who want the works to have been written by an aristocrat, a university graduate, or an "important" person, the plays and poems seem clearly to have been produced by a man from Stratford-upon-Avon with a very good "grammar-school" education and a life of experience in London and in the world of the London theater. How this particular man produced the works that dominate the cultures of much of the world almost four hundred years after his death is one of life's mysteries—and one that will continue to tease our imaginations as we continue to delight in his plays and poems.

Shakespeare's Theater

The actors of Shakespeare's time are known to have performed plays in a great variety of locations. They played at court (that is, in the great halls of such royal residences as Whitehall, Hampton Court, and Greenwich); they played in halls at the universities of Oxford and Cambridge, and at the Inns of Court (the residences in London of the legal societies); and they also played in the private houses of great lords and civic officials. Sometimes acting companies went on tour from London into the provinces, often (but not only) when outbreaks of bubonic plague in the capital forced the closing of theaters to reduce the possibility of contagion in crowded audiences. In the provinces the actors usually staged their plays in churches (until around 1600) or in guildhalls. While surviving records show only a handful of occasions when actors played at inns while on tour, London inns were important playing places up until the 1590s.

The building of theaters in London had begun only shortly before Shakespeare wrote his first plays in the 1590s. These theaters were of two kinds: outdoor or public playhouses that could accommodate large numbers of playgoers, and indoor or private theaters for much smaller audiences. What is usually regarded as the first London outdoor public playhouse was called simply the Theatre. James Burbage—the father of Richard Burbage, who was perhaps the most famous actor in Shakespeare's company—built it in 1576 in an area north of the city of London called Shoreditch. Among the more famous of the other public playhouses that capitalized on the new fashion were the Curtain and the Fortune (both also built north of the city), the Rose,

A stylized representation of the Globe theater.
From Claes Jansz Visscher, *Londinum florentissima
Britanniae urbs . . .* [c.1625].

the Swan, the Globe, and the Hope (all located on the Bankside, a region just across the Thames south of the city of London). All these playhouses had to be built outside the jurisdiction of the city of London because many civic officials were hostile to the performance of drama and repeatedly petitioned the royal council to abolish it.

The theaters erected on the Bankside (a region under the authority of the Church of England, whose head was the monarch) shared the neighborhood with houses of prostitution and with the Paris Garden, where the blood sports of bearbaiting and bullbaiting were carried on. There may have been no clear distinction between playhouses and buildings for such sports, for we know that the Hope was used for both plays and baiting and that Philip Henslowe, owner of the Rose and, later, partner in the ownership of the Fortune, was also a partner in a monopoly on baiting. All these forms of entertainment were easily accessible to Londoners by boat across the Thames or over London Bridge.

Evidently Shakespeare's company prospered on the Bankside. They moved there in 1599. Threatened by difficulties in renewing the lease on the land where their first theater (the Theatre) had been built, Shakespeare's company took advantage of the Christmas holiday in 1598 to dismantle the Theatre and transport its timbers across the Thames to the Bankside, where, in 1599, these timbers were used in the building of the Globe. The weather in late December 1598 is recorded as having been especially harsh. It was so cold that the Thames was "nigh [nearly] frozen," and there was heavy snow. Perhaps the weather aided Shakespeare's company in eluding their landlord, the snow hiding their activity and the freezing of the Thames allowing them to slide the timbers across to the Bankside without paying tolls for repeated trips over London Bridge.

Attractive as this narrative is, it remains just as likely that the heavy snow hampered transport of the timbers in wagons through the London streets to the river. It also must be remembered that the Thames was, according to report, only "nigh frozen," and therefore did not necessarily provide solid footing. Whatever the precise circumstances of this fascinating event in English theater history, Shakespeare's company was able to begin playing at their new Globe theater on the Bankside in 1599. After this theater burned down in 1613 during the staging of Shakespeare's *Henry VIII* (its thatch roof was set alight by cannon fire called for in performance), Shakespeare's company immediately rebuilt on the same location. The second Globe seems to have been a grander structure than its predecessor. It remained in use until the beginning of the English Civil War in 1642, when Parliament officially closed the theaters. Soon thereafter it was pulled down.

The public theaters of Shakespeare's time were very different buildings from our theaters today. First of all, they were open-air playhouses. As recent excavations of the Rose and the Globe confirm, some were polygonal or roughly circular in shape; the Fortune, however, was square. The most recent estimates of their size put the diameter of these buildings at 72 feet (the Rose) to 100 feet (the Globe), but we know that they held vast audiences of two or three thousand, who must have been squeezed together quite tightly. Some of these spectators paid extra to sit or stand in the two or three levels of roofed galleries that extended, on the upper levels, all the way around the theater and surrounded an open space. In this space were the stage and, perhaps, the tiring house (what we would call dressing rooms), as well as the so-called yard. In the yard stood the spectators who chose to pay less, the ones whom Hamlet contemptuously called "groundlings." For a roof they had only the sky, and so they were exposed to all kinds of weather. They stood on a floor that was sometimes made of mortar and sometimes of ash mixed with the shells of hazelnuts, which, it has recently been discovered, were standard flooring material in the period.

Unlike the yard, the stage itself was covered by a roof. Its ceiling, called "the heavens," is thought to have been elaborately painted to depict the sun, moon, stars, and planets. The exact size of the stage remains hard to determine. We have a single sketch of part of the interior of the Swan. A Dutchman named Johannes de Witt visited this theater around 1596 and sent a sketch of it back to his friend, Arend van Buchel. Because van Buchel found de Witt's letter and sketch of interest, he copied both into a book. It is van Buchel's copy, adapted, it seems, to the shape and size of the page in his book, that survives. In this sketch, the stage appears to be a large rectangular platform that thrusts far out into the yard, perhaps even as far as the center of the circle formed by the surrounding galleries. This drawing, combined with the specifications for the size of the stage in the building contract for the Fortune, has led scholars to conjecture that the stage on which Shakespeare's plays were performed must have measured approximately 43 feet in width and 27 feet in depth, a vast acting area. But the digging up of a large part of the Rose by late-twentieth-century archaeologists has provided evidence of a quite different stage design. The Rose stage was a platform tapered at the corners and much shallower than what seems to be depicted in the van Buchel sketch. Indeed, its measurements seem to be about 37.5 feet across at its widest point and only 15.5 feet deep. Because the surviving indications of stage size and design differ from each other so much, it is possible that the stages in other theaters, like the Theatre, the Curtain, and the Globe (the outdoor playhouses where we know that Shakespeare's plays were performed), were different from those at both the Swan and the Rose.

After about 1608 Shakespeare's plays were staged not only at the Globe but also at an indoor or private playhouse in Blackfriars. This theater had been constructed in 1596 by James Burbage in an upper hall of a former Dominican priory or monastic house. Although Henry VIII had dissolved all English monasteries in the 1530s (shortly after he had founded the Church of England), the area remained under church, rather than hostile civic, control. The hall that Burbage had purchased and renovated was a large one in which Parliament had once met. In the private theater that he constructed, the stage, lit by candles, was built across the narrow end of the hall, with boxes flanking it. The rest of the hall offered seating room only. Because there was no provision for standing room, the largest audience it could hold was less than a thousand, or about a quarter of what the Globe could accommodate. Admission to Blackfriars was correspondingly more expensive. Instead of a penny to stand in the yard at the Globe, it cost a minimum of sixpence to get into Blackfriars. The best seats at the Globe (in the Lords' Room in the gallery above and behind the stage) cost sixpence; but the boxes flanking the stage at Blackfriars were half a crown, or five times sixpence. Some spectators who were particularly interested in displaying themselves paid even more to sit on stools on the Blackfriars stage.

Whether in the outdoor or indoor playhouses, the stages of Shakespeare's time were different from ours. They were not separated from the audience by the dropping of a curtain between acts and scenes. Therefore the playwrights of the time had to find other ways of signaling to the audience that one scene (to be imagined as occurring in one location at a given time) had ended and the next (to be imagined at perhaps a different location at a later time) had begun. The customary way used by Shakespeare and many of his contemporaries was to have everyone on stage exit at the end of one scene and have one or more different characters enter to begin the next. In a few cases, where characters remain onstage from one scene to another, the dialogue or stage action makes the change of location clear, and the characters are generally to be imagined as having moved from one place to another. For example, in *Romeo and Juliet*, Romeo and his friends remain onstage in Act 1 from scene 4 to scene 5, but they are represented as having moved between scenes from the street that leads to Capulet's house into Capulet's house itself. The new location is signaled in part by the appearance onstage of Capulet's servingmen carrying napkins, something they would not take into the streets. Playwrights had to be quite resourceful in the use of hand properties, like the napkin, or in the use of dialogue to specify where the action was taking place in their plays because, in contrast to most of today's theaters, the playhouses of Shakespeare's time did not fill the stage with scenery to make the setting precise. A consequence of this difference was that the playwrights of Shakespeare's time did not have to specify exactly where the action of their plays was set when they did not choose to do so, and much of the action of their plays is tied to no specific place.

Usually Shakespeare's stage is referred to as a "bare stage," to distinguish it from the stages of the last two or three centuries with their elaborate sets. But the stage in Shakespeare's time was not completely bare. Philip Henslowe, owner of the Rose, lists in his inventory of stage properties a rock, three tombs, and two mossy banks. Stage directions in plays of the time also call for such things as thrones (or "states"), banquets (presumably tables with plaster replicas of food on them), and beds and tombs to be pushed onto the stage. Thus the stage often held more than the actors.

The actors did not limit their performing to the stage alone. Occasionally they went beneath the stage, as the Ghost appears to do in the first act of *Hamlet*. From there they could emerge onto the stage through a trapdoor. They could retire behind the hangings across the back of the stage, as, for example, the actor playing Polonius does when he hides behind the arras. Sometimes the hangings could be drawn back during a performance to "discover" one or more actors behind them. When performance required that an actor appear "above," as when Juliet is imagined to stand at the window of her chamber in the famous and misnamed "balcony scene," then the actor probably climbed the stairs to the gallery over the back of the stage and temporarily shared it with some of the spectators. The stage was also provided with ropes and winches so that actors could descend from, and reascend to, the "heavens."

Perhaps the greatest difference between dramatic performances in Shakespeare's time and ours was that in Shakespeare's England the roles of women were played by boys. (Some of these boys grew up to take male roles in their maturity.) There were no women in the acting companies. It had not always been so in the history of the English stage. There are records of women on English stages in the thirteenth and fourteenth centuries, two hundred years before Shakespeare's plays were performed. After the accession of James I in 1603, the queen of England and her ladies took part in entertainments at court called masques, and with the reopening of the theaters in 1660 at the restoration of Charles II, women again took their place on the public stage.

The chief competitors of such acting companies as the one to which Shakespeare belonged and for which he wrote were companies of exclusively boy actors. The competition was most intense in the early 1600s. There were then two principal children's companies: the Children of Paul's (the choirboys from St. Paul's Cathedral, whose private playhouse was near the cathedral); and the Children of the Chapel Royal (the choirboys from the monarch's private chapel, who performed at the Blackfriars theater built by Burbage in 1596). In *Hamlet* Shakespeare writes of "an aerie [nest] of children, little eyases [hawks], that cry out on the top of question and are most tyrannically clapped for 't. These are now the fashion and . . . berattle the common stages [attack the public theaters]." In the long run, the adult actors prevailed. The Children of Paul's dissolved around 1606. By about 1608 the Children of the Chapel Royal had been forced to stop playing at the Blackfriars theater, which was then taken over by the King's Men, Shakespeare's own troupe.

Acting companies and theaters of Shakespeare's time seem to have been organized in various ways. For example, with the building of the Globe, Shakespeare's company apparently managed itself, with the principal actors, Shakespeare among them, having the status of "sharers" and the right to a share in the takings, as well as the responsibility for a part of the expenses. Five of the sharers, including Shakespeare, owned the Globe. As actor, as sharer in an acting company and in ownership of theaters, and as playwright, Shakespeare was about as involved in the theatrical industry as one could imagine. Although Shakespeare and his fellows prospered, their status under the law was conditional upon the protection of powerful patrons. "Common players"—those who did not have patrons or masters—were classed in the language of the law with "vagabonds and sturdy beggars." So the actors had to secure for themselves the official rank of servants of patrons. Among the patrons under whose protection Shakespeare's company worked were the lord chamberlain and, after the accession of King James in 1603, the king himself.

In the early 1990s we seemed on the verge of learning a great deal more about the theaters in which Shakespeare and his contemporaries performed—or, at least, opening up new questions about them. At that time about 70 percent of the Rose had been excavated, as had about 10 percent of the second Globe, the one built in 1614. It was then hoped that more would become available for study. However, excavation was halted at that point, and while it is not known if or when it will resume at these sites, archaeological discoveries in Shoreditch in 2008 in the vicinity of the Theatre may yield new information about the playhouses of Shakespeare's London.

The Publication of Shakespeare's Plays

Eighteen of Shakespeare's plays found their way into print during the playwright's lifetime, but there is nothing to suggest that he took any interest in their publication. These eighteen appeared separately in editions in quarto or, in the case of *Henry VI, Part 3*, octavo format. The quarto pages are not much larger than a modern mass-market paperback book, and the octavo pages are even smaller; these little books were sold unbound for a few pence. The earliest of the quartos that still survive were printed in 1594, the year that both *Titus Andronicus* and a version of the play now called *Henry VI, Part 2* became available. While almost every one of these early quartos displays on its title page the name of the acting company that performed the play, only about half provide the name of the playwright, Shakespeare. The first quarto edition to bear the name Shakespeare on its title page is *Love's Labor's Lost* of 1598. A few of the quartos were popular with the book-buying public of Shakespeare's lifetime; for example, quarto *Richard II* went through five editions between 1597 and 1615. But most of the quartos were far from best sellers; *Love's Labor's Lost* (1598), for instance, was not reprinted in quarto until 1631. After Shakespeare's death, two more of his plays appeared in quarto format: *Othello* in 1622 and *The Two Noble Kinsmen*, coauthored with John Fletcher, in 1634.

In 1623, seven years after Shakespeare's death, *Mr. William Shakespeares Comedies, Histories, & Tragedies* was published. This printing offered readers in a single book thirty-six of the thirty-eight plays now thought to have been written by Shakespeare, including eighteen that had never been printed before. And it offered them in a style that was then reserved for serious literature and scholarship. The plays were arranged in double columns on pages nearly a foot high. This large page size is called "folio," as opposed to the smaller "quarto," and the 1623 volume is usually called the Shakespeare First Folio. It is reputed to have sold for the lordly price of a pound. (One copy at the Folger Shakespeare Library is marked fifteen shillings—that is, three-quarters of a pound.)

In a preface to the First Folio entitled "To the great Variety of Readers," two of Shakespeare's former fellow actors in the King's Men, John Heminge and Henry Condell, wrote that they themselves had collected their dead companion's plays. They suggested that they had seen his own papers: "we have scarce received from him a blot in his papers." The title page of the Folio declared that the plays within it had been printed "according to the True Original Copies." Comparing the Folio to the quartos, Heminge and Condell disparaged the quartos, advising their readers that "before you were abused with divers stolen and surreptitious copies, maimed, and deformed by the frauds and stealths of injurious impostors." Many Shakespeareans of the eighteenth and nineteenth centuries believed Heminge and Condell and regarded the Folio plays as superior to anything in the quartos.

Once we begin to examine the Folio plays in detail, it becomes less easy to take at face value the word of Heminge and Condell about the superiority of the Folio texts. For example, of the first nine plays in the Folio (one-quarter of the entire collection), four were essentially reprinted from earlier quarto printings that Heminge and Condell had disparaged, and four have now been identified as printed from copies written in the hand of a professional scribe of the 1620s named Ralph Crane; the ninth, *The Comedy of Errors*, was apparently also printed from a manuscript, but one whose origin cannot be readily identified. Evidently, then, eight of the first nine plays in the First Folio were not printed, in spite of what the Folio title page announces, "according to the True Original Copies," or Shakespeare's own papers, and the source of the ninth is unknown. Since today's editors have been forced to treat Heminge and Condell's pronouncements with skepticism, they must choose whether to base their own editions upon quartos or the Folio on grounds other than Heminge and Condell's story of where the quarto and Folio versions originated.

Editors have often fashioned their own narratives to explain what lies behind the quartos and Folio. They have said that Heminge and Condell meant to criticize only a few of the early quartos, the ones that offer much shorter and sometimes quite different, often garbled, versions of plays. Among the examples of these are the 1600 quarto of *Henry V* (the Folio offers a much fuller version) or the 1603 *Hamlet* quarto. (In 1604 a different, much longer form of the play got into print as a quarto.) Early twentieth-century editors speculated that these questionable texts were produced when someone in the audience took notes from the plays' dialogue during performances and then employed "hack poets" to fill out the notes. The poor results were then sold to a publisher and presented in print as Shakespeare's plays. More recently this story has given way to another in which the shorter versions are said to be re-creations from memory of Shakespeare's plays by actors who wanted to stage them in the provinces but lacked manuscript copies. Most of the quartos offer much better texts than these so-called bad quartos. Indeed, in most of the quartos we find texts that are at least equal to or better than what is printed in the Folio. Many Shakespeare enthusiasts persuaded themselves that most of the quartos were set into type directly from Shakespeare's own papers, although there is nothing on which to base this conclusion except the desire for it to be true. Thus speculation continues about how the Shakespeare plays got to be printed. All that we have are the printed texts.

The book collector who was most successful in bringing together copies of the quartos and the First Folio was Henry Clay Folger, founder of the Folger Shakespeare Library in Washington, D.C. While it is estimated that there survive around the world only about 230 copies of the First Folio, Mr. Folger was able to acquire more than seventy-five copies, as well as a large number of fragments, for the library that bears his name. He also amassed a substantial number of quartos. For example, only fourteen copies of the First Quarto of *Love's Labor's Lost* are known to exist, and three are at the Folger Shakespeare Library. As a consequence of Mr. Folger's labors, scholars visiting the Folger Shakespeare Library have been able to learn a great deal about sixteenth- and seventeenth-century printing and, particularly, about the printing of Shakespeare's plays. And Mr. Folger did not stop at the First Folio, but collected many copies of later editions of Shakespeare, beginning with the Second Folio (1632), the Third (1663–64), and the Fourth (1685). Each of these later folios was based on its immediate predecessor and was edited anonymously. The first editor of Shakespeare whose name we know was Nicholas Rowe, whose first edition came out in 1709. Mr. Folger collected this edition and many, many more by Rowe's successors, and the collecting continues.

An Introduction to This Text

The play we call *Hamlet* was printed in three different versions in the first quarter of the seventeenth century.

In 1603 appeared *The Tragicall Historie of Hamlet Prince of Denmark by William Shake-speare*, a quarto or pocket-size book that provides a version of the play markedly different from the two subsequent printings and from the play most readers know. This version is little more than half as long as the others. Some of the characters have different names; for example, Polonius is called Corambis and his servant Reynaldo appears as Montano. The action of the play also varies considerably. Most scholars have found many passages in this version extremely difficult to read and have concluded that it is so full of errors that it is generally unreliable as a witness to what was written for the stage. This First Quarto has therefore been dubbed a "bad quarto."

The Second Quarto, often called the "good quarto," is dated in some copies 1604, in others 1605. Although it has exactly the same title as the First Quarto, the Second Quarto's title page goes on to represent it as "Newly imprinted and enlarged to almost as much againe as it was, according to the true and perfect Coppie."

The third version to see print is found in the First Folio of Shakespeare's plays, published in 1623. Entitled *The Tragedie of Hamlet, Prince of Denmarke*, the Folio play has some eighty-five or so lines not found in the Second Quarto; but the Folio lacks about two hundred of the Second Quarto's lines. These two versions also differ from each other in their readings of hundreds of words.

Most modern editions offer various combinations of the Second Quarto and Folio versions. It is impossible in any edition to combine the whole of these two

THE
Tragicall Historie of
HAMLET,

Prince of Denmarke.

By William Shakespeare.

Newly imprinted and enlarged to almost as much
againe as it was, according to the true and perfect
Coppie.

AT LONDON,
Printed by I. R. for N. L. and are to be sold at his
shoppe vnder Saint Dunstons Church in
1604.

Title page of *Hamlet* Second Quarto, 1604.
From the Folger Shakespeare Library collection.

forms of the play, because they often provide alternative readings that are mutually exclusive; for example, when the Second Quarto has Hamlet wish that his "too too sallied flesh would melt," the Folio prints "solid" for "sallied." In such cases (and there are a great many such cases) editors must choose whether to be guided by the Second Quarto, by the Folio, or perhaps even by the First Quarto in selecting what to print.

Twentieth-century editors made the decision about which version to prefer according to their theories about the origins of the three early printed texts. Most such editors have preferred the Second Quarto's readings in the belief that it was printed either directly from Shakespeare's own manuscript or from a scribe's copy of it. A few have, instead, adopted Folio readings in the belief that the Folio was set into type from a theater manuscript, and they wanted to give their readers the play as it was performed on Shakespeare's stage. Still fewer editors have granted the First Quarto much influence over their choices, since many believe that the First Quarto prints a manuscript put together from memory by a small-part actor who had a role in the play as it was performed outside of London. Editors who have been convinced of this story about the First Quarto sometimes have depended on it as a record of what was acted. In recent years, some editors have come to believe that the Second Quarto and Folio are distinct, independent Shakespearean versions of the play that ought never to be combined with each other in an edition. Nevertheless, as today's scholars reexamine the narratives about the origins of the printed texts, we discover that the evidence upon which they are based is questionable, and we become more skeptical about ever identifying with any certainty how the play assumed the forms in which it was printed.

The present edition is based upon a fresh examination

of the early printed texts rather than upon any modern edition. It is designed both for those who prefer the traditional text of *Hamlet*, which is the combination of Second Quarto and First Folio, and for those who prefer to regard the Second Quarto and First Folio as distinct versions of the play. The present edition resembles most other modern editions in offering its readers a text of the Second Quarto combined with as much of the First Folio as it has been possible to include. It also resembles most other editions in its efforts to correct what are believed to be errors or deficiencies in the Second Quarto by substituting or introducing alternatives either from the First Folio or from the editorial tradition. Yet the present edition is unique in marking all passages that are found only in the Second Quarto and all words and passages found only in the Folio. Thus it becomes possible for a reader to use this book to discover the major and even many of the minor differences between the Second Quarto and First Folio versions of *Hamlet*. This edition ignores the First Quarto version because the First Quarto is so widely different from the Second Quarto and the Folio.

In order to enable its readers to tell the difference between the Folio and Second Quarto versions, the present edition uses a variety of signals:

(1) All the words in this edition that are printed only in the Folio version but not in the Second Quarto appear in pointed parentheses (⟨ ⟩).

(2) All lines that are found only in the Second Quarto and not in the Folio are printed in square brackets ([ ]).

(3) Sometimes neither the Second Quarto nor the Folio seems to offer a satisfactory reading, and it is necessary to print a word different from what is offered by either. Such words (called "emendations" by editors) are printed within superior half-brackets (⌈ ⌉).

Whenever we change the wording of the Second

Quarto or add anything to its stage directions, we mark the change because we want our readers to be immediately aware that we have intervened. (Only when we correct an obvious typographical error in the Second Quarto or the First Folio does the change not get marked.) Whenever we change the Second Quarto's or First Folio's wording or their punctuation so that meaning changes, we list the change in the textual notes at the back of the book, even if all we have done is fix an obvious error. Those who wish to find the Folio's alternatives to the Second Quarto's readings will be able to find these in the textual notes.

For the convenience of the reader, we have modernized the punctuation and the spelling of both the Second Quarto and the Folio. Thus, for example, our text supplies the modern standard spelling "sullied" for the Second Quarto's variant spelling "sallied." Sometimes we go so far as to modernize certain old forms of words; for example, usually when *a* means "he," we change it to *he;* we change *mo* to *more, ye* to *you,* and *god buy to you* to *good-bye to you.* It is not our practice in editing any of the plays to modernize words that sound distinctly different from modern forms. For example, when the early printed texts read *sith* or *apricocks* or *porpentine,* we have not modernized to *since, apricots, porcupine.* When the forms *an, and,* or *and if* appear instead of the modern form *if,* we have reduced *and* to *an* but have not changed any of these forms to their modern equivalent, *if.* We also modernize and, where necessary, correct passages in foreign languages, unless an error in the early printed text can be reasonably explained as a joke.

We correct or regularize a number of the proper names in the dialogue and in the stage directions, as is the usual practice in editions of the play. For example, the Second Quarto's "Gertrard" or "Gertrad" is changed to Folio's "Gertrude" because "Gertrude" has become the familiar form of the name; and there are a number of other comparable adjustments in the names.

This edition differs from many earlier ones in its efforts to aid the reader in imagining the play as a performance. Thus stage directions are written with reference to the stage. For example, the present edition reproduces the Second Quarto direction: "Ghost cries under the stage" (1.5.168). Whenever it is reasonably certain, in our view, that a speech is accompanied by a particular action, we provide a stage direction describing the action. (Occasional exceptions to this rule occur when the action is so obvious that to add a stage direction would insult the reader.) Stage directions for the entrance of characters in mid-scene are, with rare exceptions, placed so that they immediately precede the characters' participation in the scene, even though these entrances may appear somewhat earlier in the early printed texts. Whenever we move a stage direction, we record this change in the textual notes. Latin stage directions (e.g., *Exeunt*) are translated into English (e.g., *They exit*).

We expand the often severely abbreviated forms of names used as speech headings in early printed texts into the full names of the characters. We also regularize the speakers' names in speech headings, using only a single designation for each character, even though the early printed texts sometimes use a variety of designations. Variations in the speech headings of the early printed texts are recorded in the textual notes.

In the present edition, as well, we mark with a dash any change of address within a speech, unless a stage direction intervenes. When the *-ed* ending of a word is to be pronounced, we mark it with an accent. Like editors for the last two centuries, we print metrically linked lines in the following way:

MARCELLUS
  It is offended.
BARNARDO   See, it stalks away.

However, when there are a number of short verse-lines that can be linked in more than one way, we do not, with rare exceptions, indent any of them.

The Explanatory Notes

The notes that appear on the pages facing the text are designed to provide readers with the help that they may need to enjoy the play. Whenever the meaning of a word in the text is not readily accessible in a good contemporary dictionary, we offer the meaning in a note. Sometimes we provide a note even when the relevant meaning is to be found in the dictionary but when the word has acquired since Shakespeare's time other potentially confusing meanings. In our notes, we try to offer modern synonyms for Shakespeare's words. We also try to indicate to the reader the connection between the word in the play and the modern synonym. For example, Shakespeare sometimes uses the word *head* to mean "source," but, for modern readers, there may be no connection evident between these two words. We provide the connection by explaining Shakespeare's usage as follows: "**head:** fountainhead, source." On some occasions, a whole phrase or clause needs explanation. Then, if space allows, we rephrase in our own words the difficult passage, and add at the end synonyms for individual words in the passage. When scholars have been unable to determine the meaning of a word or phrase, we acknowledge the uncertainty. Biblical quotations are from the Geneva Bible (1560), with spelling modernized.

The Tragedy of

HAMLET,

Prince of Denmark

Characters in the Play

THE GHOST
HAMLET, Prince of Denmark, son of the late King Hamlet
    and Queen Gertrude
QUEEN GERTRUDE, widow of King Hamlet, now married
    to Claudius
KING CLAUDIUS, brother to the late King Hamlet

OPHELIA
LAERTES, her brother
POLONIUS, father of Ophelia and Laertes, councillor to
    King Claudius
REYNALDO, servant to Polonius

HORATIO, Hamlet's friend and confidant

VOLTEMAND
CORNELIUS
ROSENCRANTZ
GUILDENSTERN } *courtiers at the Danish court*
OSRIC
Gentlemen
A Lord

FRANCISCO
BARNARDO } *Danish soldiers*
MARCELLUS

FORTINBRAS, Prince of Norway
A Captain in Fortinbras's army

Ambassadors to Denmark from England

Players who take the roles of Prologue, Player King,
    Player Queen, and Lucianus in *The Murder of Gonzago*

Two Messengers
Sailors
Gravedigger
Gravedigger's companion
Doctor of Divinity

Attendants, Lords, Guards, Musicians, Laertes's Followers, Soldiers, Officers

The Tragedy of

HAMLET,

Prince of Denmark

ACT 1

1.1 On the guards' platform at Elsinore, Horatio waits with Barnardo and Marcellus to question a ghost that has twice before appeared. The Ghost, in the form of the late King Hamlet of Denmark, appears but will not speak. Horatio decides to tell his fellow student, Prince Hamlet, about the Ghost's appearance.

———————

2. **unfold yourself:** disclose your identity

14. **The rivals of my watch:** my fellow sentries   **watch:** continuous lookout, for protection or defense

⟨ACT 1⟩

⟨Scene 1⟩

Enter Barnardo and Francisco, two sentinels.

BARNARDO Who's there?

FRANCISCO

  Nay, answer me. Stand and unfold yourself.

BARNARDO Long live the King!

FRANCISCO Barnardo?

BARNARDO He. 5

FRANCISCO

  You come most carefully upon your hour.

BARNARDO

  'Tis now struck twelve. Get thee to bed, Francisco.

FRANCISCO

  For this relief much thanks. 'Tis bitter cold,

  And I am sick at heart.

BARNARDO Have you had quiet guard? 10

FRANCISCO Not a mouse stirring.

BARNARDO Well, good night.

  If you do meet Horatio and Marcellus,

  The rivals of my watch, bid them make haste.

Enter Horatio and Marcellus.

FRANCISCO

  I think I hear them.—Stand ho! Who is there? 15

HORATIO Friends to this ground.

17. **the Dane:** the Danish king
18. **Give:** God **give**
23. **what:** an interjection introducing a question
30. **of us:** by us
32. **watch:** keep watch during
34. **approve our eyes:** confirm our observation
43. **pole:** Polaris, the North Star
44. **his:** its

Sledded warriors: "sledded Polacks on the ice." (1.1.74)
From Cesare Vecellio, *Habiti antichi et moderni* (1598).

MARCELLUS And liegemen to the Dane.
FRANCISCO Give you good night.
MARCELLUS
   O farewell, honest ⟨soldier.⟩ Who hath relieved
     you?   20
FRANCISCO
   Barnardo hath my place. Give you good night.
                                             Francisco exits.
MARCELLUS Holla, Barnardo.
BARNARDO Say, what, is Horatio there?
HORATIO A piece of him.
BARNARDO
   Welcome, Horatio.—Welcome, good Marcellus.   25
HORATIO
   What, has this thing appeared again tonight?
BARNARDO I have seen nothing.
MARCELLUS
   Horatio says 'tis but our fantasy
   And will not let belief take hold of him
   Touching this dreaded sight twice seen of us.   30
   Therefore I have entreated him along
   With us to watch the minutes of this night,
   That, if again this apparition come,
   He may approve our eyes and speak to it.
HORATIO
   Tush, tush, 'twill not appear.   35
BARNARDO   Sit down awhile,
   And let us once again assail your ears,
   That are so fortified against our story,
   What we have two nights seen.
HORATIO   Well, sit we down,   40
   And let us hear Barnardo speak of this.
BARNARDO Last night of all,
   When yond same star that's westward from the pole
   Had made his course t' illume that part of heaven
   Where now it burns, Marcellus and myself,   45
   The bell then beating one—

51. harrows: torments (A harrow is a farm implement used to break up the ground.) See picture, below.

56. buried Denmark: the **buried** king of **Denmark**

57. sometimes: formerly

65. on 't: of it

67. sensible: attested by the senses; **avouch:** guarantee, testimony

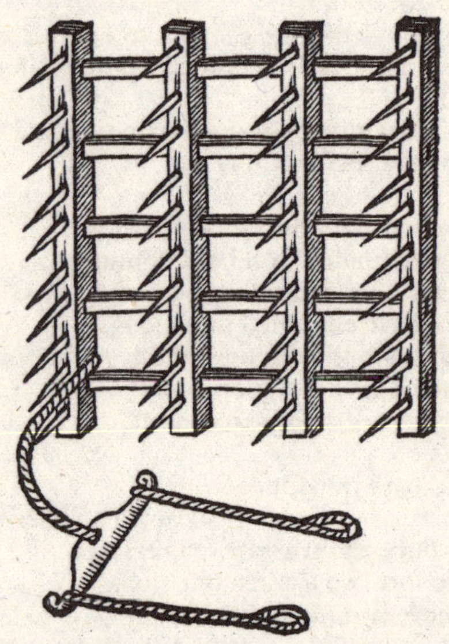

The harrow. (1.1.51; 1.5.21)
From Gervase Markham, *The English husbandman* (1613).

Enter Ghost.

MARCELLUS
  Peace, break thee off! Look where it comes again.
BARNARDO
  In the same figure like the King that's dead.
MARCELLUS, ⌜*to Horatio*⌝
  Thou art a scholar. Speak to it, Horatio.
BARNARDO
  Looks he not like the King? Mark it, Horatio.   50
HORATIO
  Most like. It ⟨harrows⟩ me with fear and wonder.
BARNARDO
  It would be spoke to.
MARCELLUS   Speak to it, Horatio.
HORATIO
  What art thou that usurp'st this time of night,
  Together with that fair and warlike form   55
  In which the majesty of buried Denmark
  Did sometimes march? By heaven, I charge thee,
    speak.
MARCELLUS
  It is offended.
BARNARDO   See, it stalks away.   60
HORATIO
  Stay! speak! speak! I charge thee, speak!
                                      Ghost exits.
MARCELLUS 'Tis gone and will not answer.
BARNARDO
  How now, Horatio, you tremble and look pale.
  Is not this something more than fantasy?
  What think you on 't?   65
HORATIO
  Before my God, I might not this believe
  Without the sensible and true avouch
  Of mine own eyes.

72. **Norway:** i.e., the king of **Norway** (the elder Fortinbras)

73. **parle:** parley, meeting

74. **smote:** attacked or, perhaps, defeated; **sledded Polacks:** Polish military riding in sleds (See picture, page 8.)

76. **jump:** exactly

78–79. **In what . . . opinion:** i.e., I cannot be precise, **but in** my general **opinion**

81. **Good now:** i.e., please, I entreat you; **tell . . . knows:** i.e., let him who **knows tell me**

82. **watch:** See note to line 14, above.

83. **toils:** causes to labor; wearies; **subject of the land:** i.e., subjects of the realm

85. **foreign mart:** international trade

86. **impress:** enforced service

88. **toward:** approaching, about to happen

95. **Thereto . . . pride:** stirred to do this (i.e., to dare King Hamlet to combat) by a proud desire to rival the Danish king

98. **sealed compact:** contract or covenant bearing a seal guaranteeing its authenticity

99. **law and heraldry:** the **law** of arms, regulating tournaments and battles

101. **stood seized of:** legally possessed

MARCELLUS   Is it not like the King?
HORATIO As thou art to thyself.   70
 Such was the very armor he had on
 When he the ambitious Norway combated.
 So frowned he once when, in an angry parle,
 He smote the sledded ⌈Polacks⌉ on the ice.
 'Tis strange.   75
MARCELLUS
 Thus twice before, and jump at this dead hour,
 With martial stalk hath he gone by our watch.
HORATIO
 In what particular thought to work I know not,
 But in the gross and scope of mine opinion
 This bodes some strange eruption to our state. 80
MARCELLUS
 Good now, sit down, and tell me, he that knows,
 Why this same strict and most observant watch
 So nightly toils the subject of the land,
 And ⟨why⟩ such daily ⟨cast⟩ of brazen cannon
 And foreign mart for implements of war, 85
 Why such impress of shipwrights, whose sore task
 Does not divide the Sunday from the week.
 What might be toward that this sweaty haste
 Doth make the night joint laborer with the day?
 Who is 't that can inform me?   90
HORATIO   That can I.
 At least the whisper goes so: our last king,
 Whose image even but now appeared to us,
 Was, as you know, by Fortinbras of Norway,
 Thereto pricked on by a most emulate pride, 95
 Dared to the combat; in which our valiant Hamlet
 (For so this side of our known world esteemed him)
 Did slay this Fortinbras, who by a sealed compact,
 Well ratified by law and heraldry,
 Did forfeit, with his life, all ⟨those⟩ his lands 100
 Which he stood seized of, to the conqueror.

102. **a moiety competent:** an appropriate por-
tion

103. **gagèd:** engaged, i.e., pledged; **which had:**
which would have

104. **inheritance:** possession

105. **comart:** perhaps, bargain

106. **carriage of the article designed:** i.e., mean-
ing carried by the agreement drawn up

108. **unimprovèd:** i.e., untested, unused

110. **Sharked up:** i.e., gathered indiscriminately

111. **For . . . to:** i.e., as means or provisions for

112. **stomach:** spirit of adventure

118. **head:** fountainhead, source

119. **posthaste:** extreme haste; **rummage:** bus-
tle, commotion

121. **Well may it sort:** i.e., it would thus be fitting

125. **palmy:** triumphant, worthy to bear the palm

127. **sheeted:** wrapped in their shrouds

129–30. **As stars . . . sun:** These lines are awk-
ward; probably some text has been lost. **Disasters:**
threatening signs

130. **moist star:** the moon, believed to be cold
and **moist** (See picture, page 26.)

131. **Upon . . . stands:** i.e., by **whose influence**
the sea is controlled **Neptune:** Roman god of the
sea

132. **doomsday:** i.e., the end of the world, Judg-
ment Day (See picture, page 68.)

133. **even . . . precurse:** the same kind of fore-
shadowing

134. **still:** always; **the fates:** that which is des-
tined to happen

135. **omen:** i.e., ominous event

Against the which a moiety competent
Was gagèd by our king, which had ⟨returned⟩
To the inheritance of Fortinbras
Had he been vanquisher, as, by the same comart   105
And carriage of the article ⌜designed,⌝
His fell to Hamlet. Now, sir, young Fortinbras,
Of unimprovèd mettle hot and full,
Hath in the skirts of Norway here and there
Sharked up a list of lawless resolutes   110
For food and diet to some enterprise
That hath a stomach in 't; which is no other
(As it doth well appear unto our state)
But to recover of us, by strong hand
And terms compulsatory, those foresaid lands   115
So by his father lost. And this, I take it,
Is the main motive of our preparations,
The source of this our watch, and the chief head
Of this posthaste and rummage in the land.

[BARNARDO
I think it be no other but e'en so.   120
Well may it sort that this portentous figure
Comes armèd through our watch so like the king
That was and is the question of these wars.

HORATIO
A mote it is to trouble the mind's eye.
In the most high and palmy state of Rome,   125
A little ere the mightiest Julius fell,
The graves stood tenantless, and the sheeted dead
Did squeak and gibber in the Roman streets;
As stars with trains of fire and dews of blood,
Disasters in the sun; and the moist star,   130
Upon whose influence Neptune's empire stands,
Was sick almost to doomsday with eclipse.
And even the like precurse of ⌜feared⌝ events,
As harbingers preceding still the fates
And prologue to the omen coming on,   135

137. **climatures:** geographic regions

138. **soft:** an exclamation requesting silence

139. **cross it:** meet it face to face, encounter it; block its path; **blast me:** shrivel or blight me, destroy me

146. **happily:** perhaps; or, fortunately

164. **fearful:** terrifying; **heard: heard** that

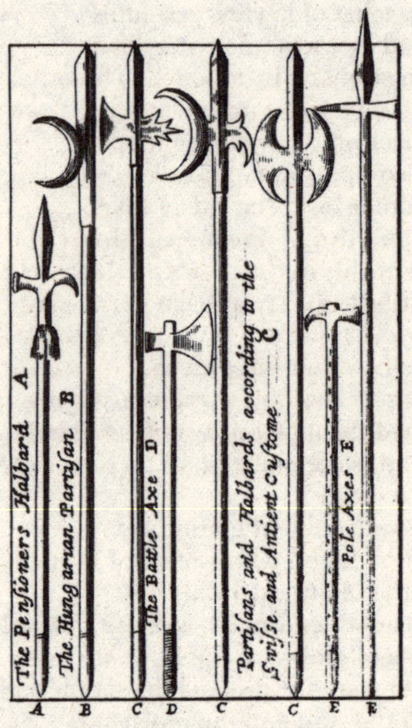

Partisans and other weapons. (1.1.153)
From Louis de Gaya, *A treatise of the arms . . .* (1678).

Have heaven and earth together demonstrated
Unto our climatures and countrymen.]

                    Enter Ghost.

But soft, behold! Lo, where it comes again!
I'll cross it though it blast me.—Stay, illusion!
                              It spreads his arms.
If thou hast any sound or use of voice,   140
Speak to me.
If there be any good thing to be done
That may to thee do ease and grace to me,
Speak to me.
If thou art privy to thy country's fate,   145
Which happily foreknowing may avoid,
O, speak!
Or if thou hast uphoarded in thy life
Extorted treasure in the womb of earth,
For which, they say, ⟨you⟩ spirits oft walk in death,   150
Speak of it.   *The cock crows.*
          Stay and speak!—Stop it, Marcellus.
MARCELLUS
  Shall I strike it with my partisan?
HORATIO Do, if it will not stand.
BARNARDO 'Tis here.   155
HORATIO 'Tis here.

                              ⟨*Ghost exits.*⟩

MARCELLUS 'Tis gone.
  We do it wrong, being so majestical,
  To offer it the show of violence,
  For it is as the air, invulnerable,   160
  And our vain blows malicious mockery.
BARNARDO
  It was about to speak when the cock crew.
HORATIO
  And then it started like a guilty thing
  Upon a fearful summons. I have heard

165. **trumpet to:** trumpeter who proclaims the arrival of

169. **extravagant . . . spirit:** a supernatural being who has wandered out of **his confine** (line 170) or place of confinement; **hies:** hurries

171. **made probation:** demonstrated

173. **'gainst:** just before

177. **strike:** destroy through malign influence

178. **takes:** puts under a magic spell

179. **gracious:** full of grace, blessed

181. **russet:** coarse homespun fabric in gray or reddish brown

A cock. (1.1.162, 165, 172)
From Konrad Gesner, *Historiae animalium . . .* (1585–1604).

The cock, that is the trumpet to the morn, 165
Doth with his lofty and shrill-sounding throat
Awake the god of day, and at his warning,
Whether in sea or fire, in earth or air,
Th' extravagant and erring spirit hies
To his confine, and of the truth herein 170
This present object made probation.

MARCELLUS
It faded on the crowing of the cock.
Some say that ever 'gainst that season comes
Wherein our Savior's birth is celebrated,
This bird of dawning singeth all night long; 175
And then, they say, no spirit dare stir abroad,
The nights are wholesome; then no planets strike,
No fairy takes, nor witch hath power to charm,
So hallowed and so gracious is that time.

HORATIO
So have I heard and do in part believe it. 180
But look, the morn in russet mantle clad
Walks o'er the dew of yon high eastward hill.
Break we our watch up, and by my advice
Let us impart what we have seen tonight
Unto young Hamlet; for, upon my life, 185
This spirit, dumb to us, will speak to him.
Do you consent we shall acquaint him with it
As needful in our loves, fitting our duty?

MARCELLUS
Let's do 't, I pray, and I this morning know
Where we shall find him most convenient. 190

They exit.

1.2 In an audience chamber in Elsinore, Claudius, the new king of Denmark, holds court. After thanking his courtiers for their recent support, he dispatches ambassadors to Norway to halt a threatened attack from Fortinbras. He gives Laertes permission to return to France but denies Hamlet's request to return to the university in Wittenberg. Hamlet, mourning for his father's death, is left alone to vent his despair at what he regards as his mother's all too hasty marriage to his uncle, Claudius. The audience learns that the marriage took place "within a month" of the former king's death.

Horatio, Barnardo, and Marcellus arrive and tell Hamlet about the Ghost. Hamlet makes plans to join them that night.

---

0 SD. **Flourish:** a trumpet sound signaling a royal entry

8. **our sometime sister:** my former sister-in-law (Claudius uses the royal "we" throughout, when he is speaking as king.)

9. **jointress:** a woman who owns property jointly with her husband

11. **With . . . eye:** as if smiling **with** one **eye** and crying **with** the other

13. **equal scale:** a perfectly balanced **scale** (See picture, page 22.) **dole:** grief

17. **that you know: that** which **you** already **know**

18. **a weak . . . worth:** i.e., a low opinion of my ability

(continued)

⟨Scene 2⟩

*Flourish. Enter Claudius, King of Denmark, Gertrude the
Queen, ⌜the⌝ Council, as Polonius, and his son Laertes,
Hamlet, with others, ⌜among them Voltemand and
Cornelius.⌝*

KING
 Though yet of Hamlet our dear brother's death
 The memory be green, and that it us befitted
 To bear our hearts in grief, and our whole kingdom
 To be contracted in one brow of woe,
 Yet so far hath discretion fought with nature   5
 That we with wisest sorrow think on him
 Together with remembrance of ourselves.
 Therefore our sometime sister, now our queen,
 Th' imperial jointress to this warlike state,
 Have we (as 'twere with a defeated joy,   10
 With an auspicious and a dropping eye,
 With mirth in funeral and with dirge in marriage,
 In equal scale weighing delight and dole)
 Taken to wife. Nor have we herein barred
 Your better wisdoms, which have freely gone   15
 With this affair along. For all, our thanks.
 Now follows that you know. Young Fortinbras,
 Holding a weak supposal of our worth
 Or thinking by our late dear brother's death
 Our state to be disjoint and out of frame,   20
 Colleaguèd with this dream of his advantage,
 He hath not failed to pester us with message
 Importing the surrender of those lands
 Lost by his father, with all bonds of law,
 To our most valiant brother—so much for him.   25
 Now for ourself and for this time of meeting.
 Thus much the business is: we have here writ
 To Norway, uncle of young Fortinbras,
 Who, impotent and bedrid, scarcely hears

21. **Colleaguèd:** i.e., in league with; **advantage:** i.e., superior position

29. **impotent:** helpless; **bedrid:** confined to bed

31. **gait:** course

31–33. **in that . . . subject:** i.e., since the troops and supplies are drawn from Norway's own subjects

37. **To business:** to negotiate

38. **these . . . articles:** this detailed account

39. **let . . . duty:** i.e., **let your** speedy departure take the place of ceremonious leave-taking

41. **nothing:** not at all

44. **Dane:** Danish king

45. **lose your voice:** i.e., waste your words

48. **native:** naturally connected

58. **leave and pardon:** permission to depart

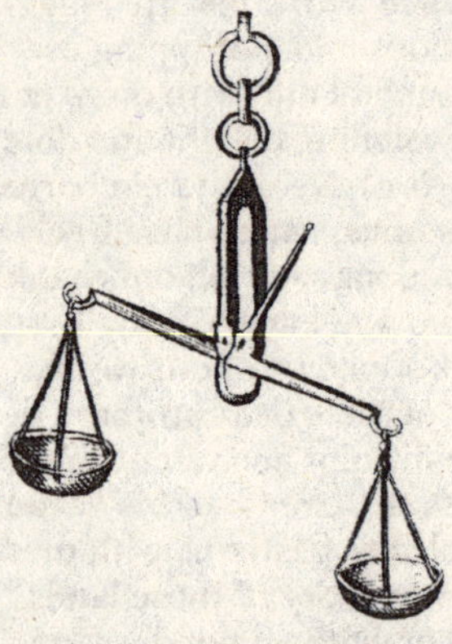

A balance. (1.2.13; 4.5.180–81)
From Silvestro Pietrasanta, . . . *Symbola heroica* . . . (1682).

Of this his nephew's purpose, to suppress   30
His further gait herein, in that the levies,
The lists, and full proportions are all made
Out of his subject; and we here dispatch
You, good Cornelius, and you, Voltemand,
For bearers of this greeting to old Norway,   35
Giving to you no further personal power
To business with the King more than the scope
Of these dilated articles allow.
                       ⌜*Giving them a paper.*⌝
Farewell, and let your haste commend your duty.

CORNELIUS/VOLTEMAND
In that and all things will we show our duty.   40

KING
We doubt it nothing. Heartily farewell.
                 ⟨*Voltemand and Cornelius exit.*⟩
And now, Laertes, what's the news with you?
You told us of some suit. What is 't, Laertes?
You cannot speak of reason to the Dane
And lose your voice. What wouldst thou beg,   45
    Laertes,
That shall not be my offer, not thy asking?
The head is not more native to the heart,
The hand more instrumental to the mouth,
Than is the throne of Denmark to thy father.   50
What wouldst thou have, Laertes?

LAERTES   My dread lord,
Your leave and favor to return to France,
From whence though willingly I came to Denmark
To show my duty in your coronation,   55
Yet now I must confess, that duty done,
My thoughts and wishes bend again toward France
And bow them to your gracious leave and pardon.

KING
Have you your father's leave? What says Polonius?

60–61. **wrung . . . petition:** i.e., finally persuaded me to allow him

62. **Upon . . . consent:** i.e., I reluctantly agreed to his wishes

64–65. **Take . . . will:** a courteous formula giving Laertes permission to return to France

66. **cousin:** kinsman

67. **more than kin:** i.e., twice related: uncle/nephew and "father"/"son"; **less than kind:** i.e., in a less-than-natural relationship

69. **in the sun:** a pun on **sun**/*son*

70. **nighted color:** i.e., black (mourning) clothing

71. **Denmark:** the king of Denmark

72. **vailèd lids:** i.e., lowered eyes

74. **common:** belonging to all human beings

78. **particular:** special, personal

80–86. **'Tis . . . truly:** i.e., it is not only my black clothes, my sighs and tears, my downcast face, and other outward signs of grief that indicate my real feelings

87. **play:** perform as on a stage

POLONIUS
  Hath, my lord, [wrung from me my slow leave   60
  By laborsome petition, and at last
  Upon his will I sealed my hard consent.]
  I do beseech you give him leave to go.
KING
  Take thy fair hour, Laertes. Time be thine,
  And thy best graces spend it at thy will.—   65
  But now, my cousin Hamlet and my son—
HAMLET, ⌜*aside*⌝
  A little more than kin and less than kind.
KING
  How is it that the clouds still hang on you?
HAMLET
  Not so, my lord; I am too much in the sun.
QUEEN
  Good Hamlet, cast thy nighted color off,   70
  And let thine eye look like a friend on Denmark.
  Do not forever with thy vailèd lids
  Seek for thy noble father in the dust.
  Thou know'st 'tis common; all that lives must die,
  Passing through nature to eternity.   75
HAMLET
  Ay, madam, it is common.
QUEEN   If it be,
  Why seems it so particular with thee?
HAMLET
  "Seems," madam? Nay, it is. I know not "seems."
  'Tis not alone my inky cloak, ⟨good⟩ mother,   80
  Nor customary suits of solemn black,
  Nor windy suspiration of forced breath,
  No, nor the fruitful river in the eye,
  Nor the dejected havior of the visage,
  Together with all forms, moods, ⌜shapes⌝ of grief,   85
  That can ⟨denote⟩ me truly. These indeed "seem,"
  For they are actions that a man might play;

96. **obsequious:** dutiful (Claudius seems to be playing on the related word *obsequy,* funeral service.)

97. **obstinate condolement:** sorrow that refuses comfort

99. **incorrect to heaven:** uncorrected by the divine will

101. **simple:** i.e., dull

103. **As . . . sense: As** anything that is **the most** familiar object of perception

108. **still:** always, habitually

109. **corse:** corpse (The **first corse,** according to Genesis, was Abel, murdered by his brother, Cain. See Genesis 4.1–16, and picture, page 184.)

111. **unprevailing:** futile, useless

113. **most immediate:** next in line of succession

116. **impart toward:** give to

118. **retrograde:** opposite, contrary

119. **bend you:** perhaps, incline or dispose yourself

"The moist star." (1.1.130)
From Laurentius Wolffgang Woyt,
. . . *Emblematischer Parnassus* . . . (1728–30).

But I have that within which passes show,
These but the trappings and the suits of woe.

KING
'Tis sweet and commendable in your nature, Hamlet,   90
To give these mourning duties to your father.
But you must know your father lost a father,
That father lost, lost his, and the survivor bound
In filial obligation for some term   95
To do obsequious sorrow. But to persever
In obstinate condolement is a course
Of impious stubbornness. 'Tis unmanly grief.
It shows a will most incorrect to heaven,
A heart unfortified, ⟨a⟩ mind impatient,   100
An understanding simple and unschooled.
For what we know must be and is as common
As any the most vulgar thing to sense,
Why should we in our peevish opposition
Take it to heart? Fie, 'tis a fault to heaven,   105
A fault against the dead, a fault to nature,
To reason most absurd, whose common theme
Is death of fathers, and who still hath cried,
From the first corse till he that died today,
"This must be so." We pray you, throw to earth   110
This unprevailing woe and think of us
As of a father; for let the world take note,
You are the most immediate to our throne,
And with no less nobility of love
Than that which dearest father bears his son   115
Do I impart toward you. For your intent
In going back to school in Wittenberg,
It is most retrograde to our desire,
And we beseech you, bend you to remain
Here in the cheer and comfort of our eye,   120
Our chiefest courtier, cousin, and our son.

129. **jocund health:** merry toast

130. **tell:** count out; report

131. **rouse:** deep drink; **bruit again:** i.e., echo

132. **earthly thunder:** the sound of **the great cannon** (line 130)

133. **sullied:** stained, defiled (The Second Quarto [Q2] reads "sallied," an alternate spelling for "sullied"; the Folio [F] reads "solid.")

136. **canon:** divine law

143. **that was to this:** in comparison **to this** king

144. **Hyperion to a satyr:** i.e., like the sun god as compared to **a** goatlike **satyr** (See pictures, pages 32 and 192.)

145. **might not beteem:** would not allow

151. **or ere:** before

Niobe. (1.2.153)
From Giovanni Battista Cavalleriis,
Antiquarum statuarum . . . (1585–94).

QUEEN
    Let not thy mother lose her prayers, Hamlet.
    I pray thee, stay with us. Go not to Wittenberg.
HAMLET
    I shall in all my best obey you, madam.
KING
    Why, 'tis a loving and a fair reply.   125
    Be as ourself in Denmark.—Madam, come.
    This gentle and unforced accord of Hamlet
    Sits smiling to my heart, in grace whereof
    No jocund health that Denmark drinks today
    But the great cannon to the clouds shall tell,   130
    And the King's rouse the heaven shall bruit again,
    Respeaking earthly thunder. Come away.
                Flourish. All but Hamlet exit.
HAMLET
    O, that this too, too sullied flesh would melt,
    Thaw, and resolve itself into a dew,
    Or that the Everlasting had not fixed   135
    His canon 'gainst ⟨self-slaughter!⟩ O God, God,
    How ⟨weary,⟩ stale, flat, and unprofitable
    Seem to me all the uses of this world!
    Fie on 't, ah fie! 'Tis an unweeded garden
    That grows to seed. Things rank and gross in nature   140
    Possess it merely. That it should come ⟨to this:⟩
    But two months dead—nay, not so much, not two.
    So excellent a king, that was to this
    Hyperion to a satyr; so loving to my mother
    That he might not beteem the winds of heaven   145
    Visit her face too roughly. Heaven and earth,
    Must I remember? Why, she ⟨would⟩ hang on him
    As if increase of appetite had grown
    By what it fed on. And yet, within a month
    (Let me not think on 't; frailty, thy name is woman!),   150
    A little month, or ere those shoes were old
    With which she followed my poor father's body,

153. **Niobe:** In Greek mythology, **Niobe,** so grief-stricken at the loss of her children that she could not cease crying, was transformed into a stone from which water continually flowed. (See picture, page 28.)

154. **wants . . . reason:** lacks the ability to reason

158. **Hercules:** in Greek mythology, a hero of extraordinary strength and courage (See picture, page 98.)

160. **Had . . . eyes:** i.e., had stopped turning **her eyes** red

161. **post:** rush (as in riding a post-horse)

162. **incestuous:** Hamlet calls the marriage of his mother and his uncle "incestuous"—i.e., a violation of the laws against intercourse between close kin. The Ghost will also make this charge (1.5.49). Other members of the Danish court seem to see the marriage of Gertrude and Claudius as legal and legitimate. Debates about the incestuousness of a marriage between a widow and her dead husband's brother were heated in the sixteenth century (especially during the divorce trial of Henry VIII and Catherine of Aragon). The Bible gives conflicting commands about such marriages. How one is to view the marriage of Gertrude and Claudius is an ongoing focus of interest for students of *Hamlet.*

169. **I'll . . . you:** i.e., instead of your calling yourself my **servant,** we'll call each other **friend**

170. **what . . . from: what** are **you** doing away **from**

Like Niobe, all tears—why she, ⟨even she⟩
(O God, a beast that wants discourse of reason
Would have mourned longer!), married with my   155
    uncle,
My father's brother, but no more like my father
Than I to Hercules. Within a month,
Ere yet the salt of most unrighteous tears
Had left the flushing in her gallèd eyes,   160
She married. O, most wicked speed, to post
With such dexterity to incestuous sheets!
It is not, nor it cannot come to good.
But break, my heart, for I must hold my tongue.

    Enter Horatio, Marcellus, and Barnardo.

HORATIO   Hail to your Lordship.   165
HAMLET   I am glad to see you well.
    Horatio—or I do forget myself!
HORATIO
    The same, my lord, and your poor servant ever.
HAMLET
    Sir, my good friend. I'll change that name with you.
    And what make you from Wittenberg, Horatio?—   170
    Marcellus?
MARCELLUS   My good lord.
HAMLET
    I am very glad to see you. ⌜*To Barnardo.*⌝ Good
    even, sir.—
    But what, in faith, make you from Wittenberg?   175
HORATIO
    A truant disposition, good my lord.
HAMLET
    I would not hear your enemy say so,
    Nor shall you do my ear that violence
    To make it truster of your own report
    Against yourself. I know you are no truant.   180
    But what is your affair in Elsinore?
    We'll teach you to drink ⟨deep⟩ ere you depart.

186. **hard upon:** soon after

188. **coldly:** served cold (as leftovers)

189. **dearest:** most grievous; bitterest

194. **goodly:** admirable, excellent

201. **Season your admiration:** i.e., control your astonishment

202. **attent:** attentive; **deliver:** narrate, describe

The sun god in his chariot.
(1.1.167; 1.2.144; 3.2.176; 3.4.66)
From Vincenzo Cartari, *Le vere e noue imagini . . .* (1615).

HORATIO
    My lord, I came to see your father's funeral.
HAMLET
    I prithee, do not mock me, fellow student.
    I think it was to ⟨see⟩ my mother's wedding.   185
HORATIO
    Indeed, my lord, it followed hard upon.
HAMLET
    Thrift, thrift, Horatio. The funeral baked meats
    Did coldly furnish forth the marriage tables.
    Would I had met my dearest foe in heaven
    Or ever I had seen that day, Horatio!   190
    My father—methinks I see my father.
HORATIO
    Where, my lord?
HAMLET   In my mind's eye, Horatio.
HORATIO
    I saw him once. He was a goodly king.
HAMLET
    He was a man. Take him for all in all,   195
    I shall not look upon his like again.
HORATIO
    My lord, I think I saw him yesternight.
HAMLET Saw who?
HORATIO
    My lord, the King your father.
HAMLET   The King my father?   200
HORATIO
    Season your admiration for a while
    With an attent ear, till I may deliver
    Upon the witness of these gentlemen
    This marvel to you.
HAMLET   For God's love, let me hear!   205
HORATIO
    Two nights together had these gentlemen,
    Marcellus and Barnardo, on their watch,

210. **at point exactly, cap-à-pie:** at every **point,** from head to foot (See picture, below.)

213. **oppressed and fear-surprisèd:** terrified

214. **truncheon's:** A truncheon is a short staff (here carried as a symbol of authority). **distilled:** melted, dissolved

215. **the act of fear: the** action **of fear** upon them

227. **methought:** it seemed to me

228–29. **did address . . . speak:** i.e., began to move **as** if **it would speak**

230. **even then:** at that very moment

"Armed at point exactly, cap-à-pie." (1.2.210)
From Henry Peacham, *Minerua Britanna* [1612].

In the dead waste and middle of the night,
Been thus encountered: a figure like your father,
Armed at point exactly, cap-à-pie,   210
Appears before them and with solemn march
Goes slow and stately by them. Thrice he walked
By their oppressed and fear-surprisèd eyes
Within his truncheon's length, whilst they, distilled
Almost to jelly with the act of fear,   215
Stand dumb and speak not to him. This to me
In dreadful secrecy impart they did,
And I with them the third night kept the watch,
⌈Where, as⌉ they had delivered, both in time,
Form of the thing (each word made true and good),   220
The apparition comes. I knew your father;
These hands are not more like.
HAMLET   But where was this?
MARCELLUS
My lord, upon the platform where we watch.
HAMLET
Did you not speak to it?   225
HORATIO   My lord, I did,
But answer made it none. Yet once methought
It lifted up its head and did address
Itself to motion, like as it would speak;
But even then the morning cock crew loud,   230
And at the sound it shrunk in haste away
And vanished from our sight.
HAMLET   'Tis very strange.
HORATIO
As I do live, my honored lord, 'tis true.
And we did think it writ down in our duty   235
To let you know of it.
HAMLET Indeed, sirs, but this troubles me.
Hold you the watch tonight?
ALL   We do, my lord.
HAMLET
Armed, say you?   240

245. **beaver:** frontpiece of a helmet (See picture, below.)
248. **red:** a natural healthy color
252. **would:** wish
255. **tell:** count
259. **grizzled:** gray

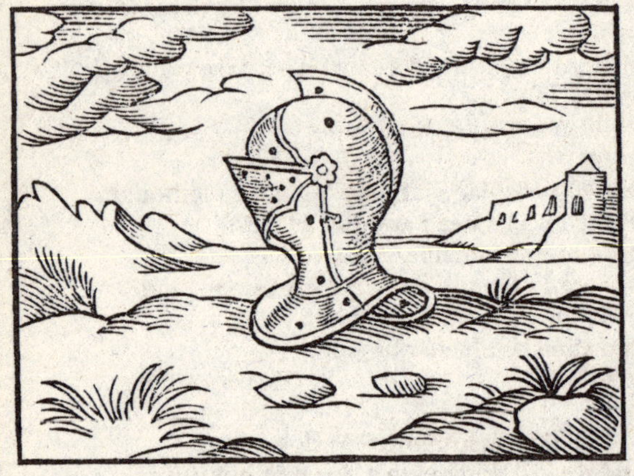

Helmet with beaver down. (1.2.245)
From Henry Peacham, *Minerua Britanna* [1612].

ALL   Armed, my lord.
HAMLET   From top to toe?
ALL My lord, from head to foot.
HAMLET Then saw you not his face?
HORATIO
  O, yes, my lord, he wore his beaver up.   245
HAMLET What, looked he frowningly?
HORATIO
  A countenance more in sorrow than in anger.
HAMLET Pale or red?
HORATIO
  Nay, very pale.
HAMLET   And fixed his eyes upon you?   250
HORATIO
  Most constantly.
HAMLET   I would I had been there.
HORATIO It would have much amazed you.
HAMLET Very like. Stayed it long?
HORATIO
  While one with moderate haste might tell a   255
    hundred.
BARNARDO/MARCELLUS Longer, longer.
HORATIO
  Not when I saw 't.
HAMLET   His beard was grizzled, no?
HORATIO
  It was as I have seen it in his life,   260
  A sable silvered.
HAMLET   I will watch ⌜tonight.⌝
  Perchance 'twill walk again.
HORATIO   I warrant it will.
HAMLET
  If it assume my noble father's person,   265
  I'll speak to it, though hell itself should gape
  And bid me hold my peace. I pray you all,
  If you have hitherto concealed this sight,

269. **tenable:** withheld, kept secret

278. **doubt . . . play:** suspect some unfair or treacherous dealing

280. **o'erwhelm:** cover, bury

1.3 In Polonius's chambers, Laertes says good-bye to his sister, Ophelia, and tells her not to trust Hamlet's promises of love. Polonius joins them, sends Laertes off, then echoes Laertes's warnings to Ophelia, finally ordering her not to see Hamlet again.

---

3. **convey is assistant:** transport is available

6. **For:** as **for; trifling . . . favor:** i.e., his flirting or dallying with you

7. **fashion:** a temporary enthusiasm; **toy in blood:** amorous flirtation

8. **in . . . nature: in the** early days **of** its prime

9. **Forward:** ardent, eager

10. **perfume . . . minute:** that which makes the moment sweet and fills it with pleasure

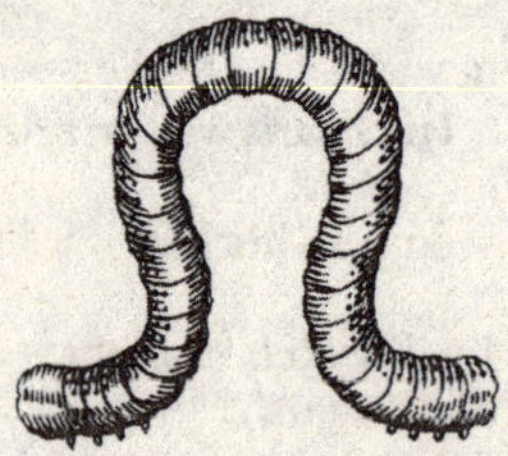

A cankerworm. (1.3.43)
From John Johnstone, *Opera aliquot . . .* (1650–62).

Let it be tenable in your silence still;
And whatsomever else shall hap tonight, 270
Give it an understanding but no tongue.
I will requite your loves. So fare you well.
Upon the platform, 'twixt eleven and twelve,
I'll visit you.

ALL   Our duty to your Honor. 275

HAMLET
Your loves, as mine to you. Farewell.

          ⌜*All but Hamlet*⌝ *exit.*

My father's spirit—in arms! All is not well.
I doubt some foul play. Would the night were come!
Till then, sit still, my soul. ⟨Foul⟩ deeds will rise,
Though all the earth o'erwhelm them, to men's 280
    eyes.

          He exits.

⟨Scene 3⟩

Enter Laertes and Ophelia, his sister.

LAERTES
My necessaries are embarked. Farewell.
And, sister, as the winds give benefit
And convey ⟨is⟩ assistant, do not sleep,
But let me hear from you.

OPHELIA   Do you doubt that? 5

LAERTES
For Hamlet, and the trifling of his favor,
Hold it a fashion and a toy in blood,
A violet in the youth of primy nature,
Forward, not permanent, sweet, not lasting,
The perfume and suppliance of a minute, 10
No more.

OPHELIA   No more but so?

LAERTES   Think it no more.

14–15. **nature . . . bulk:** i.e., a growing human **does not** increase only in strength and size

15. **this temple:** the body; **waxes:** grows larger

17. **withal:** at the same time

18. **soil:** moral stain; **cautel:** deceit

20. **greatness:** high rank

21. **birth:** noble lineage

23. **Carve:** i.e., choose

26. **voice and yielding:** judgment and consent; **that body:** i.e., the Danish state

31. **give his saying deed:** put his words into action

32. **withal:** along with

34. **credent:** gullible; **list:** listen to

35–36. **your chaste . . . importunity:** i.e., surrender **your** chastity **to his** uncontrolled pleading

38. **keep . . . affection:** i.e., hold yourself back from actions your feelings would lead you into (The metaphor is from warfare, and is continued in the next line.)

40. **chariest:** most careful; **maid:** maiden, virgin

42. **strokes:** blows

43. **The canker . . . spring:** i.e., the cankerworm destroys the early spring blossoms (See picture, page 38.)

44. **buttons be disclosed:** buds have opened

46. **Contagious:** noxious, pernicious; **blastments:** withering blights

48. **Youth . . . else near:** i.e., **youth** loses self-control even without a tempter

For nature, crescent, does not grow alone
In thews and ⟨bulk,⟩ but, as this temple waxes,   15
The inward service of the mind and soul
Grows wide withal. Perhaps he loves you now,
And now no soil nor cautel doth besmirch
The virtue of his will; but you must fear,
His greatness weighed, his will is not his own,   20
⟨For he himself is subject to his birth.⟩
He may not, as unvalued persons do,
Carve for himself, for on his choice depends
The safety and ⌜the⌝ health of this whole state.
And therefore must his choice be circumscribed   25
Unto the voice and yielding of that body
Whereof he is the head. Then, if he says he loves
    you,
It fits your wisdom so far to believe it
As he in his particular act and place   30
May give his saying deed, which is no further
Than the main voice of Denmark goes withal.
Then weigh what loss your honor may sustain
If with too credent ear you list his songs
Or lose your heart or your chaste treasure open   35
To his unmastered importunity.
Fear it, Ophelia; fear it, my dear sister,
And keep you in the rear of your affection,
Out of the shot and danger of desire.
The chariest maid is prodigal enough   40
If she unmask her beauty to the moon.
Virtue itself 'scapes not calumnious strokes.
The canker galls the infants of the spring
Too oft before their buttons be disclosed,
And, in the morn and liquid dew of youth,   45
Contagious blastments are most imminent.
Be wary, then; best safety lies in fear.
Youth to itself rebels, though none else near.

OPHELIA
I shall the effect of this good lesson keep

51. **ungracious:** ungodly

52–54. **Show me . . . treads:** i.e., **show me** how to live a strict and virtuous life while he **himself** follows a life of self-indulgence (See Matthew 7.13–14.)

55. **recks not his own rede:** does **not** heed **his own** advice

58. **A double . . . grace:** i.e., to receive one's father's **blessing** twice is a **double** favor from heaven

59. **Occasion smiles upon:** i.e., opportunity (personified as **Occasion**) kindly grants me; **leave:** leave-taking

65. **Look thou character:** see that you inscribe

66. **unproportioned:** immoderate; **his:** its

67. **familiar:** friendly; **vulgar:** i.e., indiscriminate

71. **unfledged courage:** spirited youngster

74. **voice:** approval, support

75. **censure:** synonymous with **judgment**

76. **habit:** clothing

80. **Are . . . in that:** This puzzling line reads, in Q2, "Or of a most select and generous, chiefe in that"; in F it reads, "Are of a most . . . cheff in that." The line seems to mean, generally: the French show their refinement chiefly in the way they choose their apparel.

As watchman to my heart. But, good my brother, 50
Do not, as some ungracious pastors do,
Show me the steep and thorny way to heaven,
Whiles, ⟨like⟩ a puffed and reckless libertine,
Himself the primrose path of dalliance treads
And recks not his own rede. 55
LAERTES   O, fear me not.

Enter Polonius.

I stay too long. But here my father comes.
A double blessing is a double grace.
Occasion smiles upon a second leave.
POLONIUS
Yet here, Laertes? Aboard, aboard, for shame! 60
The wind sits in the shoulder of your sail,
And you are stayed for. There, my blessing with
 thee.
And these few precepts in thy memory
Look thou character. Give thy thoughts no tongue, 65
Nor any unproportioned thought his act.
Be thou familiar, but by no means vulgar.
Those friends thou hast, and their adoption tried,
Grapple them unto thy soul with hoops of steel,
But do not dull thy palm with entertainment 70
Of each new-hatched, unfledged courage. Beware
Of entrance to a quarrel, but, being in,
Bear 't that th' opposèd may beware of thee.
Give every man thy ear, but few thy voice.
Take each man's censure, but reserve thy judgment. 75
Costly thy habit as thy purse can buy,
But not expressed in fancy (rich, not gaudy),
For the apparel oft proclaims the man,
And they in France of the best rank and station
⟨Are⟩ of a most select and generous chief in that. 80
Neither a borrower nor a lender ⟨be,⟩
For ⟨loan⟩ oft loses both itself and friend,

83. **husbandry:** management of one's money

89. **invests:** i.e., presses upon (Many editors prefer the Folio's "invites.") **tend:** i.e., await you

98. **Marry:** a mild oath derived from "By the Virgin Mary"; **bethought:** considered

103. **so 'tis put on me:** so I have been told

108–9. **tenders . . . to me:** offers **to me of his affection**

110. **green:** gullible; inexperienced

111. **Unsifted in:** i.e., naive about

Woodcocks in a springe. (1.3.124; 5.2.336)
From Henry Parrot, *Laquei ridiculosi . . .* (1613).

And borrowing ⟨dulls the⟩ edge of husbandry.
This above all: to thine own self be true,
And it must follow, as the night the day,   85
Thou canst not then be false to any man.
Farewell. My blessing season this in thee.

LAERTES
Most humbly do I take my leave, my lord.

POLONIUS
The time invests you. Go, your servants tend.

LAERTES
Farewell, Ophelia, and remember well   90
What I have said to you.

OPHELIA   'Tis in my memory locked,
And you yourself shall keep the key of it.

LAERTES   Farewell.   *Laertes exits.*

POLONIUS
What is 't, Ophelia, he hath said to you?   95

OPHELIA
So please you, something touching the Lord
    Hamlet.

POLONIUS   Marry, well bethought.
'Tis told me he hath very oft of late
Given private time to you, and you yourself   100
Have of your audience been most free and
    bounteous.
If it be so (as so 'tis put on me,
And that in way of caution), I must tell you
You do not understand yourself so clearly   105
As it behooves my daughter and your honor.
What is between you? Give me up the truth.

OPHELIA
He hath, my lord, of late made many tenders
Of his affection to me.

POLONIUS
Affection, puh! You speak like a green girl   110
Unsifted in such perilous circumstance.
Do you believe his "tenders," as you call them?

115. **tenders:** coins that should be "legal tender" but are not because they **are not sterling** (line 116)

116. **Tender yourself more dearly:** regard yourself at a higher rate

117–18. **not to . . . thus: not** to run **the phrase,** as if it were a horse, so hard that it becomes winded

118. **tender me a fool:** (1) show yourself to **me** as **a fool;** (2) make **me** look like **a fool;** (3) present me with a grandchild (The word "fool" was used as a term of endearment for a child.)

122. **given . . . to:** supported, backed up

124. **springes:** snares; **woodcocks:** birds thought to be stupid and easily captured (See picture, page 44.)

127–28. **extinct . . . a-making:** i.e., **both** the **light** and the **heat** of such **blazes** dying out almost as soon as they appear

131. **Set . . . rate:** i.e., place a greater value on your conversation

132. **command to parle:** summons to speak (**Entreatments** and **parle** usually referred to military negotiations for truce or surrender.)

135. **In few:** i.e., in short

136–40. **brokers . . . beguile:** See longer note, page 289. **brokers:** agents **investments:** clothing, vestments **implorators:** solicitors **Breathing:** speaking **beguile:** deceive; entice (**Bawds** was suggested by Lewis Theobald; Q2 and F read "bonds.")

142. **slander:** disgrace by misusing

OPHELIA
I do not know, my lord, what I should think.
POLONIUS
Marry, I will teach you. Think yourself a baby
That you have ta'en these tenders for true pay,   115
Which are not sterling. Tender yourself more dearly,
Or (not to crack the wind of the poor phrase,
⌜Running⌝ it thus) you'll tender me a fool.
OPHELIA
My lord, he hath importuned me with love
In honorable fashion—   120
POLONIUS
Ay, "fashion" you may call it. Go to, go to!
OPHELIA
And hath given countenance to his speech, my lord,
With almost all the holy vows of heaven.
POLONIUS
Ay, ⟨springes⟩ to catch woodcocks. I do know,
When the blood burns, how prodigal the soul   125
Lends the tongue vows. These blazes, daughter,
Giving more light than heat, extinct in both
Even in their promise as it is a-making,
You must not take for fire. From this time
Be something scanter of your maiden presence.   130
Set your entreatments at a higher rate
Than a command to parle. For Lord Hamlet,
Believe so much in him that he is young,
And with a larger ⟨tether⟩ may he walk
Than may be given you. In few, Ophelia,   135
Do not believe his vows, for they are brokers,
Not of that dye which their investments show,
But mere ⟨implorators⟩ of unholy suits,
Breathing like sanctified and pious ⌜bawds⌝
The better to ⟨beguile.⟩ This is for all: 140
I would not, in plain terms, from this time forth
Have you so slander any moment leisure

1.4   While Claudius drinks away the night, Hamlet, Horatio, and Marcellus are visited by the Ghost. It signals to Hamlet. Hamlet's friends try to stop his following the Ghost, but Hamlet will not be held back.

------

1. **shrewdly:** keenly, intensely
2. **eager:** sharp (from the French *aigre*)
7. **held his wont:** has been accustomed
7 SD. **pieces:** i.e., **pieces** of artillery (to create the sound of the **great cannon** promised by Claudius at 1.2.130)
9. **doth . . . rouse:** stays awake tonight drinking
10. **Keeps wassail:** carouses; **upspring:** a German dance, particularly associated with heavy drinking
11. **Rhenish:** Rhine wine
13. **triumph of his pledge:** his feat of emptying the cup in one draft
17. **to the manner born:** destined through birth to accept this **custom**
20. **taxed of:** censured by
21. **clepe:** call; **swinish phrase:** Proverbial: "as drunk as a pig"
22. **addition:** titles of honor

As to give words or talk with the Lord Hamlet.
Look to 't, I charge you. Come your ways.
OPHELIA I shall obey, my lord.   145

They exit.

⌐Scene 4⌐

Enter Hamlet, Horatio, and Marcellus.

HAMLET
The air bites shrewdly; it is very cold.
HORATIO
It is ⟨a⟩ nipping and an eager air.
HAMLET What hour now?
HORATIO I think it lacks of twelve.
MARCELLUS No, it is struck.   5
HORATIO
Indeed, I heard it not. It then draws near the season
Wherein the spirit held his wont to walk.
      A flourish of trumpets and two pieces goes off.
What does this mean, my lord?
HAMLET
The King doth wake tonight and takes his rouse,
Keeps wassail, and the swagg'ring upspring reels;   10
And, as he drains his draughts of Rhenish down,
The kettledrum and trumpet thus bray out
The triumph of his pledge.
HORATIO Is it a custom?
HAMLET Ay, marry, is 't,   15
But, to my mind, though I am native here
And to the manner born, it is a custom
More honored in the breach than the observance.
[This heavy-headed ⌐revel⌐ east and west
Makes us traduced and taxed of other nations.   20
They clepe us drunkards and with swinish phrase
Soil our addition. And, indeed, it takes

25. **pith and marrow:** essence; **attribute:** reputation

26. **So:** in the same way; **oft it chances in:** it often happens with

27. **mole of nature:** natural fault

30. **o'ergrowth . . . complexion:** i.e., the increase of one of the four humors, which were thought to control man's physical and emotional being

31. **pales and forts:** palings and ramparts

32. **o'erleavens:** radically changes

33. **plausive:** pleasing

35. **nature's livery:** i.e., something by which one is marked by nature (**as in their birth** [line 28], or **the o'ergrowth of some complexion** [line 30]); **fortune's star:** something determined by luck (as in the accidental forming of **some habit** [line 32])

36. **His virtues else:** the other **virtues** of **these men** (line 33)

37. **undergo:** experience

39–41. **The dram . . . scandal:** These difficult lines have never been satisfactorily repaired, but the general sense may be that a small amount **of evil** makes even something admirable seem disreputable.

44. **goblin:** demon

48. **questionable:** problematic

52. **canonized:** i.e., buried in accord with the canons of the church (accent on the second syllable); **hearsèd:** placed in or under a hearse (an elaborate framework covering the coffin of a distinguished person during the funeral)

53. **cerements:** a waxed cloth used to wrap a corpse for burial (pronounced as "seerments") See picture, page 52.

From our achievements, though performed at
   height,
The pith and marrow of our attribute.   25
So oft it chances in particular men
That for some vicious mole of nature in them,
As in their birth (wherein they are not guilty,
Since nature cannot choose his origin),
By ⌜the⌝ o'ergrowth of some complexion   30
(Oft breaking down the pales and forts of reason),
Or by some habit that too much o'erleavens
The form of plausive manners—that these men,
Carrying, I say, the stamp of one defect,
Being nature's livery or fortune's star,   35
His virtues else, be they as pure as grace,
As infinite as man may undergo,
Shall in the general censure take corruption
From that particular fault. The dram of ⌜evil⌝
Doth all the noble substance of a doubt   40
To his own scandal.]

Enter Ghost.

HORATIO   Look, my lord, it comes.
HAMLET
Angels and ministers of grace, defend us!
Be thou a spirit of health or goblin damned,
Bring with thee airs from heaven or blasts from   45
   hell,
Be thy intents wicked or charitable,
Thou com'st in such a questionable shape
That I will speak to thee. I'll call thee "Hamlet,"
"King," "Father," "Royal Dane." O, answer me!   50
Let me not burst in ignorance, but tell
Why thy canonized bones, hearsèd in death,
Have burst their cerements; why the sepulcher,
Wherein we saw thee quietly interred,
Hath oped his ponderous and marble jaws   55

59–61. and we . . . our souls: and causing us weak humans to agitate our minds **with thoughts** that go **beyond** what even **our souls** can reach to

64. some . . . desire: did desire to impart something

73. a pin's fee: the cost of a pin

74. And for: and as **for**

77. flood: sea

79. beetles . . . base: i.e., overhangs its **base** (as if it were a face with beetle brows—prominent jutting eyebrows)

81. deprive your sovereignty of reason: depose **reason** as ruler of **your** mind

83. toys of desperation: desperate impulses

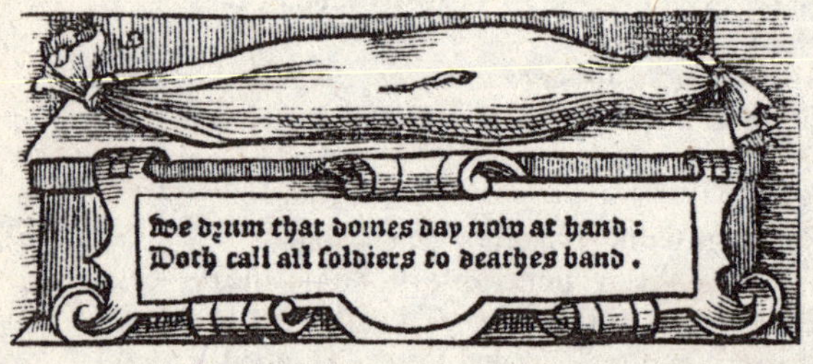

A corpse in a shrouding sheet or cerements. (1.4.53; 5.1.97)
From Richard Day, *A booke of Christian prayers . . .* (1590).

To cast thee up again. What may this mean
That thou, dead corse, again in complete steel,
Revisits thus the glimpses of the moon,
Making night hideous, and we fools of nature
So horridly to shake our disposition   60
With thoughts beyond the reaches of our souls?
Say, why is this? Wherefore? What should we do?

                                  ⟨*Ghost*⟩ *beckons.*

HORATIO
  It beckons you to go away with it
  As if it some impartment did desire
  To you alone.   65
MARCELLUS   Look with what courteous action
  It waves you to a more removèd ground.
  But do not go with it.
HORATIO   No, by no means.
HAMLET
  It will not speak. Then I will follow it.   70
HORATIO
  Do not, my lord.
HAMLET   Why, what should be the fear?
  I do not set my life at a pin's fee.
  And for my soul, what can it do to that,
  Being a thing immortal as itself?   75
  It waves me forth again. I'll follow it.
HORATIO
  What if it tempt you toward the flood, my lord?
  Or to the dreadful summit of the cliff
  That beetles o'er his base into the sea,
  And there assume some other horrible form   80
  Which might deprive your sovereignty of reason
  And draw you into madness? Think of it.
  [The very place puts toys of desperation,
  Without more motive, into every brain
  That looks so many fathoms to the sea   85
  And hears it roar beneath.]

92. **arture:** artery (Arteries were believed to carry the body's invisible vital spirits. Here, the word may have its more obscure meaning of "ligament.")
93. **the Nemean lion's nerve:** the sinews of the lion killed by Hercules as one of his twelve labors
95. **lets me:** holds me back
99. **Have after:** let's follow

1.5 The Ghost tells Hamlet a tale of horror. Saying that he is the spirit of Hamlet's father, he demands that Hamlet avenge King Hamlet's murder at the hands of Claudius. Hamlet, horrified, vows to "remember" and swears his friends to secrecy about what they have seen.

----

3. **Mark me:** pay attention to me

HAMLET
It waves me still.—Go on, I'll follow thee.
MARCELLUS
You shall not go, my lord. ⌜*They hold back Hamlet.*⌝
HAMLET   Hold off your hands.
HORATIO
Be ruled. You shall not go.   90
HAMLET   My fate cries out
And makes each petty arture in this body
As hardy as the Nemean lion's nerve.
Still am I called. Unhand me, gentlemen.
By heaven, I'll make a ghost of him that lets me!   95
I say, away!—Go on. I'll follow thee.
                      Ghost and Hamlet exit.
HORATIO
He waxes desperate with imagination.
MARCELLUS
Let's follow. 'Tis not fit thus to obey him.
HORATIO
Have after. To what issue will this come?
MARCELLUS
Something is rotten in the state of Denmark.   100
HORATIO
Heaven will direct it.
MARCELLUS   Nay, let's follow him.
                          They exit.

⌜Scene 5⌝

Enter Ghost and Hamlet.

HAMLET
Whither wilt thou lead me? Speak. I'll go no
    further.
GHOST
Mark me.

9. **lend thy serious hearing:** listen intently

10. **unfold:** reveal

11. **bound:** ready (The word also means "in duty bound" and "obligated," which is the sense to which the Ghost responds in the following line.)

16. **And for:** and during

17. **crimes:** offenses, sins

21. **harrow up:** tear up (agricultural image) For a picture of a harrow, see page 10.

22–23. **stars . . . spheres:** According to Ptolemaic astronomy, each planet (star) is carried around the earth in a crystalline sphere. (See picture, page 224.)

24. **knotted and combinèd locks:** Editors suggest that this describes Hamlet's carefully—perhaps elaborately—arranged hair.

25. **an end:** on **end**

26. **fearful porpentine:** uneasy (threatened) porcupine (See picture, below.)

27. **eternal blazon:** description of that which is **eternal**

A porcupine. (1.5.26)
From Edward Topsell,
The historie of foure-footed beastes . . . (1607).

HAMLET   I will.
GHOST   My hour is almost come   5
     When I to sulf'rous and tormenting flames
     Must render up myself.
HAMLET   Alas, poor ghost!
GHOST
     Pity me not, but lend thy serious hearing
     To what I shall unfold.   10
HAMLET   Speak. I am bound to hear.
GHOST
     So art thou to revenge, when thou shalt hear.
HAMLET   What?
GHOST   I am thy father's spirit,
     Doomed for a certain term to walk the night   15
     And for the day confined to fast in fires
     Till the foul crimes done in my days of nature
     Are burnt and purged away. But that I am forbid
     To tell the secrets of my prison house,
     I could a tale unfold whose lightest word   20
     Would harrow up thy soul, freeze thy young blood,
     Make thy two eyes, like stars, start from their
        spheres,
     Thy knotted and combinèd locks to part,
     And each particular hair to stand an end,   25
     Like quills upon the fearful porpentine.
     But this eternal blazon must not be
     To ears of flesh and blood. List, list, O list!
     If thou didst ever thy dear father love—
HAMLET   O God!   30
GHOST
     Revenge his foul and most unnatural murder.
HAMLET   Murder?
GHOST
     Murder most foul, as in the best it is,
     But this most foul, strange, and unnatural.
HAMLET
     Haste me to know 't, that I, with wings as swift   35

39. **duller . . . be:** you would **be duller; fat:** thick

40. **Lethe wharf:** bank of the river **Lethe** (the river of forgetfulness)

41. **Wouldst thou not:** if you did **not**

42. **orchard:** palace garden (See picture, below.)

44. **forgèd process:** false story

45. **Rankly abused:** grossly deceived

57–58. **decline / Upon:** to turn to (with the sense of *declining* as falling, bending downward)

60. **moved:** affected, stirred

65. **soft:** "enough," or "wait a minute"

68. **Upon . . . hour:** at a time I felt safe

69. **hebona:** a poison (perhaps a name for the poisonous weed called "henbane")

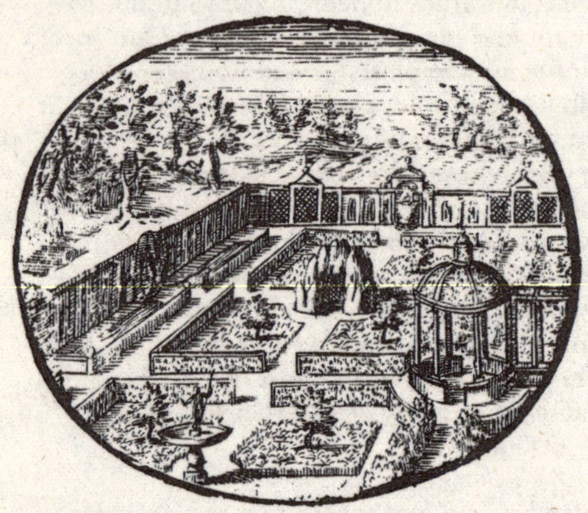

Orchard. (1.5.42)
From Octavio Boldoni, *Theatrum temporaneum* (1636).

As meditation or the thoughts of love
May sweep to my revenge.
GHOST   I find thee apt;
And duller shouldst thou be than the fat weed
That roots itself in ease on Lethe wharf,   40
Wouldst thou not stir in this. Now, Hamlet, hear.
'Tis given out that, sleeping in my orchard,
A serpent stung me. So the whole ear of Denmark
Is by a forgèd process of my death
Rankly abused. But know, thou noble youth,   45
The serpent that did sting thy father's life
Now wears his crown.
HAMLET   O, my prophetic soul! My uncle!
GHOST
Ay, that incestuous, that adulterate beast,
With witchcraft of his wits, with traitorous gifts—   50
O wicked wit and gifts, that have the power
So to seduce!—won to his shameful lust
The will of my most seeming-virtuous queen.
O Hamlet, what ⟨a⟩ falling off was there!
From me, whose love was of that dignity   55
That it went hand in hand even with the vow
I made to her in marriage, and to decline
Upon a wretch whose natural gifts were poor
To those of mine.
But virtue, as it never will be moved,   60
Though lewdness court it in a shape of heaven,
So, ⟨lust,⟩ though to a radiant angel linked,
Will ⟨sate⟩ itself in a celestial bed
And prey on garbage.
But soft, methinks I scent the morning air.   65
Brief let me be. Sleeping within my orchard,
My custom always of the afternoon,
Upon my secure hour thy uncle stole
With juice of cursèd hebona in a vial
And in the porches of my ears did pour   70

71. **leprous distilment:** distillation causing a condition like leprosy

75. **posset:** clot

76. **eager:** acid

78–80. **a most instant tetter . . . body:** i.e., sores and scabs, as on a leper, covered **my body with** a **vile crust** like the bark of a tree   **tetter:** a skin disease marked by sores and scabs   **lazar-like:** like a leper (*Lazar* is a word that refers to Lazarus the beggar in Luke 16.19–31. See picture, page 62.)

82. **dispatched:** dispossessed

84. **Unhouseled . . . unaneled:** without having received final rites

85. **No reck'ning made:** i.e., **no** chance to ask forgiveness for my sins (literally, no rendering an account of my conduct); **my account:** i.e., God's judgment of me

90. **luxury:** lust; **incest:** See note to 1.2.162, above.

96. **matin:** morning

104. **globe:** Hamlet perhaps gestures to his head.

105. **table:** i.e., erasable writing tablet (See longer note, page 289.)

The leprous distilment, whose effect
Holds such an enmity with blood of man
That swift as quicksilver it courses through
The natural gates and alleys of the body,
And with a sudden vigor it doth ⟨posset⟩   75
And curd, like eager droppings into milk,
The thin and wholesome blood. So did it mine,
And a most instant tetter barked about,
Most lazar-like, with vile and loathsome crust
All my smooth body.   80
Thus was I, sleeping, by a brother's hand
Of life, of crown, of queen at once dispatched,
Cut off, even in the blossoms of my sin,
Unhouseled, disappointed, unaneled,
No reck'ning made, but sent to my account   85
With all my imperfections on my head.
O horrible, O horrible, most horrible!
If thou hast nature in thee, bear it not.
Let not the royal bed of Denmark be
A couch for luxury and damnèd incest.   90
But, howsomever thou pursues this act,
Taint not thy mind, nor let thy soul contrive
Against thy mother aught. Leave her to heaven
And to those thorns that in her bosom lodge
To prick and sting her. Fare thee well at once.   95
The glowworm shows the matin to be near
And 'gins to pale his uneffectual fire.
Adieu, adieu, adieu. Remember me.   ⟨*He exits.*⟩
HAMLET
O all you host of heaven! O Earth! What else?
And shall I couple hell? O fie! Hold, hold, my heart, 100
And you, my sinews, grow not instant old,
But bear me ⟨stiffly⟩ up. Remember thee?
Ay, thou poor ghost, whiles memory holds a seat
In this distracted globe. Remember thee?
Yea, from the table of my memory   105

106. **fond records:** foolish jottings (**Records** is accented on the second syllable.)

107. **saws of:** sayings or commonplaces from; **pressures:** impressions

108. **youth and observation:** youthful **observation**

114. **tables:** a word used interchangeably with **table** (See note to line 105, above.)   **meet it is: it is** appropriate that

117. **word:** perhaps, promise; or, perhaps, the **commandment** (line 109) given Hamlet by the Ghost (line 98)

125. **Hillo, ho . . . bird, come:** Hamlet mocks Marcellus's call, as if it were the call of a falconer.

The beggar Lazarus: "lazar-like." (1.5.79)
From [Guillaume Guéroult,] *Figures de la Bible* (1565–70).

I'll wipe away all trivial, fond records,
All saws of books, all forms, all pressures past,
That youth and observation copied there,
And thy commandment all alone shall live
Within the book and volume of my brain,   110
Unmixed with baser matter. Yes, by heaven!
O most pernicious woman!
O villain, villain, smiling, damnèd villain!
My tables—meet it is I set it down
That one may smile and smile and be a villain. 115
At least I am sure it may be so in Denmark.
          ⌜*He writes.*⌝
So, uncle, there you are. Now to my word.
It is "adieu, adieu, remember me."
I have sworn 't.

    Enter Horatio and Marcellus.

HORATIO My lord, my lord!   120
MARCELLUS Lord Hamlet.
HORATIO Heavens secure him!
HAMLET So be it.
MARCELLUS Illo, ho, ho, my lord!
HAMLET Hillo, ho, ho, boy! Come, ⟨bird,⟩ come! 125
MARCELLUS
 How is 't, my noble lord?
HORATIO   What news, my lord?
HAMLET O, wonderful!
HORATIO
 Good my lord, tell it.
HAMLET   No, you will reveal it. 130
HORATIO
 Not I, my lord, by heaven.
MARCELLUS   Nor I, my lord.
HAMLET
 How say you, then? Would heart of man once think
  it?
But you'll be secret?   135

138. **arrant:** complete

142. **circumstance:** ceremony

154. **honest:** genuine

165. **sword:** an appropriate object on which to swear an oath, in that the hilt and guard form a cross (See picture, page 66.)

Fortune. (2.2.247, 260, 536–37; 3.2.71)
From Charles de Bouelles,
Que hoc volumine continentur . . . [1510].

HORATIO/MARCELLUS   Ay, by heaven, ⟨my lord.⟩
HAMLET
  There's never a villain dwelling in all Denmark
  But he's an arrant knave.
HORATIO
  There needs no ghost, my lord, come from the grave
  To tell us this.   140
HAMLET   Why, right, you are in the right.
  And so, without more circumstance at all,
  I hold it fit that we shake hands and part,
  You, as your business and desire shall point you
  (For every man hath business and desire,   145
  Such as it is), and for my own poor part,
  I will go pray.
HORATIO
  These are but wild and whirling words, my lord.
HAMLET
  I am sorry they offend you, heartily;
  Yes, faith, heartily.   150
HORATIO   There's no offense, my lord.
HAMLET
  Yes, by Saint Patrick, but there is, Horatio,
  And much offense, too. Touching this vision here,
  It is an honest ghost—that let me tell you.
  For your desire to know what is between us,   155
  O'ermaster 't as you may. And now, good friends,
  As you are friends, scholars, and soldiers,
  Give me one poor request.
HORATIO What is 't, my lord? We will.
HAMLET
  Never make known what you have seen tonight.   160
HORATIO/MARCELLUS My lord, we will not.
HAMLET Nay, but swear 't.
HORATIO In faith, my lord, not I.
MARCELLUS Nor I, my lord, in faith.
HAMLET
  Upon my sword.   165

170. **truepenny:** honest fellow

177. **Hic et ubique:** here and everywhere (Latin)

184. **pioner:** a foot soldier who digs trenches; a digger or miner; **remove:** move to another spot

186. **as a stranger give it welcome:** welcome **it as** one should welcome **a stranger**

188. **your philosophy:** i.e., **philosophy** in general

189–202. **never . . . help you:** i.e., **swear never to note,** even through gestures and hints, that **you know** anything about **me,** no matter **how** strangely I act

190. **How . . . some'er:** howsoever **strange or odd**

191–92. **As I . . . on:** since **I** may in the future **think** it appropriate to act bizarrely

194. **With arms . . . headshake: with** your **arms** folded or shaking your head in a knowing way

195. **doubtful:** ambiguous

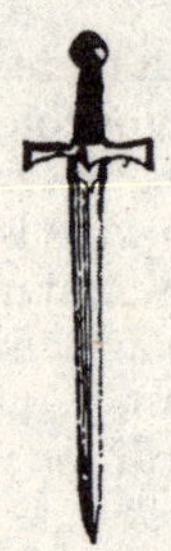

A sword. (1.5.165)
From Jacobus a. Bruck, *Emblemata moralia & bellica* (1615).

MARCELLUS   We have sworn, my lord, already.
HAMLET Indeed, upon my sword, indeed.
GHOST *cries under the stage* Swear.
HAMLET
 Ha, ha, boy, sayst thou so? Art thou there,
  truepenny?—   170
 Come on, you hear this fellow in the cellarage.
 Consent to swear.
HORATIO   Propose the oath, my lord.
HAMLET
 Never to speak of this that you have seen,
 Swear by my sword.   175
GHOST, ⌜*beneath*⌝ Swear.
HAMLET
 Hic et ubique? Then we'll shift our ground.
 Come hither, gentlemen,
 And lay your hands again upon my sword.
 Swear by my sword   180
 Never to speak of this that you have heard.
GHOST, ⌜*beneath*⌝ Swear by his sword.
HAMLET
 Well said, old mole. Canst work i' th' earth so fast?—
 A worthy pioner! Once more remove, good friends.
HORATIO
 O day and night, but this is wondrous strange. 185
HAMLET
 And therefore as a stranger give it welcome.
 There are more things in heaven and earth, Horatio,
 Than are dreamt of in your philosophy. But come.
 Here, as before, never, so help you mercy,
 How strange or odd some'er I bear myself 190
 (As I perchance hereafter shall think meet
 To put an antic disposition on)
 That you, at such times seeing me, never shall,
 With arms encumbered thus, or this headshake,
 Or by pronouncing of some doubtful phrase, 195

196. **an if: if**

197. **would:** wished to

198. **list:** should choose

200. **giving-out:** expression; **note:** indicate

204. **Rest, rest, perturbèd spirit:** These words suggest that Horatio and Marcellus have sworn the oath demanded by Hamlet and the Ghost; Q2 and F give no stage direction to indicate when they do so.

209. **still . . . lips:** i.e., always keep the secret (as you swore)

210. **spite:** malicious fate or fortune

212. **Nay, come:** Horatio and Marcellus perhaps wait for Hamlet to precede them.

The Last Judgment, or Doomsday.
(1.1.132; 2.2.257; 3.4.59; 5.1.61, 237).
From *A Series . . . of Ancient . . . Paintings . . .
on the Walls of the Chapel . . . at Stratford-upon-Avon*
(etched and published by Thomas Fisher in 1807).

As "Well, well, we know," or "We could an if we
   would,"
Or "If we list to speak," or "There be an if they
   might,"
Or such ambiguous giving-out, to note   200
That you know aught of me—this do swear,
So grace and mercy at your most need help you.
GHOST, ⌜*beneath*⌝ Swear.
HAMLET
Rest, rest, perturbèd spirit.—So, gentlemen,
With all my love I do commend me to you,   205
And what so poor a man as Hamlet is
May do t' express his love and friending to you,
God willing, shall not lack. Let us go in together,
And still your fingers on your lips, I pray.
The time is out of joint. O cursèd spite   210
That ever I was born to set it right!
Nay, come, let's go together.

                                     They exit.

The Tragedy of

HAMLET,

Prince of Denmark

ACT 2

2.1   Polonius sends his servant Reynaldo to Paris to question Laertes's acquaintances. Ophelia enters, deeply disturbed about a visit she has just had from an apparently mad Hamlet. Polonius decides that Hamlet has been made insane by Ophelia's refusing to see him. Polonius rushes off to tell the king.

----

0 SD. **man:** servant

4–5. **make inquire / Of:** ask questions about

8. **Inquire me:** i.e., **inquire** on my behalf; **Danskers:** Danes

9. **what means:** **what** is their supply of money

10. **keep:** live

12. **encompassment and drift of question:** roundabout conversation (Polonius's language itself tends to be roundabout.)

13–14. **come you . . . touch it:** i.e., **you will come** closer (to getting answers) than you would by specific questions

15. **Take you, as 'twere:** assume, **as** it were

<ACT 2>

⌜Scene 1⌝

Enter old Polonius with his man ⟨Reynaldo.⟩

POLONIUS
  Give him this money and these notes, Reynaldo.
REYNALDO   I will, my lord.
POLONIUS
  You shall do marvelous wisely, good Reynaldo,
  Before you visit him, to make inquire
  Of his behavior.   5
REYNALDO   My lord, I did intend it.
POLONIUS
  Marry, well said, very well said. Look you, sir,
  Inquire me first what Danskers are in Paris;
  And how, and who, what means, and where they
    keep,   10
  What company, at what expense; and finding
  By this encompassment and drift of question
  That they do know my son, come you more nearer
  Than your particular demands will touch it.
  Take you, as 'twere, some distant knowledge of him,   15
  As thus: "I know his father and his friends
  And, in part, him." Do you mark this, Reynaldo?
REYNALDO   Ay, very well, my lord.
POLONIUS
  "And, in part, him, but," you may say, "not well.

73

21. **put on him:** accuse him of

22. **forgeries:** invented faults; **rank:** great; offensive

24. **wanton:** rebellious

25–26. **are companions . . . liberty: are known to** accompany youthful activity

27. **gaming:** gambling

29. **drabbing:** dealing with prostitutes

31. **season . . . charge:** make **the charge** seem less serious by your way of stating it **season:** temper

33. **open to incontinency:** habitually inclined to sexual indulgence

34. **breathe:** speak

35. **quaintly:** cunningly

36. **taints of liberty:** slight faults that accompany independence

38–39. **A savageness . . . assault:** i.e., a wildness **in** untamed **blood,** which all young people can be accused of

41. **Wherefore:** why

44. **fetch of wit:** clever trick

46. **soiled i' th' working:** i.e., **soiled** by handling as it is being made

48. **sound: sound** out or question

49. **prenominate crimes:** before-named wrongdoings

51. **closes . . . consequence:** agrees **with you** as follows

53. **addition:** form of address

But if 't be he I mean, he's very wild,   20
Addicted so and so." And there put on him
What forgeries you please—marry, none so rank
As may dishonor him, take heed of that,
But, sir, such wanton, wild, and usual slips
As are companions noted and most known   25
To youth and liberty.

REYNALDO   As gaming, my lord.

POLONIUS   Ay, or drinking, fencing, swearing,
Quarreling, drabbing—you may go so far.

REYNALDO   My lord, that would dishonor him.   30

POLONIUS
Faith, ⟨no,⟩ as you may season it in the charge.
You must not put another scandal on him
That he is open to incontinency;
That's not my meaning. But breathe his faults so
   quaintly   35
That they may seem the taints of liberty,
The flash and outbreak of a fiery mind,
A savageness in unreclaimèd blood,
Of general assault.

REYNALDO   But, my good lord—   40

POLONIUS   Wherefore should you do this?

REYNALDO   Ay, my lord, I would know that.

POLONIUS   Marry, sir, here's my drift,
And I believe it is a fetch of wit.
You, laying these slight sullies on my son,   45
As 'twere a thing a little soiled ⟨i' th'⟩ working,
Mark you, your party in converse, him you would
   sound,
Having ever seen in the prenominate crimes
The youth you breathe of guilty, be assured   50
He closes with you in this consequence:
"Good sir," or so, or "friend," or "gentleman,"
According to the phrase or the addition
Of man and country—

66. **o'ertook in 's rouse:** overcome by drink

69. **Videlicet:** namely, that is to say (Latin)

69–70. **See . . . truth:** i.e., **you** can **see** this deceptive **bait** capture a real fish

71. **reach:** mental ability

72. **windlasses . . . bias:** indirect approaches (A *windlass* is an indirect course in hunting, and the **bias** is the curve that brings the ball to the desired point in the game of bowls. See picture, below.)

75. **Shall you my son: you shall** (find out) **my son**

79. **in yourself:** yourself (instead of in reports)

The game of bowls. (2.1.72; 3.1.73)
From *Le centre de l'amour* (1650).

REYNALDO   Very good, my lord.   55
POLONIUS And then, sir, does he this, he does—what
    was I about to say? By the Mass, I was about to say
    something. Where did I leave?
REYNALDO At "closes in the consequence," ⟨at "friend,
    or so," and "gentleman."⟩   60
POLONIUS
    At "closes in the consequence"—ay, marry—
    He closes thus: "I know the gentleman.
    I saw him yesterday," or "th' other day"
    (Or then, or then, with such or such), "and as you
        say,   65
    There was he gaming, there ⟨o'ertook⟩ in 's rouse,
    There falling out at tennis"; or perchance
    "I saw him enter such a house of sale"—
    Videlicet, a brothel—or so forth. See you now
    Your bait of falsehood take this carp of truth;   70
    And thus do we of wisdom and of reach,
    With windlasses and with assays of bias,
    By indirections find directions out.
    So by my former lecture and advice
    Shall you my son. You have me, have you not?   75
REYNALDO
    My lord, I have.
POLONIUS   God be wi' you. Fare you well.
REYNALDO Good my lord.
POLONIUS
    Observe his inclination in yourself.
REYNALDO I shall, my lord.   80
POLONIUS And let him ply his music.
REYNALDO Well, my lord.
POLONIUS
    Farewell.   *Reynaldo exits.*

                    Enter Ophelia.

        How now, Ophelia, what's the matter?

87. **closet:** private room

88. **doublet:** close-fitting jacket; **unbraced:** unfastened

89. **fouled:** dirty

90. **down-gyvèd to his ankle:** fallen down around his ankles like gyves or chains (See picture, below.)

114. **ecstasy:** madness

115. **violent property:** characteristic violence; **fordoes:** destroys

A man in gyves. (2.1.90; 4.7.23)
From Cesare Vecellio, *Degli habiti antichi et moderni* (1590).

OPHELIA
  O, my lord, my lord, I have been so affrighted!   85
POLONIUS With what, i' th' name of God?
OPHELIA
  My lord, as I was sewing in my closet,
  Lord Hamlet, with his doublet all unbraced,
  No hat upon his head, his stockings fouled,
  Ungartered, and down-gyvèd to his ankle,   90
  Pale as his shirt, his knees knocking each other,
  And with a look so piteous in purport
  As if he had been loosèd out of hell
  To speak of horrors—he comes before me.
POLONIUS
  Mad for thy love?   95
OPHELIA   My lord, I do not know,
  But truly I do fear it.
POLONIUS   What said he?
OPHELIA
  He took me by the wrist and held me hard.
  Then goes he to the length of all his arm,   100
  And, with his other hand thus o'er his brow,
  He falls to such perusal of my face
  As he would draw it. Long stayed he so.
  At last, a little shaking of mine arm,
  And thrice his head thus waving up and down,   105
  He raised a sigh so piteous and profound
  As it did seem to shatter all his bulk
  And end his being. That done, he lets me go,
  And, with his head over his shoulder turned,
  He seemed to find his way without his eyes,   110
  For out o' doors he went without their helps
  And to the last bended their light on me.
POLONIUS
  Come, go with me. I will go seek the King.
  This is the very ecstasy of love,
  Whose violent property fordoes itself   115

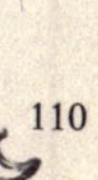

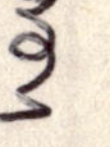

125. **coted:** observed

126. **wrack:** destroy; **beshrew my jealousy:** curse my suspicious thoughts

127. **proper to our age:** characteristic of the old

128. **cast beyond ourselves:** i.e., go too far (**Cast** could mean—among other things—calculate, predict, and throw.)

130. **discretion:** good judgment

131. **close:** hidden

131–33. **might . . . love: this love might** cause **more grief** if hidden **than** hatred if spoken of

2.2 Claudius and Gertrude set Rosencrantz and Guildenstern, two boyhood friends of Hamlet, to spy on him.

When Hamlet himself enters, he is confronted first by Polonius and then by Rosencrantz and Guildenstern, whom he quickly identifies as Claudius's spies. As they talk, a company of touring actors enters. Hamlet persuades one of them to deliver a speech, and recognizes, to his shame, that he has shown less intensity in avenging his father's murder than the actor has done in performance. Hamlet hopes that when the players stage *The Murder of Gonzago* for the court, he can determine whether Claudius is guilty of King Hamlet's death.

———————

6. **Sith:** since; **nor . . . nor:** neither . . . nor

And leads the will to desperate undertakings
As oft as any passions under heaven
That does afflict our natures. I am sorry.
What, have you given him any hard words of late?

OPHELIA
No, my good lord, but as you did command　　　　　120
I did repel his letters and denied
His access to me.

POLONIUS　　　　　　　That hath made him mad.
I am sorry that with better heed and judgment
I had not coted him. I feared he did but trifle　　　125
And meant to wrack thee. But beshrew my jealousy!
By heaven, it is as proper to our age
To cast beyond ourselves in our opinions
As it is common for the younger sort
To lack discretion. Come, go we to the King.　　　130
This must be known, which, being kept close, might
　move
More grief to hide than hate to utter love.
Come.

　　　　　　　　　　　　　　　　They exit.

〈Scene 2〉

*Flourish. Enter King and Queen, Rosencrantz and
　　Guildenstern ⌜and Attendants.⌝*

KING
Welcome, dear Rosencrantz and Guildenstern.
Moreover that we much did long to see you,
The need we have to use you did provoke
Our hasty sending. Something have you heard
Of Hamlet's transformation, so call it,　　　　　5
Sith nor th' exterior nor the inward man
Resembles that it was. What it should be,
More than his father's death, that thus hath put him

12. **neighbored to:** acquainted with; **youth and havior:** perhaps, youthful manners or behavior

13. **vouchsafe your rest:** agree to stay

18. **opened:** laid bare, revealed

22. **gentry:** generosity (or, perhaps, courtesy)

24. **supply . . . hope:** support and benefit of what we hope for

32. **in the full bent:** fully, totally (The term suggests an archer's bow, bent to its limit.) See picture, below.

40. **practices:** actions (with perhaps a suggestion of intrigues, maneuvers, and plots)

A bow "in the full bent." (2.2.32)
From Jacobus a. Bruck, *Emblemata moralia & bellica* (1615).

So much from th' understanding of himself
I cannot dream of. I entreat you both 10
That, being of so young days brought up with him
And sith so neighbored to his youth and havior,
That you vouchsafe your rest here in our court
Some little time, so by your companies
To draw him on to pleasures, and to gather 15
So much as from occasion you may glean,
[Whether aught to us unknown afflicts him thus]
That, opened, lies within our remedy.

QUEEN
Good gentlemen, he hath much talked of you,
And sure I am two men there is not living 20
To whom he more adheres. If it will please you
To show us so much gentry and goodwill
As to expend your time with us awhile
For the supply and profit of our hope,
Your visitation shall receive such thanks 25
As fits a king's remembrance.

ROSENCRANTZ   Both your Majesties
Might, by the sovereign power you have of us,
Put your dread pleasures more into command
Than to entreaty. 30

GUILDENSTERN   But we both obey,
And here give up ourselves in the full bent
To lay our service freely at your feet,
To be commanded.

KING
Thanks, Rosencrantz and gentle Guildenstern. 35

QUEEN
Thanks, Guildenstern and gentle Rosencrantz.
And I beseech you instantly to visit
My too much changèd son.—Go, some of you,
And bring these gentlemen where Hamlet is.

GUILDENSTERN
Heavens make our presence and our practices 40
Pleasant and helpful to him!

45. **still:** always

50. **Hunts . . . sure:** i.e., does not follow **so** successfully **the trail of** statecraft (See picture, below.)

55. **fruit:** dessert

56. **do grace to:** honor

58. **head and source:** fountainhead, origin; **distemper:** derangement, illness

59. **doubt:** suspect; **the main:** the central point

61. **sift:** examine closely (as if through a sieve) (See picture, page 86.)

A dog hunting the trail. (2.2.50)
From George Turberville, *The noble art of venerie* (1611).

QUEEN   Ay, amen!
                              Rosencrantz and Guildenstern exit
                                   「*with some Attendants.*」

                              Enter Polonius.

POLONIUS
  Th' ambassadors from Norway, my good lord,
  Are joyfully returned.
KING
  Thou still hast been the father of good news.   45
POLONIUS
  Have I, my lord? I assure my good liege
  I hold my duty as I hold my soul,
  Both to my God and to my gracious king,
  And I do think, or else this brain of mine
  Hunts not the trail of policy so sure   50
  As it hath used to do, that I have found
  The very cause of Hamlet's lunacy.
KING
  O, speak of that! That do I long to hear.
POLONIUS
  Give first admittance to th' ambassadors.
  My news shall be the fruit to that great feast.   55
KING
  Thyself do grace to them and bring them in.
                                   「*Polonius exits.*」
  He tells me, my dear Gertrude, he hath found
  The head and source of all your son's distemper.
QUEEN
  I doubt it is no other but the main—
  His father's death and our ⟨o'erhasty⟩ marriage.   60
KING
  Well, we shall sift him.

  Enter Ambassadors ⟨Voltemand and Cornelius 「with」
                    Polonius.⟩

63. **our brother:** i.e., my fellow king of
65. **first:** i.e., **first** making known our business
70. **impotence:** helplessness
71. **falsely borne in hand:** systematically deceived; **arrests:** orders to desist
73. **in fine:** in conclusion
75. **give ... against:** attack, assault
84. **On such ... allowance:** according to **such** terms **of safety** for Denmark and of permission for Fortinbras
86. **likes:** pleases
93. **expostulate:** make a speech about

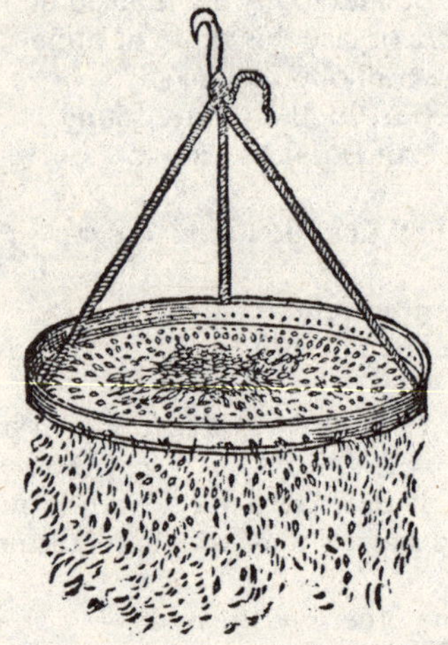

A sieve. (2.2.61)
From Geoffrey Whitney, *A choice of emblemes* (1586).

                              Welcome, my good friends.
      Say, Voltemand, what from our brother Norway?
VOLTEMAND
      Most fair return of greetings and desires.
      Upon our first, he sent out to suppress   65
      His nephew's levies, which to him appeared
      To be a preparation 'gainst the Polack,
      But, better looked into, he truly found
      It was against your Highness. Whereat, grieved
      That so his sickness, age, and impotence   70
      Was falsely borne in hand, sends out arrests
      On Fortinbras, which he, in brief, obeys,
      Receives rebuke from Norway, and, in fine,
      Makes vow before his uncle never more
      To give th' assay of arms against your Majesty.   75
      Whereon old Norway, overcome with joy,
      Gives him three-score thousand crowns in annual
        fee
      And his commission to employ those soldiers,
      So levied as before, against the Polack,   80
      With an entreaty, herein further shown,
                              ⌜*He gives a paper.*⌝
      That it might please you to give quiet pass
      Through your dominions for this enterprise,
      On such regards of safety and allowance
      As therein are set down.   85
KING   It likes us well,
      And, at our more considered time, we'll read,
      Answer, and think upon this business.
      Meantime, we thank you for your well-took labor.
      Go to your rest. At night we'll feast together.   90
      Most welcome home!
                         ⌜*Voltemand and Cornelius*⌝ *exit.*
POLONIUS   This business is well ended.
      My liege, and madam, to expostulate
      What majesty should be, what duty is,

97. **brevity . . . wit:** i.e., in a wise speech, a few words carry the central meaning

98. **flourishes:** ornaments

103. **More . . . art:** i.e., get to the point more quickly by cutting out the rhetorical ornamentations

104. **I use no art:** i.e., my language is natural

106. **figure: figure** of speech

113. **Perpend:** consider carefully

115. **mark:** note, notice this

116. **gather:** i.e., listen (literally, collect by observation, infer); **surmise:** form an idea

117–18. **To . . . Ophelia:** These lines, along with line 121, form the superscription, the address written on the outer leaf of the letter.

121. **In her . . . these, etc.:** This part of the superscription is unusual in two ways. See longer note, page 289.   **these:** i.e., this (letter) The plural word **these** was often used to refer to a single piece of correspondence, following the Latin *litterae*, a plural form meaning "an epistle."

123. **stay:** wait; **be faithful:** fulfill my duty

124–27. **Doubt . . . I love:** Hamlet's poem plays on different meanings of **doubt:** (1) to be skeptical about (e.g., the ancient truths about **the stars** and **the sun**); (2) to suspect (that, e.g., **truth** might **be a liar**); (3) to disbelieve (e.g., Hamlet's love).

Why day is day, night night, and time is time 95
Were nothing but to waste night, day, and time.
Therefore, ⟨since⟩ brevity is the soul of wit,
And tediousness the limbs and outward flourishes,
I will be brief. Your noble son is mad.
"Mad" call I it, for, to define true madness, 100
What is 't but to be nothing else but mad?
But let that go.
QUEEN   More matter with less art.
POLONIUS
Madam, I swear I use no art at all.
That he's mad, 'tis true; 'tis true 'tis pity, 105
And pity 'tis 'tis true—a foolish figure,
But farewell it, for I will use no art.
Mad let us grant him then, and now remains
That we find out the cause of this effect,
Or, rather say, the cause of this defect, 110
For this effect defective comes by cause.
Thus it remains, and the remainder thus.
Perpend.
I have a daughter (have while she is mine)
Who, in her duty and obedience, mark, 115
Hath given me this. Now gather and surmise.
    ⌜*He reads.*⌝ *To the celestial, and my soul's idol, the*
    most beautified Ophelia—
    That's an ill phrase, a vile phrase; "beautified" is a
    vile phrase. But you shall hear. Thus: ⌜*He reads.*⌝ 120
    In her excellent white bosom, these, etc.—
QUEEN   Came this from Hamlet to her?
POLONIUS
Good madam, stay awhile. I will be faithful.
    ⌜*He reads the*⌝ *letter.*
            Doubt thou the stars are fire,
                Doubt that the sun doth move, 125
            Doubt truth to be a liar,
                But never doubt I love.

128. **ill . . . numbers:** unskilled at writing verse

129. **art:** skill; artistic ability; **reckon:** i.e., express in poetic meter (literally, count)

131–32. **whilst . . . to him:** i.e., while I still occupy this body

134. **above:** besides

135. **fell out:** happened, occurred

140. **fain:** gladly

145. **played . . . table-book:** remained silent, keeping this knowledge hidden as **if I had** put it in a **desk** or a diary

146. **given . . . winking:** made **my heart** close its eyes to what was going on

149. **my young mistress:** this **young** lady (i.e., Ophelia); **bespeak:** speak to

150. **out of thy star:** a Polonian construction for "beyond your sphere" (See note to 1.5.22–23, and picture, page 224.)

151. **prescripts:** instructions

152. **resort:** i.e., visits (literally, recourse to her)

153. **tokens:** things given as an expression of affection

155–59. **he . . . Fell into . . . madness:** Polonius lists what were supposed to be the classic stages of the **declension** (decline) into love-madness: from **sadness,** to **a fast** (failure to eat), to **a watch** (insomnia), to **weakness,** to **lightness** (light-headedness), to insanity.

> *O dear Ophelia, I am ill at these numbers. I have not*
> *art to reckon my groans, but that I love thee best, O*
> *most best, believe it. Adieu.*   130
>   *Thine evermore, most dear lady, whilst*
>   *this machine is to him, Hamlet.*

This, in obedience, hath my daughter shown me,
And more ⟨above,⟩ hath his solicitings,
As they fell out by time, by means, and place,   135
All given to mine ear.

KING   But how hath she received his love?

POLONIUS   What do you think of me?

KING
As of a man faithful and honorable.

POLONIUS
I would fain prove so. But what might you think,   140
When I had seen this hot love on the wing
(As I perceived it, I must tell you that,
Before my daughter told me), what might you,
Or my dear Majesty your queen here, think,
If I had played the desk or table-book   145
Or given my heart a ⟨winking,⟩ mute and dumb,
Or looked upon this love with idle sight?
What might you think? No, I went round to work,
And my young mistress thus I did bespeak:
"Lord Hamlet is a prince, out of thy star.   150
This must not be." And then I prescripts gave her,
That she should lock herself from ⟨his⟩ resort,
Admit no messengers, receive no tokens;
Which done, she took the fruits of my advice,
And he, repelled (a short tale to make),   155
Fell into a sadness, then into a fast,
Thence to a watch, thence into a weakness,
Thence to ⟨a⟩ lightness, and, by this declension,
Into the madness wherein now he raves
And all we mourn for.   160

KING, ⌜*to Queen*⌝   Do you think ⟨'tis⟩ this?

168. **Take this from this:** Polonius gestures to his head and his shoulder (or to his chain of office and his neck, or to his staff of office and his hand), indicating that he would yield up his life (or his office) if proved wrong.

171. **center:** the earth's **center,** which, in the Ptolemaic system, is also the **center** of the universe (See picture, page 224.)

172. **try:** test

174. **lobby:** anteroom

176. **loose:** turn her loose (The figure is that of releasing an animal from its chains, either for the hunt or for purposes of mating.)

177. **arras:** a hanging screen of rich tapestry fabric

179. **thereon:** because of that, thereat

180. **assistant for a state:** perhaps, one who helps run a government

181. **keep . . . carters:** i.e., manage **a farm and** its workers (such as men who drive carts)

186. **board:** i.e., speak to; **presently:** immediately

QUEEN   It may be, very like.

POLONIUS
Hath there been such a time (I would fain know
    that)
That I have positively said "'Tis so,"   165
When it proved otherwise?

KING   Not that I know.

POLONIUS
Take this from this, if this be otherwise.
If circumstances lead me, I will find
Where truth is hid, though it were hid, indeed,   170
Within the center.

KING   How may we try it further?

POLONIUS
You know sometimes he walks four hours together
Here in the lobby.

QUEEN   So he does indeed.   175

POLONIUS
At such a time I'll loose my daughter to him.
⌜*To the King.*⌝ Be you and I behind an arras then.
Mark the encounter. If he love her not,
And be not from his reason fall'n thereon,
Let me be no assistant for a state,   180
But keep a farm and carters.

KING   We will try it.

Enter Hamlet (reading on a book.)

QUEEN
But look where sadly the poor wretch comes
    reading.

POLONIUS
Away, I do beseech you both, away.   185
I'll board him presently. O, give me leave.
         King and Queen exit ⌜*with Attendants.*⌝
How does my good Lord Hamlet?

HAMLET   Well, God-a-mercy.

198. **a good kissing carrion:** perhaps, **a good** piece of **dead** flesh for **the sun** to kiss

216. **purging:** issuing forth, discharging

218. **wit:** understanding; **hams:** buttocks and thighs

220. **honesty:** good manners

221. **old:** as **old**

224. **out of the air:** indoors (The open Elizabethan stage allowed the scene to shift from the anteroom of line 174 to the outdoor setting suggested here.)

". . . thou strumpet Fortune."
(2.2.518; see also 2.2.253–54; 3.2.75)
From *Fortunes tennis-ball: a warning . . .* (1640).

POLONIUS Do you know me, my lord?

HAMLET Excellent well. You are a fishmonger. 190

POLONIUS Not I, my lord.

HAMLET Then I would you were so honest a man.

POLONIUS Honest, my lord?

HAMLET Ay, sir. To be honest, as this world goes, is to be one man picked out of ten thousand. 195

POLONIUS That's very true, my lord.

HAMLET For if the sun breed maggots in a dead dog, being a good kissing carrion—Have you a daughter?

POLONIUS I have, my lord. 200

HAMLET Let her not walk i' th' sun. Conception is a blessing, but, as your daughter may conceive, friend, look to 't.

POLONIUS, ⌜*aside*⌝ How say you by that? Still harping on my daughter. Yet he knew me not at first; he said I was a fishmonger. He is far gone. And truly, in my youth, I suffered much extremity for love, very near this. I'll speak to him again.—What do you read, my lord? 205

HAMLET Words, words, words. 210

POLONIUS What is the matter, my lord?

HAMLET Between who?

POLONIUS I mean the matter that you read, my lord.

HAMLET Slanders, sir; for the satirical rogue says here that old men have gray beards, that their faces are wrinkled, their eyes purging thick amber and plum-tree gum, and that they have a plentiful lack of wit, together with most weak hams; all which, sir, though I most powerfully and potently believe, yet I hold it not honesty to have it thus set down; for yourself, sir, shall grow old as I am, if, like a crab, you could go backward. 215 220

POLONIUS, ⌜*aside*⌝ Though this be madness, yet there is method in 't.—Will you walk out of the air, my lord?

227. **pregnant:** full of meaning; **happiness:** aptness of phrasing

229. **so . . . delivered of:** i.e., **so** successfully give birth to

234. **withal:** with

245. **As . . . earth:** like the general run of mortals

247. **Fortune's:** The goddess Fortuna was said to control a person's luck and therefore happiness. (See picture, page 64.) **the very button:** the topmost spot

252. **privates:** intimates, with a pun on living within Fortune's "private parts" (This sexual wordplay begins with Hamlet's reference to Fortune's **favors** [line 251] and continues with his question about **the secret parts of Fortune** and his calling Fortune **a strumpet** [lines 253–54]. See picture, page 94, and note to 2.2.518.)

HAMLET Into my grave? 225
POLONIUS Indeed, that's out of the air. ⌜*Aside.*⌝ How
pregnant sometimes his replies are! A happiness
that often madness hits on, which reason and
⟨sanity⟩ could not so prosperously be delivered of. I
will leave him ⟨and suddenly contrive the means of 230
meeting between him⟩ and my daughter.—My lord,
I will take my leave of you.
HAMLET You cannot, ⟨sir,⟩ take from me anything that I
will more willingly part withal—except my life,
except my life, except my life. 235
POLONIUS Fare you well, my lord.
HAMLET, ⌜*aside*⌝ These tedious old fools.

Enter Guildenstern and Rosencrantz.

POLONIUS You go to seek the Lord Hamlet. There he is.
ROSENCRANTZ, ⌜*to Polonius*⌝ God save you, sir.
⌜*Polonius exits.*⌝

GUILDENSTERN My honored lord. 240
ROSENCRANTZ My most dear lord.
HAMLET My ⟨excellent⟩ good friends! How dost thou,
Guildenstern? Ah, Rosencrantz! Good lads, how do
you both?
ROSENCRANTZ
As the indifferent children of the earth. 245
GUILDENSTERN
Happy in that we are not ⟨overhappy.⟩
On Fortune's ⟨cap,⟩ we are not the very button.
HAMLET Nor the soles of her shoe?
ROSENCRANTZ Neither, my lord.
HAMLET Then you live about her waist, or in the 250
middle of her favors?
GUILDENSTERN Faith, her privates we.
HAMLET In the secret parts of Fortune? O, most true!
She is a strumpet. What news?
ROSENCRANTZ None, my lord, but ⟨that⟩ the world's 255
grown honest.

257. **doomsday:** See note to 1.1.132.
264. **goodly:** large
264–65. **confines:** places of confinement
282–84. **beggars bodies . . . beggars' shadows:** i.e., if **ambition is but a shadow's shadow,** then **beggars** (who are without **ambition**) are the only humans with substantial **bodies,** and kings **and heroes** (ruled by **ambition**) are only **the beggars' shadows outstretched:** i.e., outsized, larger-than-life (literally, distended)
284. **fay:** faith
286. **wait upon:** accompany; serve
287. **sort you with:** put **you** in the same class **with**
290. **what make you at:** i.e., why did you come to
292. **occasion:** reason

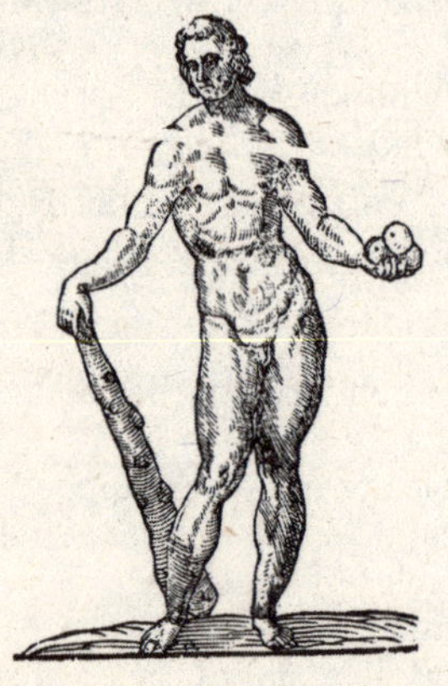

Hercules. (1.2.158; 2.2.384; 5.1.310)
From Vincenzo Cartari, *Le vere e noue imagini . . .* (1615).

HAMLET Then is doomsday near. But your news is not
true. ⟨Let me question more in particular. What
have you, my good friends, deserved at the hands of
Fortune that she sends you to prison hither?   260
GUILDENSTERN Prison, my lord?
HAMLET Denmark's a prison.
ROSENCRANTZ Then is the world one.
HAMLET A goodly one, in which there are many con-
fines, wards, and dungeons, Denmark being one o'   265
th' worst.
ROSENCRANTZ We think not so, my lord.
HAMLET Why, then, 'tis none to you, for there is
nothing either good or bad but thinking makes it
so. To me, it is a prison.   270
ROSENCRANTZ Why, then, your ambition makes it one.
'Tis too narrow for your mind.
HAMLET O God, I could be bounded in a nutshell and
count myself a king of infinite space, were it not
that I have bad dreams.   275
GUILDENSTERN Which dreams, indeed, are ambition,
for the very substance of the ambitious is merely
the shadow of a dream.
HAMLET A dream itself is but a shadow.
ROSENCRANTZ Truly, and I hold ambition of so airy   280
and light a quality that it is but a shadow's shadow.
HAMLET Then are our beggars bodies, and our mon-
archs and outstretched heroes the beggars' shad-
ows. Shall we to th' court? For, by my fay, I cannot
reason.   285
ROSENCRANTZ/GUILDENSTERN We'll wait upon you.
HAMLET No such matter. I will not sort you with the
rest of my servants, for, to speak to you like an
honest man, I am most dreadfully attended.⟩ But,
in the beaten way of friendship, what make you at   290
Elsinore?
ROSENCRANTZ To visit you, my lord, no other occasion.

294. **sure:** surely

295. **too dear a halfpenny:** not worth **a half-penny**

300. **but ... purpose:** except a straight answer

307–8. **the consonancy of our youth:** the harmony we enjoyed when we were younger

309. **by ... dear: by** whatever is **more** valuable

310. **proposer:** speaker; **charge you withal:** urge you with; **even:** straightforward

313. **of:** on

316–17. **my anticipation ... discovery:** my saying it first will keep you from having to reveal it

317–18. **your secrecy ... molt no feather: your** promise of **secrecy** not be diminished

319. **wherefore:** why

320–21. **it goes ... disposition:** my mood is **so** somber

321. **frame:** structure

323–24. **canopy, firmament, roof:** Each of these words refers to the sky or heavens overhead. **look you:** an imperative used to request someone's attention **brave:** splendid

324. **fretted:** adorned

328. **faculties:** abilities, capacities

HAMLET Beggar that I am, I am ⟨even⟩ poor in thanks;
but I thank you, and sure, dear friends, my thanks
are too dear a halfpenny. Were you not sent for? 295
Is it your own inclining? Is it a free visitation?
Come, come, deal justly with me. Come, come; nay,
speak.

GUILDENSTERN What should we say, my lord?

HAMLET Anything but to th' purpose. You were sent 300
for, and there is a kind of confession in your looks
which your modesties have not craft enough to
color. I know the good king and queen have sent for
you.

ROSENCRANTZ To what end, my lord? 305

HAMLET That you must teach me. But let me conjure
you by the rights of our fellowship, by the conso-
nancy of our youth, by the obligation of our ever-
preserved love, and by what more dear a better
proposer can charge you withal: be even and direct 310
with me whether you were sent for or no.

ROSENCRANTZ, ⌜to Guildenstern⌝ What say you?

HAMLET, ⌜aside⌝ Nay, then, I have an eye of you.—If
you love me, hold not off.

GUILDENSTERN My lord, we were sent for. 315

HAMLET I will tell you why; so shall my anticipation
prevent your discovery, and your secrecy to the
King and Queen molt no feather. I have of late, but
wherefore I know not, lost all my mirth, forgone all
custom of exercises, and, indeed, it goes so heavily 320
with my disposition that this goodly frame, the
Earth, seems to me a sterile promontory; this most
excellent canopy, the air, look you, this brave o'er-
hanging firmament, this majestical roof, fretted
with golden fire—why, it appeareth nothing to me 325
but a foul and pestilent congregation of vapors.
What ⟨a⟩ piece of work is a man, how noble in
reason, how infinite in faculties, in form and mov-

329. **express:** well framed
330. **apprehension:** understanding
332. **quintessence:** very essence (The word is usually used to describe that which transcends the four earthly essences, but here is used ironically to describe mankind as, in essence, **dust**—made from dust to return to dust. See Genesis 2.7, 3.19.)
340. **Lenten entertainment:** i.e., meager or dismal welcome
341. **coted:** passed
344. **tribute on:** tokens of homage from
345. **foil and target:** blunted smallsword and shield
346. **gratis:** without payment; **the humorous man:** the actor playing the eccentric character
347. **the clown:** the actor who plays the comic roles
348. **tickle o' th' sear:** i.e., easily made to laugh **sear:** the catch in a gunlock that keeps the hammer cocked (When the sear is **tickle** or loose, the gun goes off easily.) **the lady:** the actor playing the female role
350. **halt:** limp; go awkwardly or irregularly
353. **Their residence:** their remaining in the city
355–56. **their . . . innovation:** The **inhibition** that forces the tragedians from the city and **the innovation** that caused it may reflect London theatrical or political happenings.
358. **followed:** i.e., admired, sought out
361–62. **keeps . . . pace:** continues as usual
362. **aerie:** nest
363. **eyases:** hawks; **cry out . . . question:** speak their lines in loud, shrill voices

ing how express and admirable; in action how like an angel, in apprehension how like a god: the 330 beauty of the world, the paragon of animals—and yet, to me, what is this quintessence of dust? Man delights not me, ⟨no,⟩ nor women neither, though by your smiling you seem to say so.

ROSENCRANTZ My lord, there was no such stuff in my 335 thoughts.

HAMLET Why did you laugh, then, when I said "man delights not me"?

ROSENCRANTZ To think, my lord, if you delight not in man, what Lenten entertainment the players shall 340 receive from you. We coted them on the way, and hither are they coming to offer you service.

HAMLET He that plays the king shall be welcome—his Majesty shall have tribute on me. The adventurous knight shall use his foil and target, the lover shall 345 not sigh gratis, the humorous man shall end his part in peace, ⟨the clown shall make those laugh whose lungs are ⌜tickle⌝ o' th' sear,⟩ and the lady shall say her mind freely, or the ⟨blank⟩ verse shall halt for 't. What players are they? 350

ROSENCRANTZ Even those you were wont to take such delight in, the tragedians of the city.

HAMLET How chances it they travel? Their residence, both in reputation and profit, was better both ways.

ROSENCRANTZ I think their inhibition comes by the 355 means of the late innovation.

HAMLET Do they hold the same estimation they did when I was in the city? Are they so followed?

ROSENCRANTZ No, indeed are they not.

⟨HAMLET How comes it? Do they grow rusty? 360

ROSENCRANTZ Nay, their endeavor keeps in the wonted pace. But there is, sir, an aerie of children, little eyases, that cry out on the top of question and are most tyrannically clapped for 't. These are now the

365. **berattle the common stages:** berate the public theaters

366. **many wearing rapiers:** i.e., fashionable gentlemen

366–67. **are afraid ... thither:** fear the satirical pens of children's company poets if they attend the public theaters

369. **escoted:** financially supported

369–70. **pursue ... sing:** follow the acting profession only until their voices change in adolescence

371–72. **to common players:** to be adult actors

374. **exclaim ... succession:** i.e., attack the careers they will follow

376. **tar:** provoke, incite

377–79. **There was ... in the question:** i.e., no plays were salable that did not take up the quarrel between the children's poets and the adult players

383. **carry it away: carry** off the victory

384–85. **Hercules and his load too:** i.e., the boy actors win over the whole world of playgoers (Hercules' **load** was the globe, which he bore on his shoulders for Atlas. The sign of the Globe theater is said to have been a picture of Hercules bearing the globe.)

387. **mouths:** contorted faces

389. **picture in little:** miniature portrait

390. **'Sblood:** a strong oath (by God's blood)

394. **Th' appurtenance of:** that which belongs to

395–96. **comply ... garb:** use courteous action **with you in this** way

396. **my extent:** i.e., what I show

fashion and so ⌜berattle⌝ the common stages (so 365
they call them) that many wearing rapiers are afraid
of goose quills and dare scarce come thither.

HAMLET What, are they children? Who maintains 'em?
How are they escoted? Will they pursue the quality
no longer than they can sing? Will they not say 370
afterwards, if they should grow themselves to com-
mon players (as it is ⌜most like,⌝ if their means are
no better), their writers do them wrong to make
them exclaim against their own succession?

ROSENCRANTZ Faith, there has been much ⌜to-do⌝ on 375
both sides, and the nation holds it no sin to tar
them to controversy. There was for a while no
money bid for argument unless the poet and the
player went to cuffs in the question.

HAMLET Is 't possible? 380

GUILDENSTERN O, there has been much throwing
about of brains.

HAMLET Do the boys carry it away?

ROSENCRANTZ Ay, that they do, my lord—Hercules
and his load too.⟩ 385

HAMLET It is not very strange; for my uncle is King of
Denmark, and those that would make mouths at
him while my father lived give twenty, forty, fifty,
a hundred ducats apiece for his picture in little.
'Sblood, there is something in this more than nat- 390
ural, if philosophy could find it out.

A flourish ⟨for the Players.⟩

GUILDENSTERN There are the players.

HAMLET Gentlemen, you are welcome to Elsinore.
Your hands, come then. Th' appurtenance of wel-
come is fashion and ceremony. Let me comply 395
with you in this garb, ⟨lest my⟩ extent to the players,
which, I tell you, must show fairly outwards, should
more appear like entertainment than yours. You are
welcome. But my uncle-father and aunt-mother are
deceived. 400

402. **mad north-north-west:** only at certain times (**when the wind** sits in certain directions)

403. **I know . . . a handsaw:** a proverb that means "I can distinguish between things that do not resemble each other"

407. **swaddling clouts:** cloth for swaddling a newborn baby

408. **Haply:** perhaps

409. **twice a child: a child** for the second time (proverbial)

414. **Roscius:** a Roman actor in the first century B.C.E.

417. **Buzz, buzz:** a rude response, suggesting that Polonius's news is old news

423–24. **scene . . . unlimited:** perhaps, plays that observe the classical unities of time and place, as well as those that pay no attention to such limits

424. **Seneca:** a Roman philosopher and writer of tragedies; **heavy:** serious

425. **Plautus:** a Roman writer of comedies; **For the law . . . liberty:** i.e., for plays that follow the rules of composition and those that do not

427. **Jephthah:** According to the biblical story (Judges 11.29–40), Jephthah, because of a rash vow, had to sacrifice his daughter. Hamlet goes on to sing lines from a popular ballad based on Jephthah's story.

432. **passing:** surpassingly, exceedingly

GUILDENSTERN In what, my dear lord?

HAMLET I am but mad north-north-west. When the wind is southerly, I know a hawk from a handsaw.

Enter Polonius.

POLONIUS Well be with you, gentlemen.

HAMLET Hark you, Guildenstern, and you too—at each ear a hearer! That great baby you see there is not yet out of his swaddling clouts. 405

ROSENCRANTZ Haply he is the second time come to them, for they say an old man is twice a child.

HAMLET I will prophesy he comes to tell me of the players; mark it.—You say right, sir, a Monday morning, 'twas then indeed. 410

POLONIUS My lord, I have news to tell you.

HAMLET My lord, I have news to tell you: when Roscius was an actor in Rome— 415

POLONIUS The actors are come hither, my lord.

HAMLET Buzz, buzz.

POLONIUS Upon my honor—

HAMLET Then came each actor on his ass.

POLONIUS The best actors in the world, either for tragedy, comedy, history, pastoral, pastoral-comical, historical-pastoral, ⟨tragical-historical, tragical-comical-historical-pastoral,⟩ scene individable, or poem unlimited. Seneca cannot be too heavy, nor Plautus too light. For the law of writ and the liberty, these are the only men. 420 425

HAMLET O Jephthah, judge of Israel, what a treasure hadst thou!

POLONIUS What a treasure had he, my lord?

HAMLET Why, 430
    One fair daughter, and no more,
    The which he lovèd passing well.

POLONIUS, ⌜*aside*⌝ Still on my daughter.

HAMLET Am I not i' th' right, old Jephthah?

440. **lot:** chance; **wot:** knows

443. **row:** stanza; **chanson:** ballad

444. **my abridgment:** that which cuts short my recitation

447. **valanced:** fringed (i.e., with a beard)

448. **beard:** defy, confront; **What:** an interjection introducing an exclamation or question

449. **my young lady and mistress:** addressed to the boy actor who plays the women's parts; **By'r Lady:** a mild oath on the Virgin Mary

451. **the altitude of a chopine:** the height of the thick sole of a shoe called a **chopine**—i.e., the boy has grown several inches in height

451–53. **a piece . . . ring:** Hamlet thus expresses his hope that the boy's **voice** is **not cracked** but is still suitable for female parts. (A coin is not lawful money if it has a crack that extends inward from the edge into **the ring** that surrounds the image of the sovereign's head.)

453. **e'en to 't:** go at it

454. **fly at anything we see:** i.e., undertake **anything,** no matter how difficult

455. **straight:** straightaway, at once

456. **quality:** professional ability

461. **caviary to the general:** i.e., like caviar, too exotic for average tastes

463. **cried . . . of:** spoke with more authority than

464. **digested:** ordered, arranged

465. **modesty:** restraint; **cunning:** skill

466. **sallets:** i.e., spicy (indelicate) words

467. **no matter:** nothing

468. **affection:** artificiality, affectation

POLONIUS   If you call me "Jephthah," my lord: I have a   435
  daughter that I love passing well.
HAMLET   Nay, that follows not.
POLONIUS   What follows then, my lord?
HAMLET   Why,

> As by lot, God wot   440

and then, you know,

> It came to pass, as most like it was—

the first row of the pious chanson will show you
more, for look where my abridgment comes.

Enter the Players.

You are welcome, masters; welcome all.—I am glad   445
to see thee well.—Welcome, good friends.—O ⟨my⟩
old friend! Why, thy face is valanced since I saw thee
last. Com'st thou to beard me in Denmark?—What,
my young lady and mistress! ⟨By'r⟩ Lady, your lady-
ship is nearer to heaven than when I saw you last, by   450
the altitude of a chopine. Pray God your voice, like a
piece of uncurrent gold, be not cracked within the
ring. Masters, you are all welcome. We'll e'en to 't
like ⟨French⟩ falconers, fly at anything we see. We'll
have a speech straight. Come, give us a taste of your   455
quality. Come, a passionate speech.
⟨FIRST⟩ PLAYER   What speech, my good lord?
HAMLET   I heard thee speak me a speech once, but it
  was never acted, or, if it was, not above once; for
  the play, I remember, pleased not the million: 460
  'twas caviary to the general. But it was (as I
  received it, and others whose judgments in such
  matters cried in the top of mine) an excellent play,
  well digested in the scenes, set down with as much
  modesty as cunning. I remember one said there   465
  were no sallets in the lines to make the matter
  savory, nor no matter in the phrase that might indict
  the author of affection, but called it an honest

470. **fine:** gaudy

471–73. **Aeneas' tale . . . of Priam's slaughter:** Aeneas, hero of Virgil's *Aeneid,* tells **Dido,** queen of Carthage, stories of the Trojan War. Among them is that of Priam, king of Troy, who was killed by Pyrrhus seeking revenge for the death of his father, Achilles. **thereabout of it:** near that part **of it**

475. **Hyrcanian beast:** a tiger (Hyrcania, in Roman times, was the name of a region now in Iran at the southern end of the Caspian Sea. In the *Aeneid,* it is associated with tigers.)

477. **arms:** armor

479. **horse:** the wooden **horse** in which the Greeks hid themselves to gain entry into Troy

480. **this . . . complexion:** i.e., **this** (already) dreadful and dark appearance

482. **gules:** red (a heraldic term); **tricked:** decorated

484. **impasted:** formed into a crust; **parching:** scorching (because Troy is on fire) See picture, page 114.

485. **tyrannous:** oppressive

486. **their lord's murder:** the (impending) **murder** of Priam, lord of Troy, and hence of its **streets** (line 484)

487. **o'ersizèd:** covered as with *size,* a glaze or filler

488. **carbuncles:** deep red jewels that in myth were said to glow in the dark

492. **discretion:** judgment, discernment

496. **Repugnant to:** opposing, resisting

498. **fell:** cruel

(continued)

method, [as wholesome as sweet and, by very much,
more handsome than fine.] One speech in 't I 470
chiefly loved. 'Twas Aeneas' ⟨tale⟩ to Dido, and
thereabout of it especially when he speaks of
Priam's slaughter. If it live in your memory, begin at
this line—let me see, let me see:

The rugged Pyrrhus, like th' Hyrcanian beast— 475
'tis not so; it begins with Pyrrhus:
The rugged Pyrrhus, he whose sable arms,
Black as his purpose, did the night resemble
When he lay couchèd in th' ominous horse,
Hath now this dread and black complexion smeared 480
With heraldry more dismal. Head to foot,
Now is he total gules, horridly tricked
With blood of fathers, mothers, daughters, sons,
Baked and impasted with the parching streets,
That lend a tyrannous and a damnèd light 485
To their lord's murder. Roasted in wrath and fire,
And thus o'ersizèd with coagulate gore,
With eyes like carbuncles, the hellish Pyrrhus
Old grandsire Priam seeks.
 So, proceed you. 490
POLONIUS 'Fore God, my lord, well spoken, with good
 accent and good discretion.
⟨FIRST⟩ PLAYER   *Anon he finds him*
Striking too short at Greeks. His antique sword,
Rebellious to his arm, lies where it falls, 495
Repugnant to command. Unequal matched,
Pyrrhus at Priam drives, in rage strikes wide;
But with the whiff and wind of his fell sword
Th' unnervèd father falls. ⟨Then senseless Ilium,⟩
Seeming to feel this blow, with flaming top 500
Stoops to his base, and with a hideous crash
Takes prisoner Pyrrhus' ear. For lo, his sword,
Which was declining on the milky head
Of reverend Priam, seemed i' th' air to stick.

499. **senseless:** without human senses; **Ilium:** the royal citadel within Troy

501. **his base:** its foundation

503. **declining:** descending

506. **will and matter:** perhaps, desire and means of accomplishing it

508. **against:** i.e., just before

509. **rack:** high clouds driven by the wind

510. **orb:** i.e., Earth

514. **Cyclops':** The Cyclops were Titans who forged thunderbolts for Jove, king of the Roman gods. (See picture of Jove, page 160.)

515. **Mars's:** Mars was the Roman god of war; **for proof eterne:** to stand the test of eternity

518. **Out:** an exclamation of indignant reproach; **strumpet: Fortune** is called a **strumpet** because she gives her favors whimsically and she is faithful to no man. (See picture, page 94.)

520. **fellies:** sections of the wheel's rim; **wheel:** Fortune was often pictured as controlling human life by turning a great wheel on which she stood or sat. (See picture, page 124.)

521. **nave:** hub of the wheel

525. **jig:** a lively, mocking song

526. **Hecuba:** the wife of Priam and queen of Troy

527. **moblèd:** To moble oneself is to muffle one's head or face.

531. **bisson rheum:** blinding tears; **clout:** cloth

533. **lank and all o'erteemèd:** shrunken and worn out with childbearing

536–37. **'Gainst . . . pronounced: would have** uttered treasonous statements against **Fortune's** rule (See picture, page 64.)

So as a painted tyrant Pyrrhus stood 505
⟨And,⟩ like a neutral to his will and matter,
Did nothing.
But as we often see against some storm
A silence in the heavens, the rack stand still,
The bold winds speechless, and the orb below 510
As hush as death, anon the dreadful thunder
Doth rend the region; so, after Pyrrhus' pause,
Aroused vengeance sets him new a-work,
And never did the Cyclops' hammers fall
On Mars's armor, forged for proof eterne, 515
With less remorse than Pyrrhus' bleeding sword
Now falls on Priam.
Out, out, thou strumpet Fortune! All you gods
In general synod take away her power,
Break all the spokes and ⌜fellies⌝ from her wheel, 520
And bowl the round nave down the hill of heaven
As low as to the fiends!

POLONIUS This is too long.

HAMLET It shall to the barber's with your beard.—
 Prithee say on. He's for a jig or a tale of bawdry, or 525
 he sleeps. Say on; come to Hecuba.

⟨FIRST⟩ PLAYER
But who, ah woe, had seen the mobled queen—

HAMLET "The mobled queen"?

POLONIUS That's good. ⟨⌜"Mobled⌝ queen" is good.⟩

⟨FIRST⟩ PLAYER
Run barefoot up and down, threat'ning the flames 530
With ⟨bisson rheum,⟩ a clout upon that head
Where late the diadem stood, and for a robe,
About her lank and all o'erteemed loins
A blanket, in the alarm of fear caught up—
Who this had seen, with tongue in venom steeped, 535
'Gainst Fortune's state would treason have
 pronounced.
But if the gods themselves did see her then

543. **milch:** wet with tears, milky
544. **passion:** i.e., (aroused) deep emotion
545. **whe'er:** whether
549. **bestowed:** lodged, housed
550. **abstract:** summary
552. **ill:** bad, unfavorable
555. **God's bodykins:** a mild oath (by **God's** little body)

Burning Troy. (2.2.484, 530)
From Thomas Heywood, *The Iron Age . . .* (1632).

114

When she saw Pyrrhus make malicious sport
In mincing with his sword her ⟨husband's⟩ limbs,   540
The instant burst of clamor that she made
(Unless things mortal move them not at all)
Would have made milch the burning eyes of heaven
And passion in the gods.

POLONIUS   Look whe'er he has not turned his color and   545
has tears in 's eyes. Prithee, no more.

HAMLET   'Tis well. I'll have thee speak out the rest of
this soon.—Good my lord, will you see the players
well bestowed? Do you hear, let them be well used,
for they are the abstract and brief chronicles of the   550
time. After your death you were better have a bad
epitaph than their ill report while you live.

POLONIUS   My lord, I will use them according to their
desert.

HAMLET   God's ⟨bodykins,⟩ man, much better! Use ev-   555
ery man after his desert and who shall 'scape
whipping? Use them after your own honor and
dignity. The less they deserve, the more merit is in
your bounty. Take them in.

POLONIUS   Come, sirs.   560

HAMLET   Follow him, friends. We'll hear a play tomor-
row. ⌜*As Polonius and Players exit, Hamlet speaks to*
the First Player.⌝ Dost thou hear me, old friend? Can
you play "The Murder of Gonzago"?

⌜FIRST⌝ PLAYER   Ay, my lord.   565

HAMLET   We'll ha 't tomorrow night. You could, for ⟨a⟩
need, study a speech of some dozen or sixteen
lines, which I would set down and insert in 't,
could you not?

⌜FIRST⌝ PLAYER   Ay, my lord.   570

HAMLET   Very well. Follow that lord—and look you
mock him not. ⌜*First Player exits.*⌝ My good friends,
I'll leave you till night. You are welcome to Elsinore.

ROSENCRANTZ   Good my lord.

579. **But:** merely

580–81. **Could . . . wanned:** i.e., **could** work **his soul** into such accord with **his** thought that, from his soul's **working** on his body, **his** face grew pale

582. **aspect:** face, facial expression

583–84. **his whole function . . . conceit:** i.e., all the bodily powers that express emotion responding with outward appearances to match his thoughts

591. **Make mad . . . free:** i.e., madden guilty spectators and terrify those who are innocent

592. **Confound the ignorant:** dumbfound those previously ignorant; **amaze:** astound

594. **muddy-mettled:** dull-spirited; **peak:** mope

595. **John-a-dreams:** a proverbial name for an absent-minded dreamer; **unpregnant of:** unfilled by, and therefore never to give birth (to action)

598. **defeat:** overthrow

601–2. **gives me . . . lungs:** i.e., calls me an absolute liar

603. **'Swounds:** a strong oath (by Christ's wounds)

604–5. **I am . . . bitter:** For the complicated wordplay in these lines, see longer note, page 290.

606. **kites:** birds of prey (See picture, page 118.)

608. **kindless:** unnatural

HAMLET
  Ay, so, good-bye to you. 575
                ⌜*Rosencrantz and Guildenstern*⌝ *exit.*
                 Now I am alone.
O, what a rogue and peasant slave am I!
Is it not monstrous that this player here,
But in a fiction, in a dream of passion,
Could force his soul so to his own conceit 580
That from her working all ⟨his⟩ visage wanned,
Tears in his eyes, distraction in his aspect,
A broken voice, and his whole function suiting
With forms to his conceit—and all for nothing!
For Hecuba! 585
What's Hecuba to him, or he to ⟨Hecuba,⟩
That he should weep for her? What would he do
Had he the motive and ⟨the cue⟩ for passion
That I have? He would drown the stage with tears
And cleave the general ear with horrid speech, 590
Make mad the guilty and appall the free,
Confound the ignorant and amaze indeed
The very faculties of eyes and ears. Yet I,
A dull and muddy-mettled rascal, peak
Like John-a-dreams, unpregnant of my cause, 595
And can say nothing—no, not for a king
Upon whose property and most dear life
A damned defeat was made. Am I a coward?
Who calls me "villain"? breaks my pate across?
Plucks off my beard and blows it in my face? 600
Tweaks me by the nose? gives me the lie i' th' throat
As deep as to the lungs? Who does me this?
Ha! 'Swounds, I should take it! For it cannot be
But I am pigeon-livered and lack gall
To make oppression bitter, or ere this 605
I should ⟨have⟩ fatted all the region kites
With this slave's offal. Bloody, bawdy villain!
Remorseless, treacherous, lecherous, kindless
  villain!

611. **brave:** admirable
615. **drab:** prostitute
616. **stallion:** courtesan
617. **About:** i.e., turn around
619. **cunning:** art, skill; **scene:** performance
620. **presently:** instantly
626. **tent:** probe (as into a wound)
631. **spirits:** i.e., emotional states (such as **mel-
ancholy**)
632. **Abuses:** deceives, deludes
633. **relative:** pertinent

A kite. (2.2.606)
From Konrad Gesner, *Historiae animalium . . .* (1585–1604).

⟨O vengeance!⟩   610
Why, what an ass am I! This is most brave,
That I, the son of a dear ⌜father⌝ murdered,
Prompted to my revenge by heaven and hell,
Must, like a whore, unpack my heart with words
And fall a-cursing like a very drab,   615
A stallion! Fie upon 't! Foh!
About, my brains!—Hum, I have heard
That guilty creatures sitting at a play
Have, by the very cunning of the scene,
Been struck so to the soul that presently   620
They have proclaimed their malefactions;
For murder, though it have no tongue, will speak
With most miraculous organ. I'll have these players
Play something like the murder of my father
Before mine uncle. I'll observe his looks;   625
I'll tent him to the quick. If he do blench,
I know my course. The spirit that I have seen
May be a ⟨devil,⟩ and the ⟨devil⟩ hath power
T' assume a pleasing shape; yea, and perhaps,
Out of my weakness and my melancholy,   630
As he is very potent with such spirits,
Abuses me to damn me. I'll have grounds
More relative than this. The play's the thing
Wherein I'll catch the conscience of the King.

He exits.

The Tragedy of

HAMLET,

Prince of Denmark

ACT 3

3.1 After Rosencrantz and Guildenstern report their failure to find the cause of Hamlet's madness, Polonius places Ophelia where he and Claudius may secretly observe a meeting between her and Hamlet. Hamlet is at first courteous to Ophelia, but suddenly he turns on her: he denies having loved her, asks where her father is, attacks womankind, and tells her she should enter a nunnery. After Hamlet exits, Claudius decides that Hamlet's erratic behavior is not caused by love and announces a plan to send Hamlet on an embassy to England. Polonius persuades Claudius to take no action until Gertrude talks with Hamlet after the play, which is scheduled for that evening.

---

1. **drift:** conscious direction, steering; **conference:** discourse, conversation
2. **puts . . . confusion:** acts in this distracted way
3. **Grating:** i.e., afflicting, vexing
5. **distracted:** perturbed, unsettled
7. **forward . . . sounded:** i.e., eager **to be** questioned
14–15. **Niggard . . . reply:** not inclined to talk, but willing to answer fully our questions
16. **assay:** tempt
17. **fell out:** happened

⌜*ACT 3*⌝

⌜Scene 1⌝

Enter King, Queen, Polonius, Ophelia, Rosencrantz,
Guildenstern, ⟨and⟩ Lords.

KING
And can you by no drift of conference
Get from him why he puts on this confusion,
Grating so harshly all his days of quiet
With turbulent and dangerous lunacy?

ROSENCRANTZ
He does confess he feels himself distracted,
But from what cause he will by no means speak.

GUILDENSTERN
Nor do we find him forward to be sounded,
But with a crafty madness keeps aloof
When we would bring him on to some confession
Of his true state.

QUEEN   Did he receive you well?

ROSENCRANTZ   Most like a gentleman.

GUILDENSTERN
But with much forcing of his disposition.

ROSENCRANTZ
Niggard of question, but of our demands
Most free in his reply.

QUEEN   Did you assay him to any pastime?

ROSENCRANTZ
Madam, it so fell out that certain players

123

18. **o'erraught:** overtook
21. **order:** instruction
28. **give . . . edge:** i.e., sharpen his desire
32. **closely:** privately
34. **Affront:** meet face to face
35. **espials:** spies
38. **as he is behaved:** according to how he acts

Fortune turning her wheel. (2.2.520)
From Gregor Reisch, *Margarita philosophica . . .* [1503].

We o'erraught on the way. Of these we told him,
And there did seem in him a kind of joy
To hear of it. They are here about the court,   20
And, as I think, they have already order
This night to play before him.
POLONIUS   'Tis most true,
And he beseeched me to entreat your Majesties
To hear and see the matter.   25
KING
With all my heart, and it doth much content me
To hear him so inclined.
Good gentlemen, give him a further edge
And drive his purpose into these delights.
ROSENCRANTZ
We shall, my lord.   *Rosencrantz and Guildenstern*   30
                        ⌜*and Lords*⌝ *exit.*
KING   Sweet Gertrude, leave us ⟨too,⟩
For we have closely sent for Hamlet hither,
That he, as 'twere by accident, may here
Affront Ophelia.
Her father and myself, ⟨lawful espials,⟩   35
⟨Will⟩ so bestow ourselves that, seeing unseen,
We may of their encounter frankly judge
And gather by him, as he is behaved,
If 't be th' affliction of his love or no
That thus he suffers for.   40
QUEEN   I shall obey you.
And for your part, Ophelia, I do wish
That your good beauties be the happy cause
Of Hamlet's wildness. So shall I hope your virtues
Will bring him to his wonted way again,   45
To both your honors.
OPHELIA   Madam, I wish it may.
                         ⌜*Queen exits.*⌝
POLONIUS
Ophelia, walk you here.—Gracious, so please you,

51–52. show . . . loneliness: i.e., the apparent reading of a Bible or prayer book would give a pretext for Ophelia's being alone

52. to blame: i.e., guilty, blameworthy

59–61. The harlot's . . . word: i.e., the pockmarked **cheek** of the whore **is not** uglier, when compared to the illusion of beauty she creates with cosmetics, than is what I have done in comparison to my artful language

64. the question: the matter to be debated (See longer note, page 291.)

71. That flesh . . . to: that we inherit as mortals; **consummation:** condition that fulfills desires and aims

73. rub: obstacle (a technical term from the game of bowls, where a **rub** is any obstruction that hinders or deflects the course of the bowl) See picture, page 76.

75. shuffled off this mortal coil: i.e., untangled ourselves from the flesh; also, detached ourselves from the turmoil of human affairs

76. respect: consideration

77. makes calamity of so long life: i.e., **makes** us put up with unhappiness for such a **long** time

78. time: perhaps, the times, the age we live in; or, perhaps, the damages that **time** inflicts on us

We will bestow ourselves. ⌜*To Ophelia.*⌝ Read on this
    book,   50
That show of such an exercise may color
Your ⟨loneliness.⟩—We are oft to blame in this
('Tis too much proved), that with devotion's visage
And pious action we do sugar o'er
The devil himself.   55
KING, ⌜*aside*⌝   O, 'tis too true!
How smart a lash that speech doth give my
    conscience.
The harlot's cheek beautied with plast'ring art
Is not more ugly to the thing that helps it   60
Than is my deed to my most painted word.
O heavy burden!
POLONIUS
I hear him coming. ⟨Let's⟩ withdraw, my lord.
    ⌜*They withdraw.*⌝

    Enter Hamlet.

HAMLET
To be or not to be—that is the question:
Whether 'tis nobler in the mind to suffer
The slings and arrows of outrageous fortune,   65
Or to take arms against a sea of troubles
And, by opposing, end them. To die, to sleep—
No more—and by a sleep to say we end
The heartache and the thousand natural shocks   70
That flesh is heir to—'tis a consummation
Devoutly to be wished. To die, to sleep—
To sleep, perchance to dream. Ay, there's the rub,
For in that sleep of death what dreams may come,
When we have shuffled off this mortal coil,   75
Must give us pause. There's the respect
That makes calamity of so long life.
For who would bear the whips and scorns of time,
Th' oppressor's wrong, the proud man's contumely,

80. **despised:** unrequited (accent on the first syl-
lable)

81. **office:** i.e., those in **office**

83. **his quietus make:** settle his own account (from *quietus est,* a legal term meaning "he is quit")

84. **bare bodkin:** a mere dagger; or, an un-sheathed dagger; **fardels:** burdens, loads

87. **undiscovered:** unexplored; **bourn:** frontier

88. **puzzles:** i.e., paralyzes

91. **conscience:** i.e., knowledge, consciousness

92. **native hue:** natural color

93. **cast:** shade

94. **pitch:** height (the **pitch** is the highest point in a falcon's flight); **moment:** importance

95. **With this regard:** on this account; **their currents turn awry:** i.e., the great enterprises are like rivers that, turned aside from their main channels, **lose** momentum and become stagnant

96. **Soft you now:** an exclamation to interrupt speech ("wait a moment," "hold," "enough")

A falcon in flight. (3.1.94; 4.7.70)
From George Turberville, *The booke of faulconrie* ... (1575).

The pangs of despised love, the law's delay,   80
The insolence of office, and the spurns
That patient merit of th' unworthy takes,
When he himself might his quietus make
With a bare bodkin? Who would fardels bear,
To grunt and sweat under a weary life,   85
But that the dread of something after death,
The undiscovered country from whose bourn
No traveler returns, puzzles the will
And makes us rather bear those ills we have
Than fly to others that we know not of?   90
Thus conscience does make cowards ⟨of us all,⟩
And thus the native hue of resolution
Is ⟨sicklied⟩ o'er with the pale cast of thought,
And enterprises of great pitch and moment
With this regard their currents turn awry   95
And lose the name of action.—Soft you now,
The fair Ophelia.—Nymph, in thy orisons
Be all my sins remembered.
OPHELIA   Good my lord,
How does your Honor for this many a day?   100
HAMLET   I humbly thank you, well.
OPHELIA
My lord, I have remembrances of yours
That I have longèd long to redeliver.
I pray you now receive them.
HAMLET
No, not I. I never gave you aught.   105
OPHELIA
My honored lord, you know right well you did,
And with them words of so sweet breath composed
As made ⟨the⟩ things more rich. Their perfume
   lost,
Take these again, for to the noble mind   110
Rich gifts wax poor when givers prove unkind.
There, my lord.

113. **honest:** chaste (the usual meaning of this word in Shakespeare when applied to a woman)

115. **fair:** beautiful

117. **honesty:** chastity

118. **discourse to:** conversation with

123. **his:** its

124. **sometime:** formerly; **paradox:** a statement contrary to what is generally thought

125. **the time:** the present age

127–29. **virtue ... relish of it:** The metaphor here is of grafting a bud or branch to produce better fruit. (See picture, below.) **Virtue,** Hamlet says, may be grafted onto (may **inoculate**) sinful human nature (**our old stock**), but the fruit produced will still taste (**relish**) **of** the original sinfulness.

131. **nunnery:** convent (The word was sometimes used mockingly to refer to a brothel.)

132–33. **indifferent honest:** reasonably virtuous

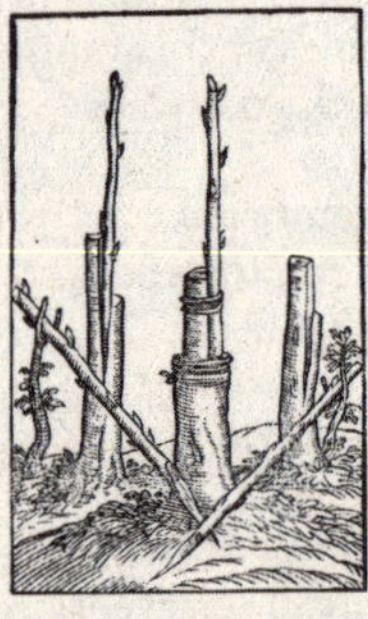

Grafting ("inoculating") tree stock. (3.1.128)
From Marco Bussato, *Giardino di agricoltura* (1599).

HAMLET Ha, ha, are you honest?

OPHELIA My lord?

HAMLET Are you fair? 115

OPHELIA What means your Lordship?

HAMLET That if you be honest and fair, ⟨your honesty⟩ should admit no discourse to your beauty.

OPHELIA Could beauty, my lord, have better commerce than with honesty? 120

HAMLET Ay, truly, for the power of beauty will sooner transform honesty from what it is to a bawd than the force of honesty can translate beauty into his likeness. This was sometime a paradox, but now the time gives it proof. I did love you once. 125

OPHELIA Indeed, my lord, you made me believe so.

HAMLET You should not have believed me, for virtue cannot so ⟨inoculate⟩ our old stock but we shall relish of it. I loved you not.

OPHELIA I was the more deceived. 130

HAMLET Get thee ⟨to⟩ a nunnery. Why wouldst thou be a breeder of sinners? I am myself indifferent honest, but yet I could accuse me of such things that it were better my mother had not borne me: I am very proud, revengeful, ambitious, with more of- 135 fenses at my beck than I have thoughts to put them in, imagination to give them shape, or time to act them in. What should such fellows as I do crawling between earth and heaven? We are arrant knaves ⟨all;⟩ believe none of us. Go thy ways to a nunnery. 140 Where's your father?

OPHELIA At home, my lord.

HAMLET Let the doors be shut upon him that he may play the fool nowhere but in 's own house. Farewell.

OPHELIA O, help him, you sweet heavens! 145

HAMLET If thou dost marry, I'll give thee this plague for thy dowry: be thou as chaste as ice, as pure as snow, thou shalt not escape calumny. Get thee to a

151. **monsters:** cuckolds (In the standard joke, a cuckold—a man whose wife was unfaithful—grew horns on his forehead. See picture, page 212.)

157. **nickname:** call by the wrong name

157–58. **make . . . ignorance:** call **your** immorality **ignorance** (The word **wantonness** may here have the less frequent meaning of "affectation.")

159. **on 't:** of it

164–65. **courtier's . . . sword:** i.e., **the courtier's eye, the scholar's tongue, the soldier's sword**

166. **expectancy:** i.e., hope; **rose:** paragon

167. **glass of fashion:** mirror of proper behavior; **mold of form:** model of attractiveness

172. **out of time: out of** correct rhythm

173. **blown:** vigorous, fresh (The word, applied to flowers in bloom, picks up the earlier **rose of the . . . state** [line 166].)

174. **Blasted with ecstasy:** blighted by madness

176. **affections:** emotions, mental state

180. **doubt:** fear; **the hatch and the disclose:** Both **hatch** and **disclose** mean to break out of the egg—here, the "egg" on which Hamlet's **melancholy sits on brood** (line 179).

nunnery, farewell. Or if thou wilt needs marry,
marry a fool, for wise men know well enough what 150
monsters you make of them. To a nunnery, go, and
quickly too. Farewell.

OPHELIA Heavenly powers, restore him!

HAMLET I have heard of your paintings ⟨too,⟩ well
enough. God hath given you one face, and you 155
make yourselves another. You jig and amble, and
you ⟨lisp;⟩ you nickname God's creatures and make
your wantonness ⟨your⟩ ignorance. Go to, I'll no
more on 't. It hath made me mad. I say we will have
no more marriage. Those that are married already, 160
all but one, shall live. The rest shall keep as they are.
To a nunnery, go.　　　　　　　　　　　*He exits.*

OPHELIA
O, what a noble mind is here o'erthrown!
The courtier's, soldier's, scholar's, eye, tongue,
　　sword,　　　　　　　　　　　　　　　　　　165
⟨Th' expectancy⟩ and rose of the fair state,
The glass of fashion and the mold of form,
Th' observed of all observers, quite, quite down!
And I, of ladies most deject and wretched,
That sucked the honey of his musicked vows, 170
Now see ⟨that⟩ noble and most sovereign reason,
Like sweet bells jangled, out of time and harsh;
That unmatched form and stature of blown youth
Blasted with ecstasy. O, woe is me
T' have seen what I have seen, see what I see! 175

KING, ⌜*advancing with*⌝ *Polonius*
Love? His affections do not that way tend;
Nor what he spake, though it lacked form a little,
Was not like madness. There's something in his soul
O'er which his melancholy sits on brood,
And I do doubt the hatch and the disclose 180
Will be some danger; which for to prevent,
I have in quick determination

184. **For . . . tribute:** i.e., to demand that England pay the overdue money it sends to Denmark (as a sign of submission or for protection or peace)

187. **something-settled:** somehow fixed

197. **round:** plainspoken

199. **find him not:** i.e., does not discover his secret

3.2 Hamlet gives direction to the actors and asks Horatio to help him observe Claudius's reaction to the play. When the court arrive, Hamlet makes bawdy and bitter comments to Ophelia. The traveling actors perform, in dumb show and then with dialogue, a story that includes many elements of Claudius's alleged seduction of Gertrude and murder of King Hamlet. At the moment that the Player King is murdered in his garden by his nephew, Claudius stops the play and rushes out. Hamlet is exuberant that the Ghost's word has been proved true. Rosencrantz and Guildenstern return to tell Hamlet that Claudius is furious and that Gertrude wishes to see Hamlet at once in her sitting room. Hamlet promises himself that he will not harm her, though he will "speak daggers."

---

3. **I had as lief:** I'd just as soon

Thus set it down: he shall with speed to England
For the demand of our neglected tribute.
Haply the seas, and countries different,   185
With variable objects, shall expel
This something-settled matter in his heart,
Whereon his brains still beating puts him thus
From fashion of himself. What think you on 't?
POLONIUS
It shall do well. But yet do I believe   190
The origin and commencement of his grief
Sprung from neglected love.—How now, Ophelia?
You need not tell us what Lord Hamlet said;
We heard it all.—My lord, do as you please,
But, if you hold it fit, after the play   195
Let his queen-mother all alone entreat him
To show his grief. Let her be round with him;
And I'll be placed, so please you, in the ear
Of all their conference. If she find him not,
To England send him, or confine him where   200
Your wisdom best shall think.
KING   It shall be so.
Madness in great ones must not ⟨unwatched⟩ go.
                              They exit.

⌜Scene 2⌝

Enter Hamlet and three of the Players.

HAMLET   Speak the speech, I pray you, as I pronounced
it to you, trippingly on the tongue; but if you mouth
it, as many of our players do, I had as lief the
town-crier spoke my lines. Nor do not saw the air
too much with your hand, thus, but use all gently;   5
for in the very torrent, tempest, and, as I may say,
whirlwind of your passion, you must acquire and
beget a temperance that may give it smoothness. O,

9. **robustious:** noisy, boisterous

11. **groundlings:** spectators who stood in the theater yard rather than sitting in gallery seats or around the stage, and thus paid less for their tickets (This is the first recorded use of this word.)

12. **capable of:** able to appreciate

14. **Termagant:** a figure who medieval Christians wrongly believed was worshipped by Muslims (He was probably shown onstage as ranting and unrestrained, though no plays are extant in which he appears.)

15. **Herod:** Herod of Judea, who appears in medieval drama as a raging tyrant

20. **modesty:** moderation, absence of excess

21. **from:** opposite to

22. **playing:** acting

25. **the . . . time:** i.e., the present exactly as it is

26. **his:** its; **pressure:** shape

26–27. **come tardy off:** done inadequately

27. **the unskillful:** those lacking judgment

28–29. **the censure . . . one:** the judgment of even one **of which**

29. **allowance:** estimation

32. **not to speak it profanely: not** intending **to** be profane in what I'm about to say

33. **Christians:** respectable human beings (an informal usage)

36. **journeymen:** hirelings who work for daily wages

38. **indifferently:** pretty well

41. **clowns:** comic roles

42. **of them:** i.e., some **of them**

43. **barren:** dull, unintelligent

it offends me to the soul to hear a robustious,
periwig-pated fellow tear a passion to tatters, to very　10
rags, to split the ears of the groundlings, who for the
most part are capable of nothing but inexplicable
dumb shows and noise. I would have such a fellow
whipped for o'erdoing Termagant. It out-Herods
Herod. Pray you, avoid it.　15
PLAYER　I warrant your Honor.
HAMLET　Be not too tame neither, but let your own
discretion be your tutor. Suit the action to the
word, the word to the action, with this special
observance, that you o'erstep not the modesty of　20
nature. For anything so o'erdone is from the pur-
pose of playing, whose end, both at the first and
now, was and is to hold, as 'twere, the mirror up to
nature, to show virtue her ⟨own⟩ feature, scorn her
own image, and the very age and body of the time　25
his form and pressure. Now this overdone or come
tardy off, though it makes the unskillful laugh,
cannot but make the judicious grieve, the censure
of ⟨the⟩ which one must in your allowance o'erweigh
a whole theater of others. O, there be players that I　30
have seen play and heard others ⟨praise⟩ (and that
highly), not to speak it profanely, that, neither
having th' accent of Christians nor the gait of
Christian, pagan, nor man, have so strutted and
bellowed that I have thought some of nature's　35
journeymen had made men, and not made them
well, they imitated humanity so abominably.
PLAYER　I hope we have reformed that indifferently
with us, ⟨sir.⟩
HAMLET　O, reform it altogether. And let those that play　40
your clowns speak no more than is set down for
them, for there be of them that will themselves
laugh, to set on some quantity of barren spectators
to laugh too, though in the meantime some neces-

45. **question:** matter, subject, topic

50. **presently:** immediately

57. **my conversation coped withal:** my experience has brought me into contact with

61. **revenue:** accent on the second syllable

64. **the candied . . . pomp:** i.e., the flatterer fawn on the wealthy (See longer note, page 292.)

65. **pregnant:** ready (to bend)

66. **thrift:** profit

67. **dear:** highly prized

68. **election:** choice

71. **Fortune's buffets and rewards:** See note to 2.2.247 and picture, page 64.

73. **blood:** i.e., emotions, passions

74. **commeddled:** mixed together

sary question of the play be then to be considered.   45
That's villainous and shows a most pitiful ambition
in the fool that uses it. Go make you ready.

⟨*Players exit.*⟩

Enter Polonius, Guildenstern, and Rosencrantz.

How now, my lord, will the King hear this piece of
work?

POLONIUS   And the Queen too, and that presently.   50
HAMLET   Bid the players make haste.   ⟨*Polonius exits.*⟩
Will you two help to hasten them?
ROSENCRANTZ   Ay, my lord.   *They exit.*
HAMLET   What ho, Horatio!

Enter Horatio.

HORATIO   Here, sweet lord, at your service.   55
HAMLET
  Horatio, thou art e'en as just a man
  As e'er my conversation coped withal.
HORATIO
  O, my dear lord—
⟨HAMLET⟩   Nay, do not think I flatter,
  For what advancement may I hope from thee   60
  That no revenue hast but thy good spirits
  To feed and clothe thee? Why should the poor be
   flattered?
  No, let the candied tongue lick absurd pomp
  And crook the pregnant hinges of the knee   65
  Where thrift may follow fawning. Dost thou hear?
  Since my dear soul was mistress of her choice
  And could of men distinguish, her election
  Hath sealed thee for herself. For thou hast been
  As one in suffering all that suffers nothing,   70
  A man that Fortune's buffets and rewards
  Hast ta'en with equal thanks; and blessed are those
  Whose blood and judgment are so well
   commeddled

75. **pipe:** small wind instrument, like a flute

76. **sound:** i.e., play; **stop:** i.e., note (literally, hole that the musician's finger or thumb covers to produce a given sound)

84. **comment:** observation

85. **occulted:** deliberately hidden

86. **unkennel:** a term describing the driving of a fox from its lair

89. **Vulcan's stithy:** forge of the Roman god of fire and metalworking (See picture, page 188.)

92. **censure of:** i.e., forming an opinion about; **seeming:** appearance, behavior

96. **idle:** This word could mean "out of one's mind, delerious."

97 SD. **Trumpets and Kettle Drums:** men carrying (and perhaps playing) **trumpets and** kettledrums

98. **fares:** does (In lines 99–101, Hamlet responds as if the word carried its meaning of "feeds," i.e., "eats.")

99. **chameleon's dish:** Chameleons were thought to live off **air** (line 100).

102. **have nothing with:** can make **nothing** of

103. **are not mine:** perhaps, say nothing to me

104. **now:** i.e., **now** that I've spoken them (proverbial)

105. **played:** acted onstage

That they are not a pipe for Fortune's finger   75
To sound what stop she please. Give me that man
That is not passion's slave, and I will wear him
In my heart's core, ay, in my heart of heart,
As I do thee.—Something too much of this.—
There is a play tonight before the King.   80
One scene of it comes near the circumstance
Which I have told thee of my father's death.
I prithee, when thou seest that act afoot,
Even with the very comment of thy soul
Observe my uncle. If his occulted guilt   85
Do not itself unkennel in one speech,
It is a damnèd ghost that we have seen,
And my imaginations are as foul
As Vulcan's stithy. Give him heedful note,
For I mine eyes will rivet to his face,   90
And, after, we will both our judgments join
In censure of his seeming.
HORATIO   Well, my lord.
If he steal aught the whilst this play is playing
And 'scape ⟨detecting⟩, I will pay the theft.   95
                              ⟨*Sound a flourish.*⟩
HAMLET They are coming to the play. I must be idle.
     Get you a place.

Enter Trumpets and Kettle Drums. ⟨Enter⟩ King, Queen,
Polonius, Ophelia, ⟨Rosencrantz, Guildenstern, and other
     Lords attendant with ⌜the King's⌝ guard carrying
                         torches.⟩

KING How fares our cousin Hamlet?
HAMLET Excellent, i' faith, of the chameleon's dish. I
     eat the air, promise-crammed. You cannot feed 100
     capons so.
KING I have nothing with this answer, Hamlet. These
     words are not mine.
HAMLET No, nor mine now. ⌜*To Polonius.*⌝ My lord, you
     played once i' th' university, you say?   105

113–14. **stay . . . patience:** await your pleasure

116–31. **Here's metal . . . my lord:** See longer note, page 292.

132. **your only jig-maker:** the best comic of them all

134. **within 's:** within this

137. **black:** i.e., mourning garments

138. **a suit of sables:** luxurious fur garments

A lady "painting" herself. (3.1.154–56; 5.1.199–201)
From Hannah Woolley, *The accomplish'd ladies delight . . .* (1684).

POLONIUS That did I, my lord, and was accounted a
   good actor.

HAMLET What did you enact?

POLONIUS I did enact Julius Caesar. I was killed i' th'
   Capitol. Brutus killed me.　110

HAMLET It was a brute part of him to kill so capital a
   calf there.—Be the players ready?

ROSENCRANTZ Ay, my lord. They stay upon your pa-
   tience.

QUEEN Come hither, my dear Hamlet, sit by me.　115

HAMLET No, good mother. Here's metal more
   attractive.   ⌜*Hamlet takes a place near Ophelia.*⌝

POLONIUS, ⌜*to the King*⌝ Oh, ho! Do you mark that?

HAMLET Lady, shall I lie in your lap?

OPHELIA No, my lord.　120

⟨HAMLET I mean, my head upon your lap?

OPHELIA Ay, my lord.⟩

HAMLET Do you think I meant country matters?

OPHELIA I think nothing, my lord.

HAMLET That's a fair thought to lie between maids'　125
   legs.

OPHELIA What is, my lord?

HAMLET Nothing.

OPHELIA You are merry, my lord.

HAMLET Who, I?　130

OPHELIA Ay, my lord.

HAMLET O God, your only jig-maker. What should a
   man do but be merry? For look you how cheerfully
   my mother looks, and my father died within 's two
   hours.　135

OPHELIA Nay, 'tis twice two months, my lord.

HAMLET So long? Nay, then, let the devil wear black,
   for I'll have a suit of sables. O heavens, die two
   months ago, and not forgotten yet? Then there's
   hope a great man's memory may outlive his life half　140
   a year. But, by 'r Lady, he must build churches, then,

142. **suffer not thinking on:** endure oblivion

142–43. **the hobby-horse:** a character in morris dances (The song that Hamlet quotes expresses sorrow that such figures are gone and forgotten.) See picture, below.

144 SD. **Dumb show:** a scene without words

150. **his crown:** the King's **crown**

152. **makes passionate action:** i.e., gestures as if grief-stricken

158. **miching mallecho:** skulking misdeed (**Miching** is dialect for "sneaking"; **mallecho** is the Spanish *malhecho*, "misdeed.")

160. **Belike:** perhaps; **imports:** makes known, conveys; **argument:** plot

168. **naught:** naughty, indecent; **mark:** pay attention to

A hobby horse. (3.2.143)
From *Morris dancers . . .* (Anon., n.d.).

or else shall he suffer not thinking on, with the
hobby-horse, whose epitaph is "For oh, for oh, the
hobby-horse is forgot."

The trumpets sounds. Dumb show follows.

Enter a King and a Queen, ⟨very lovingly,⟩ the Queen 145
embracing him and he her. ⟨She kneels and makes show of
protestation unto him.⟩ He takes her up and declines his
head upon her neck. He lies him down upon a bank of
flowers. She, seeing him asleep, leaves him. Anon
⟨comes⟩ in another man, takes off his crown, kisses it, pours 150
poison in the sleeper's ears, and leaves him. The Queen
returns, finds the King dead, makes passionate action. The
poisoner with some three or four come in again, seem to
condole with her. The dead body is carried away. The
poisoner woos the Queen with gifts. She seems harsh 155
awhile but in the end accepts ⟨his⟩ love.

⌜*Players exit.*⌝

OPHELIA What means this, my lord?
HAMLET Marry, this ⟨is miching⟩ mallecho. It means
    mischief.
OPHELIA Belike this show imports the argument of the 160
    play.

Enter Prologue.

HAMLET We shall know by this fellow. The players
    cannot keep ⟨counsel;⟩ they'll tell all.
OPHELIA Will he tell us what this show meant?
HAMLET Ay, or any show that you will show him. Be 165
    not you ashamed to show, he'll not shame to tell you
    what it means.
OPHELIA You are naught, you are naught. I'll mark the
    play.
PROLOGUE

> *For us and for our tragedy,* 170
> *Here stooping to your clemency,*
> *We beg your hearing patiently.*   ⌜*He exits.*⌝

173. posy of a ring: a poem inscribed in a ring

176–77. Full . . . ground: The language of this play-within-the-play is set apart from that surrounding it by rhymed couplets, complicated word order, frequent repetition, and arcane diction. **Phoebus' cart:** the chariot of the sun god, which appears to circle the Earth daily. (See longer note, page 292, and picture, page 32.) **Neptune's salt wash:** the ocean (Neptune was the Roman god of the sea and Tellus was the Roman goddess of the Earth.)

180. Hymen: god of marriage

181. commutual: mutual, reciprocal

184. of late: lately

186. distrust you: fear for you

188. For women . . . love: This line is part of an incomplete couplet; perhaps the completing line was dropped in the printing house.

189–90. women's . . . extremity: i.e., **women's love and fear** are parallel: where **they** do not **love, they** do not **fear;** where **they love** extremely, **they** suffer extreme **fear**

196. My operant powers . . . leave to do: my vital **powers** cease to function

198. haply: perhaps

200. confound the rest: i.e., don't finish your sentence **confound:** destroy

HAMLET   Is this a prologue or the posy of a ring?
OPHELIA   'Tis brief, my lord.
HAMLET   As woman's love.   175

Enter ⌜the Player⌝ King and Queen.

PLAYER KING
  Full thirty times hath Phoebus' cart gone round
  Neptune's salt wash and Tellus' ⟨orbèd⟩ ground,
  And thirty dozen moons with borrowed sheen
  About the world have times twelve thirties been
  Since love our hearts and Hymen did our hands   180
  Unite commutual in most sacred bands.
PLAYER QUEEN
  So many journeys may the sun and moon
  Make us again count o'er ere love be done!
  But woe is me! You are so sick of late,
  So far from cheer and from ⟨your⟩ former state,   185
  That I distrust you. Yet, though I distrust,
  Discomfort you, my lord, it nothing must.
  [For women fear too much, even as they love,]
  And women's fear and love hold quantity,
  In neither aught, or in extremity.   190
  Now what my ⟨love⟩ is, proof hath made you know,
  And, as my love is sized, my fear is so:
  [Where love is great, the littlest doubts are fear;
  Where little fears grow great, great love grows there.]
PLAYER KING
  Faith, I must leave thee, love, and shortly too.   195
  My operant powers their functions leave to do.
  And thou shalt live in this fair world behind,
  Honored, beloved; and haply one as kind
  For husband shalt thou—
PLAYER QUEEN   *O, confound the rest!*   200
  Such love must needs be treason in my breast.
  In second husband let me be accurst.
  None wed the second but who killed the first.

204. **wormwood:** i.e., bitter, harsh

205. **instances:** causes; **move:** prompt, actuate

206. **thrift:** worldly profit

211. **Purpose is but the slave to memory:** i.e., a **purpose** must be remembered if it is to be carried out

212. **validity:** vigor

215–16. **Most . . . debt:** i.e., **we** conveniently **forget** the promises we make **to ourselves**

220. **enactures:** enactments

222. **Grief joys:** i.e., **grief** rejoices; or, **grief** turns into **joy; on slender accident:** on the slightest impetus

223. **aye:** ever

227. **down:** fallen in esteem; **mark:** notice; **favorite:** chosen companion; **flies:** deserts him

229. **hitherto:** thus far

230. **who not needs:** he who lacks nothing

231. **try:** test (his friendship)

232. **seasons him:** turns him into

235. **devices still:** plans always

236. **ends:** outcome, result

HAMLET That's wormwood!
PLAYER QUEEN
   The instances that second marriage move   205
   Are base respects of thrift, but none of love.
   A second time I kill my husband dead
   When second husband kisses me in bed.
PLAYER KING
   I do believe you think what now you speak,
   But what we do determine oft we break.   210
   Purpose is but the slave to memory,
   Of violent birth, but poor validity,
   Which now, the fruit unripe, sticks on the tree
   But fall unshaken when they mellow be.
   Most necessary 'tis that we forget   215
   To pay ourselves what to ourselves is debt.
   What to ourselves in passion we propose,
   The passion ending, doth the purpose lose.
   The violence of either grief or joy
   Their own enactures with themselves destroy.   220
   Where joy most revels, grief doth most lament;
   Grief ⟨joys,⟩ joy grieves, on slender accident.
   This world is not for aye, nor 'tis not strange
   That even our loves should with our fortunes change;
   For 'tis a question left us yet to prove   225
   Whether love lead fortune or else fortune love.
   The great man down, you mark his favorite flies;
   The poor, advanced, makes friends of enemies.
   And hitherto doth love on fortune tend,
   For who not needs shall never lack a friend,   230
   And who in want a hollow friend doth try
   Directly seasons him his enemy.
   But, orderly to end where I begun:
   Our wills and fates do so contrary run
   That our devices still are overthrown;   235
   Our thoughts are ours, their ends none of our own.
   So think thou wilt no second husband wed,
   But die thy thoughts when thy first lord is dead.

239. **Nor Earth:** (may) neither **Earth**

242. **An anchor's . . . scope:** (may) **an** anchorite's (hermit's) food and drink **be my** prospect **in prison**

243. **opposite . . . joy:** obstacle that makes joy's **face** turn pale (or, perhaps, that deprives joy's **face of** all expression)

247. **If . . . now:** perhaps, (1) **if** the Player Queen breaks her word after placing this curse on herself; or, (2) **if** Gertrude speaks out or breaks down after hearing this speech

249. **fain:** gladly; **beguile:** while away

251. **rock:** soothe

254. **methinks:** it seems to me

256. **argument:** plot

261. **Marry:** a mild oath; **how:** perhaps, **how** are we to understand this name; **Tropically:** i.e., as a trope, a figure of speech

264. **anon:** soon; **knavish:** impertinent

265. **free:** innocent

266–67. **Let . . . unwrung:** a proverb that says, in effect: let guilty persons flinch; we have clear consciences   **galled jade:** a horse with raw skin   **withers:** ridge between the horse's shoulders   **unwrung:** not chafed

269. **a chorus:** a character who (as in Shakespeare's *Henry V*) tells the audience what they are about to see

PLAYER QUEEN
   Nor Earth to me give food, nor heaven light,
   Sport and repose lock from me day and night,   240
   [To desperation turn my trust and hope,
   ⌜An⌝ anchor's cheer in prison be my scope.]
   Each opposite that blanks the face of joy
   Meet what I would have well and it destroy.
   Both here and hence pursue me lasting strife,   245
   If, once a widow, ever I be wife.

HAMLET   If she should break it now!

PLAYER KING
   'Tis deeply sworn. Sweet, leave me here awhile.
   My spirits grow dull, and fain I would beguile
   The tedious day with sleep.   ⟨*Sleeps.*⟩   250

PLAYER QUEEN   *Sleep rock thy brain,*
   And never come mischance between us twain.

                     ⌜*Player Queen exits.*⌝

HAMLET   Madam, how like you this play?

QUEEN   The lady doth protest too much, methinks.

HAMLET   O, but she'll keep her word.   255

KING   Have you heard the argument? Is there no offense in 't?

HAMLET   No, no, they do but jest, poison in jest. No offense i' th' world.

KING   What do you call the play?   260

HAMLET   "The Mousetrap." Marry, how? Tropically. This play is the image of a murder done in Vienna. Gonzago is the duke's name, his wife Baptista. You shall see anon. 'Tis a knavish piece of work, but what of that? Your Majesty and we that have free 265 souls, it touches us not. Let the galled jade wince; our withers are unwrung.

Enter Lucianus.

   This is one Lucianus, nephew to the king.

OPHELIA   You are as good as a chorus, my lord.

270–71. **I could . . . dallying:** i.e., **I could** play the role of narrator at a puppet show in which **you and your** lover are shown making love

273–74. **take off mine edge:** make me less sharp; satisfy my desire (Hamlet gives a sexual meaning to Ophelia's **"You are keen"** [i.e., sharp, penetrating] and responds with this double entendre.)

275. **better and worse:** more witty and more offensive

276. **So you mis-take:** i.e., in the same way, you take falsely (Wives promise to "take" their husbands "for better, for worse.")

278–79. **the croaking . . . revenge:** Hamlet here amusingly condenses two lines from the anonymous *The True Tragedy of Richard III* (c. 1591): "The screeking **raven** sits croaking **for revenge.** / Whole herds of beasts comes bellowing **for revenge.**"

282. **Confederate season:** i.e., time being my ally; **else:** otherwise

284. **With Hecate's ban:** by the curse of Hecate, the goddess of sorcery and witchcraft; **blasted:** cursed, blighted

285. **dire property:** dreadful or evil attribute or quality

286. **On . . . usurp:** unjustly steal or encroach upon **wholesome life**

292. **false fire:** discharge of a gun loaded only with powder

299. **watch:** stay awake

HAMLET I could interpret between you and your love,   270
   if I could see the puppets dallying.

OPHELIA You are keen, my lord, you are keen.

HAMLET It would cost you a groaning to take off mine
   edge.

OPHELIA Still better and worse.   275

HAMLET So you mis-take your husbands.—Begin,
   murderer. ⟨Pox,⟩ leave thy damnable faces and
   begin. Come, the croaking raven doth bellow for
   revenge.

LUCIANUS
   Thoughts black, hands apt, drugs fit, and time   280
     agreeing,
   ⟨Confederate⟩ season, else no creature seeing,
   Thou mixture rank, of midnight weeds collected,
   With Hecate's ban thrice blasted, thrice ⟨infected,⟩
   Thy natural magic and dire property   285
   On wholesome life ⟨usurp⟩ immediately.
               ⟨*Pours the poison in his ears.*⟩

HAMLET He poisons him i' th' garden for his estate. His
   name's Gonzago. The story is extant and written in
   very choice Italian. You shall see anon how the
   murderer gets the love of Gonzago's wife.   290
                 ⌜*Claudius rises.*⌝

OPHELIA The King rises.

⟨HAMLET What, frighted with false fire?⟩

QUEEN How fares my lord?

POLONIUS Give o'er the play.

KING Give me some light. Away!   295

POLONIUS Lights, lights, lights!
            All but Hamlet and Horatio exit.

HAMLET
   Why, let the strucken deer go weep,
     The hart ungallèd play.
   For some must watch, while some must sleep:
     Thus runs the world away.   300

301. **feathers:** worn on actors' hats

302. **turn Turk with me: turn** against me

303. **Provincial roses:** i.e., *Roses de Provence,* double damask **roses** (probably made of fabric); **razed:** slashed decoratively

303–4. **a fellowship in a cry of players:** a partnership in a theater company

307. **Damon:** renowned, in Roman mythology, for the depth of his friendship for Pythias

308. **dismantled:** stripped

309. **Jove:** king of the Roman gods (See picture, page 160.)

310. **pajock:** possibly "peacock"

311. **rhymed:** The obvious rhyme word is *ass.*

317–18. **recorders:** wind instruments, straight like a flute but end-blown, with seven holes (or *stops*) along the top length and one stop underneath for the thumb

320. **perdy:** from the French *par dieu,* "by God"

327. **retirement:** withdrawal into seclusion

327–28. **distempered:** upset (with a second meaning of "ill" or "drunk," which is how Hamlet chooses to interpret it)

330. **choler:** biliousness (The word has a second meaning of "anger," which Hamlet plays on at line 334.)

332. **signify:** announce, tell

333. **purgation:** medical cleansing; spiritual purification

Would not this, sir, and a forest of feathers (if the
rest of my fortunes turn Turk with me) with ⟨two⟩
Provincial roses on my razed shoes, get me a
fellowship in a cry of players?

HORATIO Half a share. 305

HAMLET A whole one, I.
  For thou dost know, O Damon dear,
   This realm dismantled was
  Of Jove himself, and now reigns here
   A very very—pajock. 310

HORATIO You might have rhymed.

HAMLET O good Horatio, I'll take the ghost's word for
a thousand pound. Didst perceive?

HORATIO Very well, my lord.

HAMLET Upon the talk of the poisoning? 315

HORATIO I did very well note him.

HAMLET Ah ha! Come, some music! Come, the record-
ers!
  For if the King like not the comedy,
  Why, then, belike he likes it not, perdy. 320
Come, some music!

  Enter Rosencrantz and Guildenstern.

GUILDENSTERN Good my lord, vouchsafe me a word
with you.

HAMLET Sir, a whole history.

GUILDENSTERN The King, sir— 325

HAMLET Ay, sir, what of him?

GUILDENSTERN Is in his retirement marvelous distem-
pered.

HAMLET With drink, sir?

GUILDENSTERN No, my lord, with choler. 330

HAMLET Your wisdom should show itself more richer
to signify this to the doctor, for for me to put him to
his purgation would perhaps plunge him into more
choler.

336. **frame:** order; **start:** shy away (like a nervous or wild horse)

344. **wholesome:** sane

345. **pardon:** permission to depart

351. **as you . . . mother:** Hamlet calls attention to their presumption in referring to the Queen as "your **mother.**"

355. **admiration:** wonder

360. **closet:** private chamber

362. **trade:** Shakespeare generally uses this word in connection with lower-class occupations, sex workers, and merchants.

364. **by these . . . stealers:** i.e., **by these** hands (The phrase borrows from the catechism, where one is told "to keep [one's] hands from picking and stealing.")

367. **deny your griefs:** refuse to disclose the cause of your suffering

GUILDENSTERN Good my lord, put your discourse into 335
 some frame and ⟨start⟩ not so wildly from my
 affair.
HAMLET I am tame, sir. Pronounce.
GUILDENSTERN The Queen your mother, in most great
 affliction of spirit, hath sent me to you. 340
HAMLET You are welcome.
GUILDENSTERN Nay, good my lord, this courtesy is not
 of the right breed. If it shall please you to make me
 a wholesome answer, I will do your mother's
 commandment. If not, your pardon and my return 345
 shall be the end of ⟨my⟩ business.
HAMLET Sir, I cannot.
ROSENCRANTZ What, my lord?
HAMLET Make you a wholesome answer. My wit's
 diseased. But, sir, such answer as I can make, you 350
 shall command—or, rather, as you say, my mother.
 Therefore no more but to the matter. My mother,
 you say—
ROSENCRANTZ Then thus she says: your behavior hath
 struck her into amazement and admiration. 355
HAMLET O wonderful son that can so 'stonish a moth-
 er! But is there no sequel at the heels of this
 mother's admiration? Impart.
ROSENCRANTZ She desires to speak with you in her
 closet ere you go to bed. 360
HAMLET We shall obey, were she ten times our moth-
 er. Have you any further trade with us?
ROSENCRANTZ My lord, you once did love me.
HAMLET And do still, by these pickers and stealers.
ROSENCRANTZ Good my lord, what is your cause of 365
 distemper? You do surely bar the door upon your
 own liberty if you deny your griefs to your friend.
HAMLET Sir, I lack advancement.
ROSENCRANTZ How can that be, when you have the
 voice of the King himself for your succession in 370
 Denmark?

372. **"While the grass grows"**: The rest of **the proverb** reads "the horse starves."

373. **something musty**: somewhat stale, i.e., so familiar it need not be quoted in full (The proverb, in Latin, was in use 350 years before *Hamlet* was written.)

376–77. **go . . . toil**: try to get to the windward side of me, **as if** to force **me into a** trap (Hamlet speaks as if they were hunters and he their quarry.)

381. **this pipe**: the recorder

387. **ventages**: finger holes, or **stops** (line 390), of the recorder (See note to lines 317–18 above.)

396. **sound me**: (1) play me like a musical instrument; (2) measure my depths, as with a fathom line; (3) test me for my secrets (a triple pun)

397. **compass**: (1) full range of an instrument's sound; (2) limits, scope

399. **organ**: musical instrument; **'Sblood**: a strong oath (by God's, or Christ's, blood)

402. **fret**: (1) annoy; (2) torment; (3) provide a stringed instrument with frets (the raised parts on the fingerboard that guide the fingers)

HAMLET Ay, sir, but "While the grass grows"—the proverb is something musty.

Enter the Players with recorders.

O, the recorders! Let me see one. ⌜*He takes a recorder and turns to Guildenstern.*⌝ To withdraw with you: why do you go about to recover the wind of me, as if you would drive me into a toil? 375

GUILDENSTERN O, my lord, if my duty be too bold, my love is too unmannerly.

HAMLET I do not well understand that. Will you play upon this pipe? 380

GUILDENSTERN My lord, I cannot.

HAMLET I pray you.

GUILDENSTERN Believe me, I cannot.

HAMLET I do beseech you. 385

GUILDENSTERN I know no touch of it, my lord.

HAMLET It is as easy as lying. Govern these ventages with your fingers and ⟨thumb,⟩ give it breath with your mouth, and it will discourse most eloquent music. Look you, these are the stops. 390

GUILDENSTERN But these cannot I command to any utt'rance of harmony. I have not the skill.

HAMLET Why, look you now, how unworthy a thing you make of me! You would play upon me, you would seem to know my stops, you would pluck 395 out the heart of my mystery, you would sound me from my lowest note to ⟨the top of⟩ my compass; and there is much music, excellent voice, in this little organ, yet cannot you make it speak. 'Sblood, do you think I am easier to be played on than a pipe? 400 Call me what instrument you will, though you ⟨can⟩ fret me, you cannot play upon me.

Enter Polonius.

God bless you, sir.

405. **presently:** immediately

413. **by and by:** soon, before long; or, perhaps, right away

414. **fool:** trifle with; **top of my bent:** limit of my endurance (For the source of this phrase in archery, see note to 2.2.32, above.)

420. **churchyards yawn:** graves open

425. **Soft:** i.e., wait a minute, not so fast

427. **Nero:** murderer of his mother, Agrippina

431. **How . . . somever:** however; **shent:** punished

432. **give them seals:** i.e., validate my **words** (by putting them into action)

Jove. (3.2.309; 3.4.66)
From Vincenzo Cartari, *Le vere e noue imagini . . .* (1615).

POLONIUS My lord, the Queen would speak with you,
    and presently.   405
HAMLET Do you see yonder cloud that's almost in
    shape of a camel?
POLONIUS By th' Mass, and 'tis like a camel indeed.
HAMLET Methinks it is like a weasel.
POLONIUS It is backed like a weasel.   410
HAMLET Or like a whale.
POLONIUS Very like a whale.
⟨HAMLET⟩ Then I will come to my mother by and by.
    ⌜*Aside.*⌝ They fool me to the top of my bent.—I will
    come by and by.   415
⟨POLONIUS⟩ I will say so.
⟨HAMLET⟩ "By and by" is easily said. Leave me,
    friends.
                              ⌜*All but Hamlet exit.*⌝
    'Tis now the very witching time of night,
    When churchyards yawn and hell itself ⟨breathes⟩   420
      out
    Contagion to this world. Now could I drink hot
      blood
    And do such ⟨bitter⟩ business as the day
    Would quake to look on. Soft, now to my mother.   425
    O heart, lose not thy nature; let not ever
    The soul of Nero enter this firm bosom.
    Let me be cruel, not unnatural.
    I will speak ⟨daggers⟩ to her, but use none.
    My tongue and soul in this be hypocrites: 430
    How in my words somever she be shent,
    To give them seals never, my soul, consent.
                                        He exits.

3.3 Claudius orders Rosencrantz and Guildenstern to take Hamlet to England. Polonius tells Claudius of his plans to spy on Hamlet's conversation with Gertrude. Left alone, Claudius reveals his remorse for killing his brother, and he tries to pray. Hamlet comes upon him kneeling and draws his sword, but then stops to think that if he kills Claudius at prayer, Claudius will go to heaven. Hamlet decides to kill Claudius when the king is committing a sin so that Claudius will instead go to hell. After Hamlet leaves, Claudius rises, saying that he has been unable to pray.

------

 1. **I . . . not:** i.e., **I** do **not like** the way he is acting
 3. **forthwith dispatch:** prepare at once
 5. **The terms of our estate:** my position as a king
 7. **brows:** forehead (presumably alluding to Hamlet's brain)
 8. **ourselves provide:** prepare **ourselves**
 9. **fear:** apprehension, solicitude, concern
 12. **single and peculiar:** individual and private
 14. **noyance:** injury
 16. **cess:** cessation, decease
 17. **gulf:** whirlpool
 18. **it is a: it is** like **a**
 21. **mortised:** securely fastened
 23. **Attends:** i.e., participates in; **boist'rous:** violent, savage
 25. **Arm you . . . to:** i.e., prepare yourself for
 26. **fear:** ground or reason for alarm, cause of fear

⌐Scene 3⌐

Enter King, Rosencrantz, and Guildenstern.

KING
I like him not, nor stands it safe with us
To let his madness range. Therefore prepare you.
I your commission will forthwith dispatch,
And he to England shall along with you.
The terms of our estate may not endure   5
Hazard so near 's as doth hourly grow
Out of his brows.

GUILDENSTERN   We will ourselves provide.
Most holy and religious fear it is
To keep those many many bodies safe   10
That live and feed upon your Majesty.

ROSENCRANTZ
The single and peculiar life is bound
With all the strength and armor of the mind
To keep itself from noyance, but much more
That spirit upon whose weal depends and rests   15
The lives of many. The cess of majesty
Dies not alone, but like a gulf doth draw
What's near it with it; or it is a massy wheel
Fixed on the summit of the highest mount,
To whose ⟨huge⟩ spokes ten thousand lesser things   20
Are mortised and adjoined, which, when it falls,
Each small annexment, petty consequence,
Attends the boist'rous ⟨ruin.⟩ Never alone
Did the king sigh, but ⟨with⟩ a general groan.

KING
Arm you, I pray you, to this speedy voyage,   25
For we will fetters put about this fear,
Which now goes too free-footed.

ROSENCRANTZ   We will haste us.
          ⌐*Rosencrantz and Guildenstern*⌐ *exit.*

Enter Polonius.

30. **convey:** i.e., conceal

31. **process:** discussion; **I'll warrant:** I promise

31–32. **tax him home:** reprimand him strongly

34. **meet:** appropriate

36. **of vantage:** from the vantage point of concealment

41. **primal eldest curse:** The first **curse,** which condemned Cain to a life of "a fugitive and a vagabond," was laid on him for his murder of his brother, Abel (Genesis 4.10–12). See picture, page 184.

50. **Whereto . . . mercy:** what purpose does **mercy** serve

51. **the visage of offense:** perhaps, the face of the offended Deity; or, perhaps, the sinful acts of the offender

53–54. **forestallèd . . . down:** i.e., the **twofold force** of **prayer** (line 52) is that we not be led into temptation and that we be forgiven our trespasses (See Matthew 7.13–15.)

57–58. **am still possessed / Of: still** possess

58. **effects:** i.e., rewards, acquisitions

60. **th' offense:** that which has been gained through the crime

61. **currents:** course of events

62. **Offense's gilded hand:** the golden **hand** of the offender, **gilded** through money illegally obtained; **shove by:** thrust aside

POLONIUS
  My lord, he's going to his mother's closet.
  Behind the arras I'll convey myself   30
  To hear the process. I'll warrant she'll tax him
    home;
  And, as you said (and wisely was it said),
  'Tis meet that some more audience than a mother,
  Since nature makes them partial, should o'erhear   35
  The speech of vantage. Fare you well, my liege.
  I'll call upon you ere you go to bed
  And tell you what I know.
KING   Thanks, dear my lord.
                      ⌈*Polonius*⌉ *exits.*
  O, my offense is rank, it smells to heaven;   40
  It hath the primal eldest curse upon 't,
  A brother's murder. Pray can I not,
  Though inclination be as sharp as will.
  My stronger guilt defeats my strong intent,
  And, like a man to double business bound,   45
  I stand in pause where I shall first begin
  And both neglect. What if this cursèd hand
  Were thicker than itself with brother's blood?
  Is there not rain enough in the sweet heavens
  To wash it white as snow? Whereto serves mercy   50
  But to confront the visage of offense?
  And what's in prayer but this twofold force,
  To be forestallèd ere we come to fall,
  Or ⟨pardoned⟩ being down? Then I'll look up.
  My fault is past. But, O, what form of prayer   55
  Can serve my turn? "Forgive me my foul murder"?
  That cannot be, since I am still possessed
  Of those effects for which I did the murder:
  My crown, mine own ambition, and my queen.
  May one be pardoned and retain th' offense?   60
  In the corrupted currents of this world,
  Offense's gilded hand may ⟨shove⟩ by justice,

64. **'tis not so above:** this is not the case in heaven

65. **There is no shuffling:** in heaven, one cannot escape through evasion

65–68. **the action . . . in evidence:** i.e., in God's court, **the** legal **action** must be brought in accord with the facts; **we** are forced **even** to testify against **ourselves**

68. **rests:** remains

72. **limèd:** trapped, like a bird caught in birdlime

73. **engaged:** entangled; **Make assay:** put forth all your efforts

77. **pat:** opportunely

80. **would be scanned:** i.e., needs to be examined

84. **hire and salary:** i.e., something Claudius should pay me for

85. **grossly, full of bread:** in the full enjoyment of the world (See Ezekiel 16.49: "Pride, fullness **of bread,** and abundance of idleness.")

87. **audit:** final account

88. **circumstance . . . thought:** i.e., limited circumstantial knowledge

89. **'Tis . . . him:** i.e., his spirit is in a serious condition

90. **him:** i.e., Claudius; **purging:** cleansing

93. **know thou a more horrid hent:** i.e., wait for a more horrible occasion

And oft 'tis seen the wicked prize itself
Buys out the law. But 'tis not so above:
There is no shuffling; there the action lies   65
In his true nature, and we ourselves compelled,
Even to the teeth and forehead of our faults,
To give in evidence. What then? What rests?
Try what repentance can. What can it not?
Yet what can it, when one cannot repent?   70
O wretched state! O bosom black as death!
O limèd soul, that, struggling to be free,
Art more engaged! Help, angels! Make assay.
Bow, stubborn knees, and heart with strings of steel
Be soft as sinews of the newborn babe.   75
All may be well.   ⌜*He kneels.*⌝

Enter Hamlet.

HAMLET
Now might I do it ⟨pat,⟩ now he is a-praying,
And now I'll do 't.   ⌜*He draws his sword.*⌝
                    And so he goes to heaven,
And so am I ⟨revenged.⟩ That would be scanned: 80
A villain kills my father, and for that,
I, his sole son, do this same villain send
To heaven.
Why, this is ⟨hire⟩ and ⟨salary,⟩ not revenge.
He took my father grossly, full of bread,   85
With all his crimes broad blown, as flush as May;
And how his audit stands who knows save heaven.
But in our circumstance and course of thought
'Tis heavy with him. And am I then revenged
To take him in the purging of his soul,   90
When he is fit and seasoned for his passage?
No.
Up sword, and know thou a more horrid hent.
                              ⌜*He sheathes his sword.*⌝
When he is drunk asleep, or in his rage,

100. **stays:** waits

101. **This physic:** this medicine (i.e., this postponement of the killing; or, Claudius's purging of himself through prayer)

3.4 In Gertrude's room, Polonius hides behind a tapestry. Hamlet's entrance so alarms Gertrude that she cries out for help. Polonius echoes her cry, and Hamlet, thinking Polonius to be Claudius, stabs him to death. Hamlet then verbally attacks his mother for marrying Claudius. In the middle of Hamlet's attack, the Ghost returns to remind Hamlet that his real purpose is to avenge his father's death. Gertrude cannot see the Ghost and pities Hamlet's apparent madness. After the Ghost exits, Hamlet urges Gertrude to abandon Claudius's bed. He then tells her about Claudius's plan to send him to England and reveals his suspicions that the journey is a plot against him, which he resolves to counter violently. He exits dragging out Polonius's body.

---

1. **straight:** straightaway, immediately; **lay home to him:** reprove him thoroughly

2. **pranks:** malicious deeds

7. **round:** blunt

9. **I'll warrant you:** I promise; **Fear me not:** don't doubt me

Or in th' incestuous pleasure of his bed,   95
At game, a-swearing, or about some act
That has no relish of salvation in 't—
Then trip him, that his heels may kick at heaven,
And that his soul may be as damned and black
As hell, whereto it goes. My mother stays.   100
This physic but prolongs thy sickly days.
           ⌜*Hamlet*⌝ *exits.*

KING, ⌜*rising*⌝
 My words fly up, my thoughts remain below;
 Words without thoughts never to heaven go.
             He exits.

      ⌜Scene 4⌝

   Enter ⟨Queen⟩ and Polonius.

POLONIUS
 He will come straight. Look you lay home to him.
 Tell him his pranks have been too broad to bear
  with
 And that your Grace hath screened and stood
  between   5
 Much heat and him. I'll silence me even here.
 Pray you, be round ⟨with him.
HAMLET, *within* Mother, mother, mother!⟩
QUEEN I'll ⟨warrant⟩ you. Fear me not. Withdraw,
 I hear him coming.   10
     ⌜*Polonius hides behind the arras.*⌝

     Enter Hamlet.

HAMLET Now, mother, what's the matter?
QUEEN
 Hamlet, thou hast thy father much offended.
HAMLET
 Mother, you have my father much offended.

14. **idle:** foolish

16. **how now:** an expression of reproach

18. **forgot me:** forgotten who I am

19. **by the rood:** a mild oath **rood:** cross

22. **set . . . speak:** perhaps, summon those to whom you will listen

24. **glass:** looking glass, mirror

29. **Dead for a ducat:** i.e., **dead,** I'll wager **a ducat**

"Heaven's face does glow." (3.4.57)
From Richard Day, *A booke of Christian prayers* (1590).

QUEEN
  Come, come, you answer with an idle tongue.
HAMLET
  Go, go, you question with a wicked tongue.   15
QUEEN
  Why, how now, Hamlet?
HAMLET   What's the matter now?
QUEEN
  Have you forgot me?
HAMLET   No, by the rood, not so.
  You are the Queen, your husband's brother's wife,   20
  And (would it were not so) you are my mother.
QUEEN
  Nay, then I'll set those to you that can speak.
HAMLET
  Come, come, and sit you down; you shall not budge.
  You go not till I set you up a glass
  Where you may see the ⟨inmost⟩ part of you.   25
QUEEN
  What wilt thou do? Thou wilt not murder me?
  Help, ho!
POLONIUS, ⌜*behind the arras*⌝ What ho! Help!
HAMLET
  How now, a rat? Dead for a ducat, dead.
        ⌜*He ⟨kills Polonius⟩ by thrusting a rapier*
                   through the arras.⌝
POLONIUS, ⌜*behind the arras*⌝
  O, I am slain!   30
QUEEN   O, me, what hast thou done?
HAMLET   Nay, I know not. Is it the King?
QUEEN
  O, what a rash and bloody deed is this!
HAMLET
  A bloody deed—almost as bad, good mother,
  As kill a king and marry with his brother.   35
QUEEN
  As kill a king?

41. **Leave: leave** off, cease

45. **damnèd custom:** habitual wickedness

46. **proof:** invulnerable (like armor); **sense:** feeling

50. **blurs:** stains; defiles

51–53. **takes off . . . there:** The **rose** is associated with female perfection and the **blister** with punishment threatened prostitutes (though no evidence exists that such punishment was ever carried out).

55. **contraction:** i.e., the marriage contract

57. **rhapsody:** jumble; **Heaven's . . . glow:** See picture, page 170.

58. **this . . . mass:** i.e., the Earth

59. **against the doom:** when Judgment Day comes (See note to 1.1.132.)

60. **Is thought-sick:** i.e., heaven is **thought-sick**

62. **That roars . . . index:** i.e., that receives such a violent introduction (The **index** was the table of contents or preface introducing a book.)

64. **counterfeit presentment:** representation in portraits (These are perhaps miniatures—Claudius's on a chain around Gertrude's neck, King Hamlet's around Prince Hamlet's neck—or are perhaps paintings hung upon the wall.)

66. **Hyperion's:** Hyperion is the name of the sun god, often said to be the most beautiful of the pagan deities. (See picture, page 32.) **front:** forehead (See picture of Jove, page 160.)

68. **A station . . . Mercury:** a way of standing that is like that of the winged messenger of the gods (See picture, page 178.)

HAMLET   Ay, lady, it was my word.
        ⌈*He pulls Polonius' body from behind the arras.*⌉
    Thou wretched, rash, intruding fool, farewell.
    I took thee for thy better. Take thy fortune.
    Thou find'st to be too busy is some danger.   40
    ⌈*To Queen.*⌉ Leave wringing of your hands. Peace, sit
        you down,
    And let me wring your heart; for so I shall
    If it be made of penetrable stuff,
    If damnèd custom have not brazed it so   45
    That it be proof and bulwark against sense.
QUEEN
    What have I done, that thou dar'st wag thy tongue
    In noise so rude against me?
HAMLET   Such an act
    That blurs the grace and blush of modesty,   50
    Calls virtue hypocrite, takes off the rose
    From the fair forehead of an innocent love
    And sets a blister there, makes marriage vows
    As false as dicers' oaths—O, such a deed
    As from the body of contraction plucks   55
    The very soul, and sweet religion makes
    A rhapsody of words! Heaven's face does glow
    O'er this solidity and compound mass
    With heated visage, as against the doom,
    Is thought-sick at the act.   60
QUEEN   Ay me, what act
    That roars so loud and thunders in the index?
HAMLET
    Look here upon this picture and on this,
    The counterfeit presentment of two brothers.
    See what a grace was seated on this brow,   65
    Hyperion's curls, the front of Jove himself,
    An eye like Mars' to threaten and command,
    A station like the herald Mercury
    New-lighted on a ⟨heaven⟩-kissing hill,

70. **combination:** group of features

74. **ear:** i.e., of a cereal plant like wheat

75. **Blasting:** blighting; **his:** its

76. **leave to feed:** stop feeding

77. **batten:** glut yourself; **moor:** barren land

79. **heyday:** state of excitement; **blood:** passion

81. **Sense:** perception through the senses

83. **apoplexed:** suffering from apoplexy, paralyzed

84. **sense . . . thralled:** i.e., the five senses are never so subjected by lunacy (Hamlet's argument is that even in madness, Gertrude's senses would have **reserved some quantity of choice** [line 85]—i.e., retained a trace of the power to choose.)

87. **cozened:** tricked; **hoodman-blind:** the game of blindman's buff (See picture, page 194.)

89. **sans all:** without the other senses

91. **so mope:** be so stupefied

93. **mutine:** incite rebellion

94–95. **be . . . fire:** i.e., **melt** like the **wax** in a burning candle

95–98. **Proclaim . . . will:** i.e., do not call it shameful **when** youthful passion acts impetuously, **since** the **frost** of age is **itself** aflame **and reason** is acting as a pander for desire instead of controlling it

101. **grainèd:** indelible (*Grain* was a "fast" or permanent dye.)

102. **leave their tinct:** give up their color

104. **enseamèd:** greasy

A combination and a form indeed 70
Where every god did seem to set his seal
To give the world assurance of a man.
This was your husband. Look you now what follows.
Here is your husband, like a mildewed ear
Blasting his wholesome brother. Have you eyes? 75
Could you on this fair mountain leave to feed
And batten on this moor? Ha! Have you eyes?
You cannot call it love, for at your age
The heyday in the blood is tame, it's humble
And waits upon the judgment; and what judgment 80
Would step from this to this? [Sense sure you have,
Else could you not have motion; but sure that sense
Is apoplexed; for madness would not err,
Nor sense to ecstasy was ne'er so thralled,
But it reserved some quantity of choice 85
To serve in such a difference.] What devil was 't
That thus hath cozened you at hoodman-blind?
[Eyes without feeling, feeling without sight,
Ears without hands or eyes, smelling sans all,
Or but a sickly part of one true sense 90
Could not so mope.] O shame, where is thy blush?
Rebellious hell,
If thou canst mutine in a matron's bones,
To flaming youth let virtue be as wax
And melt in her own fire. Proclaim no shame 95
When the compulsive ardor gives the charge,
Since frost itself as actively doth burn,
And reason ⟨panders⟩ will.
QUEEN O Hamlet, speak no more!
Thou turn'st my eyes into my ⟨very⟩ soul, 100
And there I see such black and ⟨grainèd⟩ spots
As will ⟨not⟩ leave their tinct.
HAMLET   Nay, but to live
In the rank sweat of an enseamèd bed,
Stewed in corruption, honeying and making love 105
Over the nasty sty!

112. **a vice of kings:** a buffoon of a king (a reference to the comic Vice of the morality plays)

113. **cutpurse:** thief

123. **lapsed in time and passion:** "suffered having **time** to slip and **passion** to cool" (Samuel Johnson)

124. **important:** importunate, urgent

128. **amazement on thy mother sits:** i.e., your **mother** is in a state of extreme shock

130. **Conceit:** imagination

135. **incorporal:** immaterial

137. **in th' alarm:** waked by the call to arms

138. **bedded hair:** smooth-lying **hair; like . . . excrements:** as if a lifeless outgrowth (*excrement*) had come to life

139. **an end:** on **end**

Jove with his thunderbolt. (3.2.309–10; 3.4.66)
From Vincenzo Cartari, *Le vere e noue imagini . . .* (1615).

QUEEN O, speak to me no more!
  These words like daggers enter in my ears.
  No more, sweet Hamlet!
HAMLET   A murderer and a villain,   110
  A slave that is not twentieth part the ⟨tithe⟩
  Of your precedent lord; a vice of kings,
  A cutpurse of the empire and the rule,
  That from a shelf the precious diadem stole
  And put it in his pocket—   115
QUEEN No more!
HAMLET A king of shreds and patches—

Enter Ghost.

  Save me and hover o'er me with your wings,
  You heavenly guards!—What would your gracious
    figure?   120
QUEEN Alas, he's mad.
HAMLET
  Do you not come your tardy son to chide,
  That, lapsed in time and passion, lets go by
  Th' important acting of your dread command?
  O, say!   125
GHOST   Do not forget. This visitation
  Is but to whet thy almost blunted purpose.
  But look, amazement on thy mother sits.
  O, step between her and her fighting soul.
  Conceit in weakest bodies strongest works.   130
  Speak to her, Hamlet.
HAMLET   How is it with you, lady?
QUEEN Alas, how is 't with you,
  That you do bend your eye on vacancy
  And with th' incorporal air do hold discourse?   135
  Forth at your eyes your spirits wildly peep,
  And, as the sleeping soldiers in th' alarm,
  Your bedded hair, like life in excrements,
  Start up and stand an end. O gentle son,

144. **capable:** responsive
147. **effects:** purposes
148. **want:** lack
155. **in . . . lived:** dressed **as he** did when **he lived**
158. **ecstasy:** madness
164. **reword:** repeat word for word
165. **gambol from:** skip away from
166. **flattering unction:** soothing salve
169. **mining:** undermining

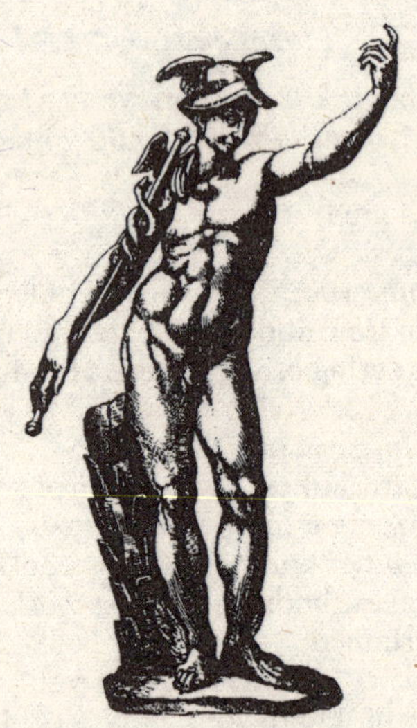

Mercury. (3.4.68)
From Giovanni Battista Cavalleriis,
Antiquarum statuarum (1585–94).

Upon the heat and flame of thy distemper　140
Sprinkle cool patience! Whereon do you look?
HAMLET
On him, on him! Look you how pale he glares.
His form and cause conjoined, preaching to stones,
Would make them capable. ⌜*To the Ghost.*⌝ Do not
　look upon me,　145
Lest with this piteous action you convert
My stern effects. Then what I have to do
Will want true color—tears perchance for blood.
QUEEN　To whom do you speak this?
HAMLET　Do you see nothing there?　150
QUEEN
Nothing at all; yet all that is I see.
HAMLET　Nor did you nothing hear?
QUEEN　No, nothing but ourselves.
HAMLET
Why, look you there, look how it steals away!
My father, in his habit as he lived!　155
Look where he goes even now out at the portal!
　　　　　　　　　　　　　　Ghost exits.
QUEEN
This is the very coinage of your brain.
This bodiless creation ecstasy
Is very cunning in.
HAMLET　　　　　　　　⟨Ecstasy?⟩　160
My pulse as yours doth temperately keep time
And makes as healthful music. It is not madness
That I have uttered. Bring me to the test,
And ⟨I⟩ the matter will reword, which madness
Would gambol from. Mother, for love of grace,　165
Lay not that flattering unction to your soul
That not your trespass but my madness speaks.
It will but skin and film the ulcerous place,
Whiles rank corruption, mining all within,
Infects unseen. Confess yourself to heaven,　170

173. **ranker:** more coarsely luxuriant
174. **fatness:** grossness; **pursy:** fat, flabby
176. **curb:** bow
182–83. **That monster . . . devil:** This passage may contain mistakes in the printing. (Editors often change "devil" to "evil.") The general meaning may be "**Custom,** a **monster** that consumes the perceptive faculties, is therefore like a **devil** in suggesting evil **habits.**"
184. **use:** habit
186. **aptly:** easily
190. **either** ⌜ . . . ⌝ **the devil:** A word seems to have been lost; Q2 reads "either the devil"; many editors (to complete the line and the thought) insert the verb "master," found in the quarto of *Hamlet* printed in 1611.
191. **potency:** strength
196. **their scourge:** heaven's lash or whip; instrument of divine punishment; **minister:** agent
197. **answer well:** perhaps, justify; or, perhaps, make amends for or suffer the consequences of
200. **remains behind:** is yet to come

Repent what's past, avoid what is to come,
And do not spread the compost on the weeds
To make them ranker. Forgive me this my virtue,
For, in the fatness of these pursy times,
Virtue itself of vice must pardon beg,   175
Yea, curb and woo for leave to do him good.

QUEEN
O Hamlet, thou hast cleft my heart in twain!

HAMLET
O, throw away the worser part of it,
And ⟨live⟩ the purer with the other half!
Good night. But go not to my uncle's bed.   180
Assume a virtue if you have it not.
[That monster, custom, who all sense doth eat,
Of habits devil, is angel yet in this,
That to the use of actions fair and good
He likewise gives a frock or livery   185
That aptly is put on.] Refrain ⟨tonight,⟩
And that shall lend a kind of easiness
To the next abstinence, [the next more easy;
For use almost can change the stamp of nature
And either ⌜ . . . ⌝ the devil or throw him out   190
With wondrous potency.] Once more, good night,
And, when you are desirous to be blest,
I'll blessing beg of you. For this same lord
                     ⌜*Pointing to Polonius.*⌝
I do repent; but heaven hath pleased it so
To punish me with this and this with me,   195
That I must be their scourge and minister.
I will bestow him and will answer well
The death I gave him. So, again, good night.
I must be cruel only to be kind.
This bad begins, and worse remains behind.   200
[One word more, good lady.]

QUEEN   What shall I do?

203. **Not . . . means . . . :** After this general state-
ment of negation, Hamlet lists the things he would
have Gertrude *not* do (e.g., go **to bed** with Claudius).
206. **reechy:** filthy
210. **mad in craft:** cunningly **mad,** pretending to
be **mad; 'Twere . . . know:** said sarcastically, as are
lines 211–18
212. **paddock:** toad; **gib:** tomcat
213. **Such dear concernings: such** important
matters
215–18. **Unpeg . . . neck down:** The story that
Hamlet alludes to here is lost. (See longer note,
page 293.) **Unpeg:** unfasten **To try conclusions:**
to experiment
229–30. **to have the enginer . . . petard: to have
the** maker of military devices blown up by **his own**
explosives (See picture, below.)
230–31. **and 't . . . I will:** i.e., and, with any luck,
I will
231. **mines:** tunnels dug under a fortress wall
234. **packing:** leaving the country; carrying off a
burden

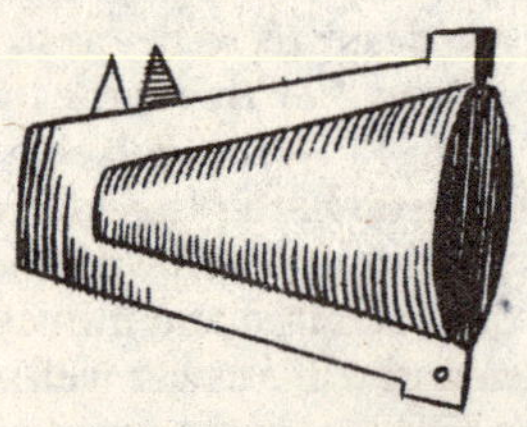

A petard. (3.4.230)
From Louis de Gaya, *A treatise of the arms* . . . (1678).

HAMLET
  Not this by no means that I bid you do:
  Let the bloat king tempt you again to bed,
  Pinch wanton on your cheek, call you his mouse,   205
  And let him, for a pair of reechy kisses
  Or paddling in your neck with his damned fingers,
  Make you to ravel all this matter out
  That I essentially am not in madness,
  But mad in craft. 'Twere good you let him know,   210
  For who that's but a queen, fair, sober, wise,
  Would from a paddock, from a bat, a gib,
  Such dear concernings hide? Who would do so?
  No, in despite of sense and secrecy,
  Unpeg the basket on the house's top,   215
  Let the birds fly, and like the famous ape,
  To try conclusions, in the basket creep
  And break your own neck down.
QUEEN
  Be thou assured, if words be made of breath
  And breath of life, I have no life to breathe   220
  What thou hast said to me.
HAMLET
  I must to England, you know that.
QUEEN   Alack,
  I had forgot! 'Tis so concluded on.
HAMLET
  [There's letters sealed; and my two schoolfellows,   225
  Whom I will trust as I will adders fanged,
  They bear the mandate; they must sweep my way
  And marshal me to knavery. Let it work,
  For 'tis the sport to have the enginer
  Hoist with his own petard; and 't shall go hard   230
  But I will delve one yard below their mines
  And blow them at the moon. O, 'tis most sweet
  When in one line two crafts directly meet.]
  This man shall set me packing.

239. **to draw toward an end with you: to** come
to the **end** of my business **with you** (with a pun on
draw, as Hamlet drags him away)

Cain murders Abel (1.2.109; 3.3.41; 5.1.79)
From Gabriel Chappuys, *Figures de la Bible . . .* (1582).

I'll lug the guts into the neighbor room.   235
Mother, good night indeed. This counselor
Is now most still, most secret, and most grave,
Who was in life a foolish prating knave.—
Come, sir, to draw toward an end with you.—
Good night, mother.   240
          ⌜*They*⌝ *exit, ⟨Hamlet tugging in Polonius.⟩*

The Tragedy of

HAMLET,

Prince of Denmark

ACT 4

4.1 Gertrude reports Polonius's death to Claudius, who sends Rosencrantz and Guildenstern to find Hamlet and recover the body.

———

   1. **matter:** significance
  11. **brainish apprehension:** brainsick belief
  12. **unseen:** hidden
  13. **heavy:** dreadful
  14. **with us:** with me (Note that Claudius uses the royal "we" throughout this largely private scene. Only in the final line does he use the first-person singular.)
  17. **answered:** justified, explained, satisfied
  18. **laid to us, whose providence:** charged against me, **whose** foresight

Vulcan in his stithy. (3.2.88–89)
From Johann Basilius Herold, *Heydenweldt* . . . [1554].

⌜ACT 4⌝

⌜Scene 1⌝

Enter King and Queen, with Rosencrantz and Guildenstern.

KING
There's matter in these sighs; these profound heaves
You must translate; 'tis fit we understand them.
Where is your son?

QUEEN
[Bestow this place on us a little while.]
⌜*Rosencrantz and Guildenstern exit.*⌝
Ah, mine own lord, what have I seen tonight!

KING What, Gertrude? How does Hamlet?

QUEEN
Mad as the sea and wind when both contend
Which is the mightier. In his lawless fit,
Behind the arras hearing something stir,
Whips out his rapier, cries "A rat, a rat,"
And in this brainish apprehension kills
The unseen good old man.

KING   O heavy deed!
It had been so with us, had we been there.
His liberty is full of threats to all—
To you yourself, to us, to everyone.
Alas, how shall this bloody deed be answered?
It will be laid to us, whose providence

189

19. **short:** i.e., on a **short** leash; **out of haunt:** away from others

23. **divulging:** coming to light

26–27. **like . . . base:** perhaps, **like** a vein of gold in a mine of **base metals;** or, perhaps, **like** gold that separates out as liquid from **base metals** when the metal is heated

32–33. **with all our majesty . . . excuse:** i.e., **with all** my royal authority I **must countenance,** and **with all** my **skill** I **must excuse**

34. **join you . . . aid:** find others to help you

41. **and what's untimely done:** Both Q2 and F print this short line; the four lines following in Q2 require that some words be inserted to provide a reference for "Whose whisper" in line 42. Many editions accept the eighteenth-century editorial insertion of "So haply slander" to complete line 41. Other editors suggest that lines 42–45 had been marked for deletion.

43. **As level . . . blank:** with as sure an aim as **the cannon** hitting its mark

Should have kept short, restrained, and out of haunt
This mad young man. But so much was our love,   20
We would not understand what was most fit,
But, like the owner of a foul disease,
To keep it from divulging, let it feed
Even on the pith of life. Where is he gone?
QUEEN
To draw apart the body he hath killed,   25
O'er whom his very madness, like some ore
Among a mineral of metals base,
Shows itself pure: he weeps for what is done.
KING   O Gertrude, come away!
The sun no sooner shall the mountains touch   30
But we will ship him hence; and this vile deed
We must with all our majesty and skill
Both countenance and excuse.—Ho, Guildenstern!

Enter Rosencrantz and Guildenstern.

Friends both, go join you with some further aid.
Hamlet in madness hath Polonius slain,   35
And from his mother's closet hath he ⟨dragged⟩ him.
Go seek him out, speak fair, and bring the body
Into the chapel. I pray you, haste in this.
                    (Rosencrantz and Guildenstern exit.)
Come, Gertrude, we'll call up our wisest friends
And let them know both what we mean to do   .   40
And what's untimely done. ⌜ . . . ⌝
[Whose whisper o'er the world's diameter,
As level as the cannon to his blank
Transports his poisoned shot, may miss our name
And hit the woundless air.] O, come away!   45
My soul is full of discord and dismay.
                                        They exit.

4.2   Hamlet refuses to tell Rosencrantz and Guild-
enstern where he has put Polonius's body.

———

3. **soft:** an exclamation here enjoining silence

6. **dust . . . kin:** "thou art **dust,** and unto **dust**
shalt thou return" (Genesis 3.19)

12–13. **to be demanded . . . what replication:**
being questioned by . . . **what** reply

15. **countenance:** favorable looks

17–18. **like an ape an apple:** as **an ape** keeps **an
apple**

23. **knavish:** mischievous; **sleeps in:** is not
understood by

A satyr. (1.2.144)
From Vincenzo Cartari, *Le vere e noue imagini . . .* (1615).

⌈Scene 2⌉

⟨*Enter Hamlet.*⟩

HAMLET Safely stowed.

⟨GENTLEMEN, *within* Hamlet! Lord Hamlet!⟩

HAMLET But soft, what noise? Who calls on Hamlet?
O, here they come.

Enter Rosencrantz, ⟨Guildenstern,⟩ and others.

ROSENCRANTZ
What have you done, my lord, with the dead body?　　5

HAMLET
⟨Compounded⟩ it with dust, whereto 'tis kin.

ROSENCRANTZ
Tell us where 'tis, that we may take it thence
And bear it to the chapel.

HAMLET Do not believe it.

ROSENCRANTZ Believe what?　　10

HAMLET That I can keep your counsel and not mine
own. Besides, to be demanded of a sponge, what
replication should be made by the son of a king?

ROSENCRANTZ Take you me for a sponge, my lord?

HAMLET Ay, sir, that soaks up the King's countenance,　　15
his rewards, his authorities. But such officers do the
King best service in the end. He keeps them like ⟨an
ape⟩ an apple in the corner of his jaw, first mouthed,
to be last swallowed. When he needs what you have
gleaned, it is but squeezing you, and, sponge, you　　20
shall be dry again.

ROSENCRANTZ I understand you not, my lord.

HAMLET I am glad of it. A knavish speech sleeps in a
foolish ear.

ROSENCRANTZ My lord, you must tell us where the　　25
body is and go with us to the King.

HAMLET The body is with the King, but the King is not
with the body. The King is a thing—

30–31. **Hide fox . . . :** perhaps a line from a child's game like hide-and-seek

4.3 Hamlet is brought to Claudius, who tells him that he is to leave immediately for England. Alone, Claudius reveals that he is sending Hamlet to his death.

---

4. **loved of: loved** by; **distracted:** unsettled

6–7. **where 'tis so . . . offense:** i.e., **where** the people love with **their eyes** instead of their reason, they judge the punishment (the **scourge**) rather than the crime (**the offense**)

7. **To bear . . . even:** to manage everything smoothly and evenly

9. **Deliberate pause:** the result of careful thought

9–10. **Diseases . . . relieved:** Proverbial: **Desperate diseases** require **desperate** remedies.

A game of hoodman-blind. (3.4.86–87)
From *Officium beate Marie v[ir] ginis ad vsum saru[m]* . . . [c. 1512].

GUILDENSTERN A "thing," my lord?

HAMLET Of nothing. Bring me to him. ⟨Hide fox, and   30
    all after!⟩

They exit.

⌈**Scene 3**⌉

Enter King and two or three.

KING
  I have sent to seek him and to find the body.
  How dangerous is it that this man goes loose!
  Yet must not we put the strong law on him.
  He's loved of the distracted multitude,
  Who like not in their judgment, but their eyes;   5
  And where 'tis so, th' offender's scourge is weighed,
  But never the offense. To bear all smooth and even,
  This sudden sending him away must seem
  Deliberate pause. Diseases desperate grown
  By desperate appliance are relieved   10
  Or not at all.

Enter Rosencrantz.

          How now, what hath befallen?

ROSENCRANTZ
  Where the dead body is bestowed, my lord,
  We cannot get from him.

KING   But where is he?   15

ROSENCRANTZ
  Without, my lord; guarded, to know your pleasure.

KING
  Bring him before us.

ROSENCRANTZ   Ho! Bring in the lord.

They enter ⌈*with Hamlet.*⌉

KING Now, Hamlet, where's Polonius?

HAMLET At supper.   20

23. **convocation of politic worms:** perhaps an allusion to the Diet of Worms, **a convocation** (council) summoned at the city of Worms by the Holy Roman Emperor in 1521

24. **Your worm:** i.e., the **worm**

26–27. **is 'but . . . service:** are merely different kinds of food

35. **progress:** royal journey

45. **Which . . . grieve: which we tender as dearly** (value as highly) **as we dearly** (deeply) **grieve**

49. **bark:** ship; **at help:** favorable

50. **tend:** attend you, wait for you; **bent:** ready

A beheading. (4.5.244; 5.2.27–28)
From [Richard Verstegen,]
Theatre des cruautez des hereticques de nostre temps . . . (1607).

KING At supper where?

HAMLET Not where he eats, but where he is eaten. A certain convocation of politic worms are e'en at him. Your worm is your only emperor for diet. We fat all creatures else to fat us, and we fat ourselves   25
for maggots. Your fat king and your lean beggar is but variable service—two dishes but to one table. That's the end.

[KING Alas, alas!

HAMLET A man may fish with the worm that hath eat   30
of a king and eat of the fish that hath fed of that worm.]

KING What dost thou mean by this?

HAMLET Nothing but to show you how a king may go a progress through the guts of a beggar.   35

KING Where is Polonius?

HAMLET In heaven. Send thither to see. If your messenger find him not there, seek him i' th' other place yourself. But if, indeed, you find him not within this month, you shall nose him as you go up   40
the stairs into the lobby.

KING, ⌜*to Attendants.*⌝ Go, seek him there.

HAMLET He will stay till you come.   ⌜*Attendants exit.*⌝

KING
Hamlet, this deed, for thine especial safety
(Which we do tender, as we dearly grieve   45
For that which thou hast done) must send thee
    hence
(With fiery quickness.) Therefore prepare thyself.
The bark is ready, and the wind at help,
Th' associates tend, and everything is bent   50
For England.

HAMLET For England?

KING Ay, Hamlet.

HAMLET Good.

KING
So is it, if thou knew'st our purposes.   55

56. **I see ... them:** Heaven's angels (cherubim), Hamlet suggests, can see Claudius's **purposes** (line 55).

63. **at foot:** at his heels; **tempt:** entice

65–66. **everything ... affair:** i.e., **everything else that** relates to the matter is completed

67. **England:** the king of **England**

68. **As ... sense: as my power** may give you a **sense thereof** (i.e., of the value of retaining **my love**)

69. **cicatrice:** scar

70–71. **thy free awe ... us:** i.e., **awe** of Denmark's power makes England pay **homage to** Denmark

71. **coldly set:** i.e., ignore

72. **Our ... process:** my royal order; **imports:** i.e., demands

73. **congruing:** agreeing (accent on the first syllable)

74. **present:** immediate

75. **the hectic:** continual fever

77. **Howe'er my haps:** whatever my fortunes

4.4 Fortinbras and his army cross Hamlet's path on their way to Poland. Hamlet finds in Fortinbras's vigorous activity a model for himself in avenging his father's murder; Hamlet resolves upon bloody action.

2–4. **by his license ... Over his kingdom:** In formal language, **Fortinbras,** having been given **license** from Claudius to march across Denmark, now asks for an escort. (See 2.2.81–85.) **conveyance of:** escort during

HAMLET
I see a cherub that sees them. But come, for
 England.
Farewell, dear mother.

KING   Thy loving father, Hamlet.

HAMLET
My mother. Father and mother is man and wife, 60
Man and wife is one flesh, ⟨and⟩ so, my mother.—
Come, for England.   *He exits.*

KING
Follow him at foot; tempt him with speed aboard.
Delay it not. I'll have him hence tonight.
Away, for everything is sealed and done 65
That else leans on th' affair. Pray you, make haste.
       ⌜*All but the King exit.*⌝
And England, if my love thou hold'st at aught
(As my great power thereof may give thee sense,
Since yet thy cicatrice looks raw and red
After the Danish sword, and thy free awe 70
Pays homage to us), thou mayst not coldly set
Our sovereign process, which imports at full,
By letters congruing to that effect,
The present death of Hamlet. Do it, England,
For like the hectic in my blood he rages, 75
And thou must cure me. Till I know 'tis done,
Howe'er my haps, my joys will ne'er begin.
        He exits.

⌜Scene 4⌝

Enter Fortinbras with his army over the stage.

FORTINBRAS
Go, Captain, from me greet the Danish king.
Tell him that by his license Fortinbras
Craves the conveyance of a promised march
Over his kingdom. You know the rendezvous.

5. **would aught with us:** wishes anything of me (Note his use of the royal "we.")

6. **in his eye: in his** presence

9. **softly:** slowly

10. **powers:** military forces

16. **the main: the main** part

18. **addition:** i.e., overstatement, exaggeration

20. **the name: the** mere **name** of conquest

21. **To pay . . . farm it: I would not pay five ducats to** rent the land for farming

23. **ranker:** higher; **in fee:** outright

27. **Will not debate . . . this straw:** are not enough to pay for settling this trifling quarrel

28. **impostume:** abscess

29. **without:** on the outside

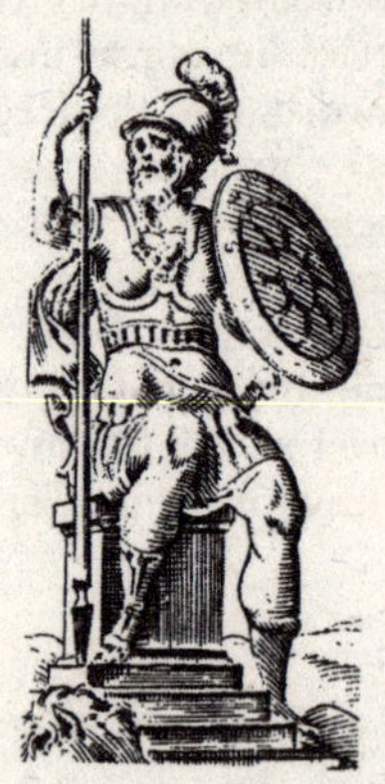

Mars. (2.2.515; 3.4.67)
From Vincenzo Cartari, *Le imagini de i dei de gli antichi . . .* (1587).

If that his Majesty would aught with us,   5
We shall express our duty in his eye;
And let him know so.
CAPTAIN I will do 't, my lord.
FORTINBRAS Go softly on.   ⌜*All but the Captain exit.*⌝

[*Enter Hamlet, Rosencrantz,* ⌜*Guildenstern,*⌝ *and others.*

HAMLET Good sir, whose powers are these?   10
CAPTAIN They are of Norway, sir.
HAMLET How purposed, sir, I pray you?
CAPTAIN Against some part of Poland.
HAMLET Who commands them, sir?
CAPTAIN
    The nephew to old Norway, Fortinbras.   15
HAMLET
    Goes it against the main of Poland, sir,
    Or for some frontier?
CAPTAIN
    Truly to speak, and with no addition,
    We go to gain a little patch of ground
    That hath in it no profit but the name.   20
    To pay five ducats, five, I would not farm it;
    Nor will it yield to Norway or the Pole
    A ranker rate, should it be sold in fee.
HAMLET
    Why, then, the Polack never will defend it.
CAPTAIN
    Yes, it is already garrisoned.   25
HAMLET
    Two thousand souls and twenty thousand ducats
    Will not debate the question of this straw.
    This is th' impostume of much wealth and peace,
    That inward breaks and shows no cause without
    Why the man dies.—I humbly thank you, sir.   30
CAPTAIN God be wi' you, sir.   ⌜*He exits.*⌝
ROSENCRANTZ Will 't please you go, my lord?

34. **inform against:** denounce

36. **market . . . time:** "that for which he sells **his time**" (Samuel Johnson)

38–39. **discourse, . . . before and after:** power of thought that looks into the past and the future

41. **fust:** become moldy

42. **Bestial oblivion:** mindlessness like the beasts'

42–43. **craven scruple / Of thinking:** cowardly hesitation that results from **thinking**

48. **Sith:** since

49. **gross as Earth:** as evident **as the Earth** itself

53. **Makes mouths at: makes** faces **at** (i.e., holds in contempt)

56–59. **Rightly . . . at the stake:** i.e., **to be** truly **great,** one should **not** fight except when the **argument** is itself **great,** unless honor is involved **at the stake:** at risk (as in gambling)

61. **Excitements of:** motives or incentives for; **blood:** passion

64. **trick of fame:** illusion of honor

66. **Whereon . . . cause:** on which **the numbers** of fighting men do not have room to fight the battle

HAMLET
I'll be with you straight. Go a little before.
⌜*All but Hamlet exit.*⌝
How all occasions do inform against me
And spur my dull revenge. What is a man   35
If his chief good and market of his time
Be but to sleep and feed? A beast, no more.
Sure He that made us with such large discourse,
Looking before and after, gave us not
That capability and godlike reason   40
To fust in us unused. Now whether it be
Bestial oblivion or some craven scruple
Of thinking too precisely on th' event
(A thought which, quartered, hath but one part
    wisdom   45
And ever three parts coward), I do not know
Why yet I live to say "This thing's to do,"
Sith I have cause, and will, and strength, and means
To do 't. Examples gross as Earth exhort me:
Witness this army of such mass and charge,   50
Led by a delicate and tender prince,
Whose spirit with divine ambition puffed
Makes mouths at the invisible event,
Exposing what is mortal and unsure
To all that fortune, death, and danger dare,   55
Even for an eggshell. Rightly to be great
Is not to stir without great argument,
But greatly to find quarrel in a straw
When honor's at the stake. How stand I, then,
That have a father killed, a mother stained,   60
Excitements of my reason and my blood,
And let all sleep, while to my shame I see
The imminent death of twenty thousand men
That for a fantasy and trick of fame
Go to their graves like beds, fight for a plot   65
Whereon the numbers cannot try the cause,

67–68. **Which is not ... hide the slain:** which **is not** large **enough to** be a **tomb** or receptacle for those who will be killed   **continent:** container
69. **bloody:** bloodthirsty

4.5   Reports reach Gertrude that Ophelia is mad. Ophelia enters singing about death and betrayal. After Ophelia has gone, Claudius agonizes over her madness and over the stir created by the return of an angry Laertes. When Laertes breaks in on Claudius and Gertrude, Claudius asserts his innocence with regard to Polonius's death. The reappearance of the mad Ophelia is devastating to Laertes.

-----

3. **distract:** distraught; **will needs be:** must **be**
6. **tricks:** plots, deception
8. **Spurns enviously at straws:** takes offense angrily at trifles; **in doubt:** obscurely
9–11. **Her speech ... to collection: her speech** makes no sense, but its very formlessness makes her **hearers** draw conclusions
11. **aim:** guess
12. **botch ... thoughts:** patch the words together to match their guesses
20. **ill-breeding:** evil-breeding
22. **as sin's true nature is:** i.e., sin, in its **true nature, is** a sickness of the **soul**
23. **toy:** trifle; **amiss:** disaster
24. **artless:** awkward, stupid; **jealousy:** unreasonable suspicions
25. **spills:** destroys; **spilt:** divulged

Which is not tomb enough and continent
To hide the slain? O, from this time forth
My thoughts be bloody or be nothing worth!
—————————————————————*He exits.*]

[*Scene 5*]

Enter Horatio, ⟨Queen,⟩ and a Gentleman.

QUEEN I will not speak with her.
GENTLEMAN She is importunate,
  Indeed distract; her mood will needs be pitied.
QUEEN What would she have?
GENTLEMAN
  She speaks much of her father, says she hears   5
  There's tricks i' th' world, and hems, and beats her
    heart,
  Spurns enviously at straws, speaks things in doubt
  That carry but half sense. Her speech is nothing,
  Yet the unshapèd use of it doth move   10
  The hearers to collection. They ⟨aim⟩ at it
  And botch the words up fit to their own thoughts;
  Which, as her winks and nods and gestures yield
    them,
  Indeed would make one think there might be   15
    thought,
  Though nothing sure, yet much unhappily.
HORATIO
  'Twere good she were spoken with, for she may
    strew
  Dangerous conjectures in ill-breeding minds.   20
[QUEEN] Let her come in.   [*Gentleman exits.*]
  [*Aside.*] To my sick soul (as sin's true nature is),
  Each toy seems prologue to some great amiss.
  So full of artless jealousy is guilt,
  It spills itself in fearing to be spilt.   25

25 SD.   **distracted:** insane, mentally disturbed

28–31.   **How should I . . . shoon:** Ophelia sings a version of a popular ballad, which continues at lines 34 and 41.   **cockle hat: A hat** with a **cockle** shell denoted a pilgrim returning from the shrine of St. James of Compostela. (See picture, below.)   **shoon:** shoes

43.   **Larded all:** strewn all over

44.   **did not go:** The word "not" has been inserted into the ballad as Ophelia's addition.

47.   **God dild you: God** yield (reward) you

47–48.   **the owl . . . daughter:** There exist an old legend and an unrelated ballad either of which could be alluded to here.

50.   **Conceit upon:** i.e., (she is) thinking about

Pilgrim with "cockle hat and staff." (4.5.30)
From Henry Peacham, *Minerua Britanna* (1612).

⟨*Enter Ophelia distracted.*⟩

OPHELIA
  Where is the beauteous Majesty of Denmark?
QUEEN How now, Ophelia?
OPHELIA ⌜*sings*⌝
        How should I your true love known
          From another one?
          By his cockle hat and staff   30
          And his sandal shoon.

QUEEN
  Alas, sweet lady, what imports this song?
OPHELIA Say you? Nay, pray you, mark.
  ⌜*Sings.*⌝ *He is dead and gone, lady,*
              He is dead and gone;   35
            At his head a grass-green turf,
              At his heels a stone.
  Oh, ho!
QUEEN Nay, but Ophelia—
OPHELIA Pray you, mark.   40
  ⌜*Sings.*⌝ *White his shroud as the mountain snow—*

              Enter King.

QUEEN Alas, look here, my lord.
OPHELIA ⌜*sings*⌝
          Larded all with sweet flowers;
        Which bewept to the ground did not go
          With true-love showers.   45
KING How do you, pretty lady?
OPHELIA Well, God dild you. They say the owl was a
  baker's daughter. Lord, we know what we are but
  know not what we may be. God be at your table.
KING Conceit upon her father.   50
OPHELIA Pray let's have no words of this, but when
  they ask you what it means, say you this:

53–60. **Tomorrow . . . more:** The song alludes to the ancient custom that the first girl a man sees on **Valentine's day** is to be his true love. The song continues in lines 63–68, 70–71. **betime:** early **dupped:** opened **maid:** virgin (This song has not been found elsewhere.)

63. **Gis:** Jesus

66. **Cock:** a substitution for "God" in oaths; **to blame:** blameworthy

71. **An:** if

74. **cannot . . . weep: cannot** help weeping

83. **spies:** individual soldiers sent by the army to scout out the territory

85–86. **most violent . . . remove:** the cause, through his violence, of his justly earned removal **author:** cause

86. **muddied:** stirred up, confused

"The ocean . . . eats . . . the flats." (4.5.109–10)
From Geoffrey Whitney, *A choice of emblemes . . .* (1586).

⌐Sings.¬ *Tomorrow is Saint Valentine's day,*
        All in the morning betime,
        And I a maid at your window,   55
        To be your Valentine.
        Then up he rose and donned his clothes
        And dupped the chamber door,
        Let in the maid, that out a maid
        Never departed more.   60
KING Pretty Ophelia—
OPHELIA
  Indeed, without an oath, I'll make an end on 't:
  ⌐Sings.¬ *By Gis and by Saint Charity,*
        Alack and fie for shame,
        Young men will do 't, if they come to 't;   65
        By Cock, they are to blame.
        Quoth she "Before you tumbled me,
        You promised me to wed."
  He answers:
        "So would I 'a done, by yonder sun,   70
        An thou hadst not come to my bed."
KING How long hath she been thus?
OPHELIA I hope all will be well. We must be patient,
  but I cannot choose but weep to think they would
  lay him i' th' cold ground. My brother shall know of   75
  it. And so I thank you for your good counsel. Come,
  my coach! Good night, ladies, good night, sweet
  ladies, good night, good night.   ⟨She exits.⟩
KING
  Follow her close; give her good watch, I pray you.
                              ⌐Horatio exits.¬
  O, this is the poison of deep grief. It springs   80
  All from her father's death, and now behold!
  O Gertrude, Gertrude,
  When sorrows come, they come not single spies,
  But in battalions: first, her father slain;
  Next, your son gone, and he most violent author   85
  Of his own just remove; the people muddied,

89–90. we have . . . greenly: I have acted foolishly

91. In hugger-mugger: without proper ceremony; secretly and hastily (See longer note, page 293.)

96. wonder: bewilderment, perplexity; **in clouds:** i.e., in a cloud of suspicion

97. wants not buzzers: does not lack gossipers

99. of matter beggared: lacking facts

100. Will nothing stick . . . arraign: will not hesitate to accuse me of the crime

101–3. this . . . superfluous death: this (battalion of troubles) kills me over and over, as if I were shot at by **a murd'ring piece,** a cannon that scatters its shots

103 SD. within: offstage

105. Attend: listen

106. Switzers: Swiss bodyguards

109–12. The ocean . . . your officers: i.e., **Laertes** and his followers are overbearing the king's **officers** as quickly and pitilessly as an **ocean** flooding its flatlands (See picture, page 208.) **overpeering of his list:** overflowing its shore   **head:** armed force

113–16. as the world . . . They cry: as if **the world were to begin** right **now,** with tradition and **custom** completely forgotten   **ratifiers and props of every word:** probably refers to **antiquity** and **custom,** the supports of words and promises

117. Caps . . . clouds: Their **caps,** that is, are thrown into the air as **hands** and voices express approval loudly.

Thick, and unwholesome in ⟨their⟩ thoughts and
　　whispers
For good Polonius' death, and we have done but
　　greenly　　　　　　　　　　　　　　　　　　90
In hugger-mugger to inter him; poor Ophelia
Divided from herself and her fair judgment,
Without the which we are pictures or mere beasts;
Last, and as much containing as all these,
Her brother is in secret come from France,　　　95
Feeds on ⟨his⟩ wonder, keeps himself in clouds,
And wants not buzzers to infect his ear
With pestilent speeches of his father's death,
Wherein necessity, of matter beggared,
Will nothing stick our person to arraign　　　　100
In ear and ear. O, my dear Gertrude, this,
Like to a murd'ring piece, in many places
Gives me superfluous death.
　　　　　　　　　　　　　　　　A noise within.
⟨QUEEN　Alack, what noise is this?⟩
KING　Attend!　　　　　　　　　　　　　　　105
　Where is my Switzers? Let them guard the door.

　　　　　　　Enter a Messenger.

　What is the matter?
MESSENGER　　　　　　Save yourself, my lord.
　The ocean, overpeering of his list,
　Eats not the flats with more impiteous haste　　110
　Than young Laertes, in a riotous head,
　O'erbears your officers. The rabble call him "lord,"
　And, as the world were now but to begin,
　Antiquity forgot, custom not known,
　The ratifiers and props of every word,　　　　115
　⟨They⟩ cry "Choose we, Laertes shall be king!"
　Caps, hands, and tongues applaud it to the clouds,
　"Laertes shall be king! Laertes king!"
　　　　　　　　　　　　　　　　A noise within.

120. **counter:** In hunting, a dog goes **counter** when it follows **the trail** (line 119) in the wrong direction; **false:** treacherous, faithless

122. **without:** outside

124. **give me leave:** i.e., please leave me

126. **Keep:** guard

132. **cuckold:** betrayed husband (See picture, below.) **brands the harlot:** See note to 3.4.51–53.

134. **true:** faithful, chaste

137. **fear our: fear** for my

138. **hedge:** surround in order to protect

139. **would:** i.e., **would** like to do

140. **his:** its

A cuckold. (3.1.151; 4.5.132)
From *Bagford Ballads* (printed in 1878).

QUEEN
  How cheerfully on the false trail they cry.
  O, this is counter, you false Danish dogs!   120
KING   The doors are broke.

            Enter Laertes with others.

LAERTES
  Where is this king?—Sirs, stand you all without.
ALL   No, let's come in!
LAERTES   I pray you, give me leave.
ALL   We will, we will.   125
LAERTES
  I thank you. Keep the door. ⌜*Followers exit.*⌝ O, thou
     vile king,
  Give me my father!
QUEEN   Calmly, good Laertes.
LAERTES
  That drop of blood that's calm proclaims me   130
     bastard,
  Cries "cuckold" to my father, brands the harlot
  Even here between the chaste unsmirchèd brow
  Of my true mother.
KING   What is the cause, Laertes,   135
  That thy rebellion looks so giant-like?—
  Let him go, Gertrude. Do not fear our person.
  There's such divinity doth hedge a king
  That treason can but peep to what it would,
  Acts little of his will.—Tell me, Laertes,   140
  Why thou art thus incensed.—Let him go,
     Gertrude.—
  Speak, man.
LAERTES   Where is my father?
KING   Dead.   145
QUEEN
  But not by him.
KING   Let him demand his fill.

148. **juggled with:** manipulated and thus deceived

152. **both . . . negligence:** i.e., **I** don't care what happens to me in this world or the next

154. **throughly:** thoroughly

157. **And for: and** as **for**

160–61. **certainty / Of:** truth or facts about

162. **swoopstake:** literally, take all the stakes on the gambling table (The metaphoric meaning of line 162 is "are you determined to take revenge on friends and enemies both?")

168. **life-rend'ring pelican:** The mother **pelican** was thought to feed her young **with** her own **blood** (line 169). (See picture, below.)

173. **sensibly:** intensely

174. **level:** intelligible, plain

176. **Let . . . in:** This line is given by Q2 to Laertes. Many editors move the line to follow "what noise is that," and some then give it to Claudius. We have chosen to have the line be part of the offstage **noise.**

179. **virtue:** power

A pelican with its young. (4.5.168–69)
From Conrad Lycosthenes, *Prodigiorum . . .* (1557).

LAERTES
  How came he dead? I'll not be juggled with.
  To hell, allegiance! Vows, to the blackest devil!
  Conscience and grace, to the profoundest pit!   150
  I dare damnation. To this point I stand,
  That both the worlds I give to negligence,
  Let come what comes, only I'll be revenged
  Most throughly for my father.
KING Who shall stay you?   155
LAERTES My will, not all the ⟨world.⟩
  And for my means, I'll husband them so well
  They shall go far with little.
KING   Good Laertes,
  If you desire to know the certainty   160
  Of your dear father, is 't writ in your revenge
  That, swoopstake, you will draw both friend and
     foe,
  Winner and loser?
LAERTES None but his enemies.   165
KING Will you know them, then?
LAERTES
  To his good friends thus wide I'll ope my arms
  And, like the kind life-rend'ring pelican,
  Repast them with my blood.
KING   Why, now you speak   170
  Like a good child and a true gentleman.
  That I am guiltless of your father's death
  And am most sensibly in grief for it,
  It shall as level to your judgment 'pear
  As day does to your eye.   175
           A noise within: ⟨"Let her come in!"
LAERTES⟩ How now, what noise is that?

         Enter Ophelia.

  O heat, dry up my brains! Tears seven times salt
  Burn out the sense and virtue of mine eye!

180–81. **paid . . . beam:** avenged (The image is of putting an excess of weight in one **scale** until it overbalances the other **scale,** or turns **the beam.** See picture, page 22.)

185. **fine in:** refined by

186. **instance of itself:** sample of its refined nature—here, Ophelia's wits

188–90. **They . . . tear:** See longer note, page 293.

193. **move thus:** be this moving

194–95. **You must sing ". . . a-down-a":** Ophelia perhaps instructs others around her to sing refrains to her song.

195. **the wheel:** perhaps, the refrain of the song; or, perhaps the turning of **the** spinning **wheel,** to which motion ballads were sung

196. **false steward:** perhaps a reference to a story or ballad no longer known

198. **This nothing's . . . matter: this** nonsense speaks **more** eloquently than does serious speech

199. **There's rosemary:** Ophelia begins here to distribute real or imaginary flowers.

202. **document:** lesson, instruction

202–3. **thoughts . . . fitted:** i.e., Ophelia has wisely linked **thoughts and remembrance**

204. **fennel:** In flower symbolism, **fennel** symbolized flattery and deceit.

205. **rue:** symbol of sorrow or repentance

207. **a difference:** a heraldic term for a variation in a coat of arms; **daisy:** symbol of dissembling

208. **violets:** symbol of faithfulness

211. **Thought:** melancholy; **passion:** suffering

By heaven, thy madness shall be paid with weight   180
Till our scale turn the beam! O rose of May,
Dear maid, kind sister, sweet Ophelia!
O heavens, is 't possible a young maid's wits
Should be as mortal as ⟨an old⟩ man's life?
⟨Nature is fine in love, and, where 'tis fine,   185
It sends some precious instance of itself
After the thing it loves.⟩
OPHELIA ⌜*sings*⌝
    They bore him barefaced on the bier,
    ⟨*Hey non nonny, nonny, hey nonny,*⟩
    And in his grave rained many a tear.   190
  Fare you well, my dove.
LAERTES
  Hadst thou thy wits and didst persuade revenge,
  It could not move thus.
OPHELIA You must sing "A-down a-down"—and you
  "Call him a-down-a."—O, how the wheel becomes   195
  it! It is the false steward that stole his master's
  daughter.
LAERTES This nothing's more than matter.
OPHELIA There's rosemary, that's for remembrance.
  Pray you, love, remember. And there is pansies,   200
  that's for thoughts.
LAERTES A document in madness: thoughts and re-
  membrance fitted.
OPHELIA There's fennel for you, and columbines.
  There's rue for you, and here's some for me; we   205
  may call it herb of grace o' Sundays. You ⟨must⟩ wear
  your rue with a difference. There's a daisy. I would
  give you some violets, but they withered all when
  my father died. They say he made a good end.
  ⌜*Sings.*⌝ *For bonny sweet Robin is all my joy.*   210
LAERTES
  Thought and afflictions, passion, hell itself
  She turns to favor and to prettiness.

213–22. **And . . . soul:** This lyric has not been
found elsewhere.   **poll:** head
226. **commune with:** share
228. **whom your:** which of your
230. **by collateral hand:** i.e., as an accessory
231. **find us touched: find** me implicated
233. **in satisfaction:** as compensation
239. **hatchment:** tablet displaying his coat of arms
240. **ostentation:** ceremony
242. **That:** so **that**

Rosemary. (4.5.199)
From *The grete herball . . .* (1529).

OPHELIA ⌜*sings*⌝
    And will he not come again?
    And will he not come again?
      No, no, he is dead.   215
      Go to thy deathbed.
    He never will come again.

    His beard was as white as snow,
    ⟨*All*⟩ *flaxen was his poll.*
      He is gone, he is gone,   220
      And we cast away moan.
    God 'a mercy on his soul.
And of all Christians' souls, ⟨I pray God.⟩ God be
wi' you.   ⟨*She exits.*⟩

LAERTES   Do you ⟨see⟩ this, O God?   225
KING
Laertes, I must commune with your grief,
Or you deny me right. Go but apart,
Make choice of whom your wisest friends you will,
And they shall hear and judge 'twixt you and me.
If by direct or by collateral hand   230
They find us touched, we will our kingdom give,
Our crown, our life, and all that we call ours,
To you in satisfaction; but if not,
Be you content to lend your patience to us,
And we shall jointly labor with your soul   235
To give it due content.
LAERTES   Let this be so.
His means of death, his obscure funeral
(No trophy, sword, nor hatchment o'er his bones,
No noble rite nor formal ostentation)   240
Cry to be heard, as 'twere from heaven to earth,
That I must call 't in question.
KING   So you shall,
And where th' offense is, let the great ax fall.
I pray you, go with me.   245
                They exit.

4.6   Horatio is given a letter from Hamlet telling of the prince's boarding of a pirate ship and his subsequent return to Denmark.

———

9. **an 't:** if it
10. **th' ambassador:** i.e., Hamlet
14. **overlooked:** read; **means: means** of access
16. **pirate . . . appointment:** pirate ship well equipped for battle
17–18. **put on a compelled valor:** became, under compulsion, courageous
21. **thieves of mercy:** merciful **thieves**
23. **repair thou:** come
25–26. **too light for the bore of the matter: too light for the** caliber **of the** gun; i.e., inadequate

Sixteenth-century ships at sea. (4.6.15–19)
From William Okeley, *Eben-ezer; or,
A small monument of great mercy . . .* (1684).

⌜Scene 6⌝

Enter Horatio and others.

HORATIO What are they that would speak with me?
GENTLEMAN Seafaring men, sir. They say they have
letters for you.
HORATIO Let them come in. ⌜*Gentleman exits.*⌝ I do not
know from what part of the world I should be 5
greeted, if not from Lord Hamlet.

Enter Sailors.

SAILOR God bless you, sir.
HORATIO Let Him bless thee too.
SAILOR He shall, sir, ⟨an 't⟩ please Him. There's a letter
for you, sir. It came from th' ambassador that was 10
bound for England—if your name be Horatio, as I
am let to know it is. ⌜*He hands Horatio a letter.*⌝
HORATIO ⟨*reads the letter*⟩ *Horatio, when thou shalt have*
overlooked this, give these fellows some means to the
King. They have letters for him. Ere we were two days 15
old at sea, a pirate of very warlike appointment gave
us chase. Finding ourselves too slow of sail, we put on
a compelled valor, and in the grapple I boarded them.
On the instant, they got clear of our ship; so I alone
became their prisoner. They have dealt with me like 20
thieves of mercy, but they knew what they did: I am to
do a ⟨good⟩ turn for them. Let the King have the letters
I have sent, and repair thou to me with as much speed
as thou wouldst fly death. I have words to speak in
thine ear will make thee dumb; yet are they much too 25
light for the ⟨bore⟩ of the matter. These good fellows
will bring thee where I am. Rosencrantz and Guilden-
stern hold their course for England; of them I have
much to tell thee. Farewell.

                           ⟨*He*⟩ *that thou knowest thine,* 30
                                        Hamlet.

32. **way:** means of access

4.7   Claudius gets a letter from Hamlet announcing the prince's return. Claudius enlists Laertes's willing help in devising another plot against Hamlet's life. Laertes agrees to kill Hamlet with a poisoned rapier in a fencing match. If he fails, Claudius will give Hamlet a poisoned cup of wine. Gertrude interrupts their plotting to announce that Ophelia has drowned.

———

1. **my acquittance seal:** ratify my acquittal, i.e., acknowledge my innocence
3. **knowing:** intelligent, understanding
7. **feats:** deeds
8. **capital:** deadly
10. **mainly:** greatly; **stirred up:** motivated
12. **unsinewed:** weak
16. **conjunctive:** closely joined
17. **star . . . sphere:** According to Ptolemaic astronomy, each planet (**star**) is inseparable from its **sphere.** (See note to 1.5.22–23.)
19. **count:** accounting, judgment
20. **the general gender:** the common people
22. **Work . . . stone:** function **like** springs of water that petrify **wood**
23. **Convert his gyves:** transform his shackles (See picture, page 78.)
25. **reverted:** returned

Come, I will ⟨give⟩ you way for these your letters
And do 't the speedier that you may direct me
To him from whom you brought them.

        They exit.

⌜Scene 7⌝

Enter King and Laertes.

KING
Now must your conscience my acquittance seal,
And you must put me in your heart for friend,
Sith you have heard, and with a knowing ear,
That he which hath your noble father slain
Pursued my life.   5
LAERTES   It well appears. But tell me
Why you ⟨proceeded⟩ not against these feats,
So criminal and so capital in nature,
As by your safety, greatness, wisdom, all things else,
You mainly were stirred up.   10
KING O, for two special reasons,
Which may to you perhaps seem much unsinewed,
But yet to me they're strong. The Queen his mother
Lives almost by his looks, and for myself
(My virtue or my plague, be it either which), 15
She is so ⟨conjunctive⟩ to my life and soul
That, as the star moves not but in his sphere,
I could not but by her. The other motive
Why to a public count I might not go
Is the great love the general gender bear him, 20
Who, dipping all his faults in their affection,
Work like the spring that turneth wood to stone,
Convert his gyves to graces, so that my arrows,
Too slightly timbered for so ⟨loud a wind,⟩
Would have reverted to my bow again,   25
But not where I have aimed them.
LAERTES
And so have I a noble father lost,

28. **terms:** condition

29. **if praises . . . again: if** I **may** praise what she used to be

30–31. **Stood   challenger . . . perfections:** her **worth** challenged **all the age** to equal **her** excellence

50. **naked:** defenseless

52. **pardon:** permission

55. **abuse:** deceit, imposture

57. **character:** handwriting

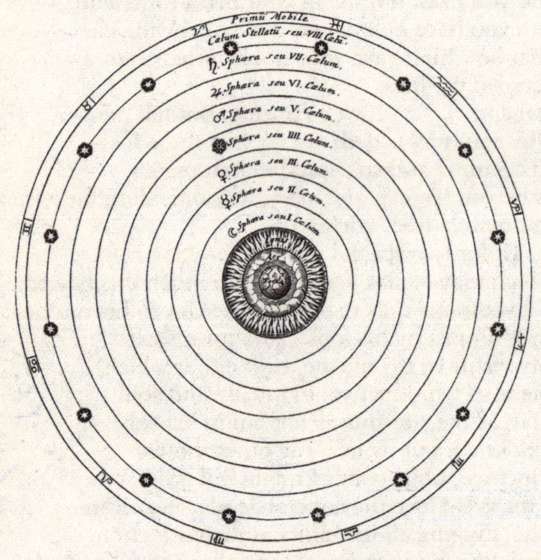

Ptolemaic universe. (1.5.22–23; 4.7.17)
From Marcus Manilius, *The sphere of . . .* (1675).

A sister driven into desp'rate terms,
Whose worth, if praises may go back again,
Stood challenger on mount of all the age   30
For her perfections. But my revenge will come.
KING
Break not your sleeps for that. You must not think
That we are made of stuff so flat and dull
That we can let our beard be shook with danger
And think it pastime. You shortly shall hear more.   35
I loved your father, and we love ourself,
And that, I hope, will teach you to imagine—

Enter a Messenger with letters.

⟨How now? What news?
MESSENGER   Letters, my lord, from
    Hamlet.⟩   40
These to your Majesty, this to the Queen.
KING From Hamlet? Who brought them?
MESSENGER
Sailors, my lord, they say. I saw them not.
They were given me by Claudio. He received them
[Of him that brought them.]   45
KING   Laertes, you shall hear
    them.—
Leave us.   ⟨*Messenger exits.*⟩
    ⌜*Reads.*⌝ *High and mighty, you shall know I am set
naked on your kingdom. Tomorrow shall I beg leave to   50
see your kingly eyes, when I shall (first asking ⟨your⟩
pardon) thereunto recount the occasion of my sudden
⟨and more strange⟩ return. ⟨Hamlet.⟩*
What should this mean? Are all the rest come back?
Or is it some abuse and no such thing?   55
LAERTES Know you the hand?
KING 'Tis Hamlet's character. "Naked"—
And in a postscript here, he says "alone."
Can you ⟨advise⟩ me?

68. **So:** provided that

70. **checking at:** refusing to continue (The image is of a falcon in flight turning away from the prey she is supposed to be pursuing.) See picture, page 128.

72. **device:** devising, planning

75. **uncharge the practice:** not blame his death on our plot **uncharge:** lift a burden from **practice:** stratagem, treachery

79. **organ:** agent, instrument

83. **Your . . . parts:** all of your qualities combined

86. **unworthiest siege:** least important rank

88. **A . . . youth:** a mere decoration in youth's **cap**

89–92. **youth no less becomes . . . graveness:** i.e., clothes worn by **youth** are as becoming to the young as the garments of **age** are to their comfortably prosperous wearers **sables:** furs; or, robes with sable trim **weeds:** garments **Importing:** signifying

A fencer in doublet and hose.
From George Silver, *Paradoxes of defence* (1599).

LAERTES
　I am lost in it, my lord. But let him come.　　　　60
　It warms the very sickness in my heart
　That I ⟨shall⟩ live and tell him to his teeth
　"Thus didst thou."
KING　　　　　　　　　　　If it be so, Laertes
　(As how should it be so? how otherwise?),　　　65
　Will you be ruled by me?
LAERTES　　　　　　　　　　Ay, my lord,
　So you will not o'errule me to a peace.
KING
　To thine own peace. If he be now returned,
　As ⟨checking⟩ at his voyage, and that he means　　70
　No more to undertake it, I will work him
　To an exploit, now ripe in my device,
　Under the which he shall not choose but fall;
　And for his death no wind of blame shall breathe,
　But even his mother shall uncharge the practice　　75
　And call it accident.
[LAERTES　My lord, I will be ruled,
　The rather if you could devise it so
　That I might be the organ.
KING　　　　　　　　　　　It falls right.　　80
　You have been talked of since your travel much,
　And that in Hamlet's hearing, for a quality
　Wherein they say you shine. Your sum of parts
　Did not together pluck such envy from him
　As did that one, and that, in my regard,　　85
　Of the unworthiest siege.
LAERTES　What part is that, my lord?
KING
　A very ribbon in the cap of youth—
　Yet needful too, for youth no less becomes
　The light and careless livery that it wears　　90
　Than settled age his sables and his weeds,
　Importing health and graveness.] Two months since

95. **can well:** are skillful

98. **As had he been: as** if **he had been;
encorpsed and demi-natured:** made into a single
body (with the horse) to form a double-natured
creature like the centaur (See picture, below.)

99. **brave:** noble; **topped:** surpassed

100. **in forgery of:** in inventing

101. **Come . . . did:** fall **short of** his actual per-
formance

108. **made confession of you:** acknowledged you

110. **art and exercise . . . defense:** theory and
practice of fencing

113. **'scrimers:** fencers (French *escrimeurs*)

119. **play:** fence

A centaur. (4.7.98)
From Gabriel Rollenhagen,
Nucleus emblematum selectissimorium (1611).

Here was a gentleman of Normandy.
I have seen myself, and served against, the French,
And they can well on horseback, but this gallant   95
Had witchcraft in 't. He grew unto his seat,
And to such wondrous doing brought his horse
As had he been encorpsed and demi-natured
With the brave beast. So far he topped ⟨my⟩ thought
That I in forgery of shapes and tricks   100
Come short of what he did.
LAERTES   A Norman was 't?
KING A Norman.
LAERTES
  Upon my life, Lamord.
KING   The very same.   105
LAERTES
  I know him well. He is the brooch indeed
  And gem of all the nation.
KING He made confession of you
  And gave you such a masterly report
  For art and exercise in your defense,   110
  And for your rapier most especial,
  That he cried out 'twould be a sight indeed
  If one could match you. [The 'scrimers of their
    nation
  He swore had neither motion, guard, nor eye,   115
  If you opposed them.] Sir, this report of his
  Did Hamlet so envenom with his envy
  That he could nothing do but wish and beg
  Your sudden coming-o'er, to play with you.
  Now out of this—   120
LAERTES   What out of this, my lord?
KING
  Laertes, was your father dear to you?
  Or are you like the painting of a sorrow,
  A face without a heart?
LAERTES   Why ask you this?   125

128. **passages of proof:** proven instances

129. **qualifies:** diminishes, lessens

131. **snuff:** the burned part of the wick of a candle

132. **is at a like goodness still:** remains always at the same level of **goodness**

133. **a pleurisy:** an excess (not to be confused with the disease of the same name)

134. **his own too-much:** its **own** excess; **That: that** which

139–40. **spendthrift . . . by easing:** According to old notions of medicine, **a sigh** eases distress but draws blood away from the heart.

140. **to . . . th' ulcer:** i.e., **to the** main point

142. **indeed:** in fact; also, in action

145. **should murder sanctuarize:** i.e., should protect a murderer (like Hamlet) from punishment

147. **Keep close:** stay in strict confinement or hidden

149. **put on those shall:** incite **those** who **shall**

151. **in fine:** in conclusion

153. **remiss:** carelessly indifferent

154. **generous:** noble-minded; **contriving:** treachery

156. **shuffling:** shifting of the foils, legerdemain

157. **unbated:** not blunted (as rapiers for such matches should be); **a pass of practice:** a treacherous thrust

KING
Not that I think you did not love your father,
But that I know love is begun by time
And that I see, in passages of proof,
Time qualifies the spark and fire of it.
[There lives within the very flame of love   130
A kind of wick or snuff that will abate it,
And nothing is at a like goodness still;
For goodness, growing to a pleurisy,
Dies in his own too-much. That we would do
We should do when we would; for this "would"   135
    changes
And hath abatements and delays as many
As there are tongues, are hands, are accidents;
And then this "should" is like a ⌜spendthrift⌝ sigh,
That hurts by easing. But to the quick of th' ulcer:]   140
Hamlet comes back; what would you undertake
To show yourself indeed your father's son
More than in words?
LAERTES   To cut his throat i' th' church.
KING
No place indeed should murder sanctuarize;   145
Revenge should have no bounds. But, good Laertes,
Will you do this? Keep close within your chamber.
Hamlet, returned, shall know you are come home.
We'll put on those shall praise your excellence
And set a double varnish on the fame   150
The Frenchman gave you; bring you, in fine, together
And wager ⟨on⟩ your heads. He, being remiss,
Most generous, and free from all contriving,
Will not peruse the foils, so that with ease,   155
Or with a little shuffling, you may choose
A sword unbated, and in a ⟨pass⟩ of practice
Requite him for your father.

161. **of a mountebank:** from a quack doctor
162. **mortal:** deadly
163. **cataplasm:** poultice
164. **Collected from:** composed of; **simples:** medicinal plants; **virtue:** medicinal power
166. **withal:** with it
167. **contagion:** poison that infects the blood
167–68. **if . . . death: if I** scratch **him** he will die
171. **May fit us to our shape: may** suit **our** plan
172. **And that:** and if
172–73. **drift . . . performance:** intention reveal itself through our bungling
175. **back or second:** backup position
176. **blast in proof:** blow up in the testing
177. **your cunnings:** Hamlet's skills and yours
179. **motion:** exertion
183. **for the nonce:** for this purpose
184. **venomed:** poisonous; **stuck:** thrust (a fencing term)
190. **askant:** aslant

LAERTES   I will do 't,
  And for ⟨that⟩ purpose I'll anoint my sword.   160
  I bought an unction of a mountebank
  So mortal that, but dip a knife in it,
  Where it draws blood no cataplasm so rare,
  Collected from all simples that have virtue
  Under the moon, can save the thing from death   165
  That is but scratched withal. I'll touch my point
  With this contagion, that, if I gall him slightly,
  It may be death.
KING   Let's further think of this,
  Weigh what convenience both of time and means   170
  May fit us to our shape. If this should fail,
  And that our drift look through our bad
     performance,
  'Twere better not assayed. Therefore this project
  Should have a back or second that might hold   175
  If this did blast in proof. Soft, let me see.
  We'll make a solemn wager on your cunnings—
  I ha 't!
  When in your motion you are hot and dry
  (As make your bouts more violent to that end)   180
  And that he calls for drink, I'll have prepared
     him
  A chalice for the nonce, whereon but sipping,
  If he by chance escape your venomed stuck,
  Our purpose may hold there.—But stay, what   185
     noise?

                      Enter Queen.

QUEEN
  One woe doth tread upon another's heel,
  So fast they follow. Your sister's drowned, Laertes.
LAERTES   Drowned? O, where?
QUEEN
  There is a willow grows askant the brook   190

191. **hoar:** gray

192. **Therewith:** i.e., with willow branches

193. **long purples:** like **dead men's fingers** (line 195), a name given to various species of *Orchis*

194. **liberal:** plainspoken; **grosser:** coarser, less decent

195. **cold:** chaste

197. **pendant:** downhanging; **coronet weeds:** weeds made into garlands

198. **envious sliver:** malicious branch

202. **lauds:** hymns

203. **incapable of:** without ability to understand

204. **endued:** naturally adapted

207. **lay:** song

213. **It . . . trick:** i.e., weeping is natural

214–15. **When these . . . out: when these** tears **are** shed, my female-like weakness **will be** spent

216. **fain:** gladly

A willow. (4.7.190)
From Henry Peacham, *Minerua Britanna* . . . [1612].

That shows his ⟨hoar⟩ leaves in the glassy stream.
Therewith fantastic garlands did she make
Of crowflowers, nettles, daisies, and long purples,
That liberal shepherds give a grosser name,
But our cold maids do "dead men's fingers" call   195
  them.
There on the pendant boughs her coronet weeds
Clamb'ring to hang, an envious sliver broke,
When down her weedy trophies and herself
Fell in the weeping brook. Her clothes spread wide,   200
And mermaid-like awhile they bore her up,
Which time she chanted snatches of old lauds,
As one incapable of her own distress
Or like a creature native and endued
Unto that element. But long it could not be   205
Till that her garments, heavy with their drink,
Pulled the poor wretch from her melodious lay
To muddy death.
LAERTES   Alas, then she is drowned.
QUEEN Drowned, drowned.   210
LAERTES
Too much of water hast thou, poor Ophelia,
And therefore I forbid my tears. But yet
It is our trick; nature her custom holds,
Let shame say what it will. When these are gone,
The woman will be out.—Adieu, my lord.   215
I have a speech o' fire that fain would blaze,
But that this folly drowns it.   *He exits.*
KING   Let's follow, Gertrude.
How much I had to do to calm his rage!
Now fear I this will give it start again.   220
Therefore, let's follow.
                                They exit.

The Tragedy of

HAMLET,

Prince of Denmark

ACT 5

5.1 Hamlet, returned from his journey, comes upon a gravedigger singing as he digs. Hamlet tries to find out who the grave is for and reflects on the skulls that are being dug up. A funeral procession approaches. Hamlet soon realizes that the corpse is Ophelia's. When Laertes in his grief leaps into her grave and curses Hamlet as the cause of Ophelia's death, Hamlet comes forward. He and Laertes struggle, with Hamlet protesting his own love and grief for Ophelia.

---

0 SD. **Enter Gravedigger and Another:** In Q2 and Folio *Hamlet,* this stage direction reads "Enter two clowns," thus indicating that the Gravedigger and his companion were played by comic actors.

1. **in Christian burial:** i.e., in consecrated ground (Suicide was considered self-murder; it was also held to be an offense against God and against the Christian church. The suicide was thus forbidden **Christian burial.**)

4. **straight:** straightaway, immediately; **crowner:** coroner; **sat on her:** conducted a formal inquest into her death; **finds it:** decided that her death warrants

9. **se offendendo:** in self-offense (the gravedigger's rendering of the common legal phrase *se defendendo,* "in self-defense")

11. **wittingly:** deliberately

12. **Argal:** a mistake for Latin *ergo,* "therefore"

14. **goodman:** a form of address prefixed, as here, to the name of an occupation

(continued)

⌜ACT 5⌝

⌜Scene 1⌝

Enter ⌜Gravedigger and Another.⌝

⌜GRAVEDIGGER⌝ Is she to be buried in Christian burial,
when she willfully seeks her own salvation?

OTHER I tell thee she is. Therefore make her grave
straight. The crowner hath sat on her and finds it
Christian burial. 5

⌜GRAVEDIGGER⌝ How can that be, unless she drowned
herself in her own defense?

OTHER Why, 'tis found so.

⌜GRAVEDIGGER⌝ It must be ⟨*se offendendo;*⟩ it cannot be
else. For here lies the point: if I drown myself 10
wittingly, it argues an act, and an act hath three
branches—it is to act, to do, to perform. ⟨Argal,⟩ she
drowned herself wittingly.

OTHER Nay, but hear you, goodman delver—

⌜GRAVEDIGGER⌝ Give me leave. Here lies the water; 15
good. Here stands the man; good. If the man go to
this water and drown himself, it is (will he, nill he)
he goes; mark you that. But if the water come to him
and drown him, he drowns not himself. Argal, he
that is not guilty of his own death shortens not his 20
own life.

OTHER But is this law?

⌜GRAVEDIGGER⌝ Ay, marry, is 't—crowner's 'quest law.

15. **Give me leave:** let me go on
17. **will he, nill he:** willy-nilly, whether wished or not
23. **'quest:** inquest
27. **there thou sayst:** you said it correctly
28. **count'nance:** legal approval
30. **even-Christian:** fellow Christians
32. **hold up:** maintain
34. **bore arms:** was given heraldic insignia (with a pun on **arms** as part of the body)
41. **Go to:** an exclamation of impatience
53. **unyoke:** i.e., quit, as a farmer does when he unyokes his team of oxen
54. **Marry:** a mild oath (See note to 1.3.98.)
56. **Mass:** by the **Mass** (another mild oath)

A gallows or gibbet. (5.1.44–45)
From *Warhafftige . . . Verrätherey . . .* (1606).

OTHER Will you ha' the truth on 't? If this had not been
a gentlewoman, she should have been buried out o'   25
Christian burial.
⌜GRAVEDIGGER⌝ Why, there thou sayst. And the more
pity that great folk should have count'nance in this
world to drown or hang themselves more than
their even-Christian. Come, my spade. There is no   30
ancient gentlemen but gard'ners, ditchers, and
grave-makers. They hold up Adam's profession.
OTHER Was he a gentleman?
⌜GRAVEDIGGER⌝ He was the first that ever bore arms.
⟨OTHER Why, he had none.   35
⌜GRAVEDIGGER⌝ What, art a heathen? How dost thou
understand the scripture? The scripture says Adam
digged. Could he dig without arms?⟩ I'll put anoth-
er question to thee. If thou answerest me not to the
purpose, confess thyself—   40
OTHER Go to!
⌜GRAVEDIGGER⌝ What is he that builds stronger than
either the mason, the shipwright, or the carpenter?
OTHER The gallows-maker; for that ⟨frame⟩ outlives a
thousand tenants.   45
⌜GRAVEDIGGER⌝ I like thy wit well, in good faith. The
gallows does well. But how does it well? It does
well to those that do ill. Now, thou dost ill to say the
gallows is built stronger than the church. Argal, the
gallows may do well to thee. To 't again, come.   50
OTHER "Who builds stronger than a mason, a ship-
wright, or a carpenter?"
⌜GRAVEDIGGER⌝ Ay, tell me that, and unyoke.
OTHER Marry, now I can tell.
⌜GRAVEDIGGER⌝ To 't.   55
OTHER Mass, I cannot tell.

⟨*Enter Hamlet and Horatio afar off.*⟩

⌜GRAVEDIGGER⌝ Cudgel thy brains no more about it,

58–59. **your . . . beating:** i.e., a stupid donkey does not move more quickly because it is beaten

61. **doomsday:** See note to 1.1.132, and picture, page 68.

63–66. **In youth . . . meet:** The words of the Gravedigger's song are found, with variations, printed in Richard Tottel's *Miscellany* (1557), entitled "The aged lover renounceth love." The "O" and "a's" (lines 65–66) may mark the breathing or grunts of the Gravedigger, or may be part of his song, which continues off and on through line 123. **behove:** benefit   **meet:** suitable

69–70. **Custom . . . easiness:** i.e., habit makes it easy for him

71. **of little employment:** not frequently used

72. **hath the daintier sense:** is more sensitive

78. **jowls:** dashes

81. **o'erreaches:** gets the better of

"An absolute gentleman." (5.2.120)
From Cesare Vecellio, *Habiti antichi et moderni* (1598).

for your dull ass will not mend his pace with
beating. And, when you are asked this question
next, say "a grave-maker." The houses he makes   60
lasts till doomsday. Go, get thee in, and fetch me a
stoup of liquor.

⌜*The Other Man exits and the Gravedigger*
digs and sings.⌝

In youth when I did love, did love,
    Methought it was very sweet
To contract—O—the time for—a—my behove,   65
    O, methought there—a—was nothing—a—meet.

HAMLET Has this fellow no feeling of his business? He
sings in grave-making.

HORATIO Custom hath made it in him a property of
easiness.   70

HAMLET 'Tis e'en so. The hand of little employment
hath the daintier sense.

⌜GRAVEDIGGER⌝ ⟨*sings*⟩
    But age with his stealing steps
    Hath clawed me in his clutch,
    And hath shipped me into the land,   75
    As if I had never been such.

⌜*He digs up a skull.*⌝

HAMLET That skull had a tongue in it and could sing
once. How the knave jowls it to the ground as if
'twere Cain's jawbone, that did the first murder!
This might be the pate of a politician which this ass   80
now o'erreaches, one that would circumvent God,
might it not?

HORATIO It might, my lord.

HAMLET Or of a courtier, which could say "Good
morrow, sweet lord! How dost thou, sweet lord?"   85
This might be my Lord Such-a-one that praised my
Lord Such-a-one's horse when he went to beg it,
might it not?

HORATIO Ay, my lord.

91. **chapless:** without a lower jaw (See picture, below.) **mazard:** head (a slang term)

94. **loggets:** a game played by throwing pieces of wood at a stake

101. **quiddities:** hair-splitting definitions

102. **quillities:** quibbles; **tenures:** holdings

103. **suffer:** allow

104. **sconce:** head (a slang term)

106–7. **his statutes, his recognizances . . . :** Hamlet begins here a list of legal terms referring to buying and holding property.

108. **the fine:** the end, the conclusion

112. **pair of indentures:** contracts (See longer note, page 294.)

113. **conveyances:** deeds; **this box:** i.e., **this** skull

114. **inheritor:** owner

120. **sirrah:** term of address to a lower-class male

A chapless skull. (5.1.91)
From Henry Peacham, *Minerua Britanna* [1612].

HAMLET Why, e'en so. And now my Lady Worm's, 90
chapless and knocked about the ⟨mazard⟩ with a
sexton's spade. Here's fine revolution, an we had
the trick to see 't. Did these bones cost no more the
breeding but to play at loggets with them? Mine
ache to think on 't. 95
⌜GRAVEDIGGER⌝ ⟨sings⟩

> A pickax and a spade, a spade,
> For and a shrouding sheet,
> O, a pit of clay for to be made
> For such a guest is meet.

⌜*He digs up more skulls.*⌝

HAMLET There's another. Why may not that be the 100
skull of a lawyer? Where be his quiddities now, his
quillities, his cases, his tenures, and his tricks? Why
does he suffer this mad knave now to knock him
about the sconce with a dirty shovel and will not tell
him of his action of battery? Hum, this fellow might 105
be in 's time a great buyer of land, with his statutes,
his recognizances, his fines, his double vouchers,
his recoveries. ⟨Is this the fine of his fines and the
recovery of his recoveries,⟩ to have his fine pate full
of fine dirt? Will ⟨his⟩ vouchers vouch him no more 110
of his purchases, and ⟨double ones too,⟩ than the
length and breadth of a pair of indentures? The very
conveyances of his lands will scarcely lie in this box,
and must th' inheritor himself have no more, ha?
HORATIO Not a jot more, my lord. 115
HAMLET Is not parchment made of sheepskins?
HORATIO Ay, my lord, and of calves' skins too.
HAMLET They are sheep and calves which seek out
assurance in that. I will speak to this fellow.—
Whose grave's this, sirrah? 120
⌜GRAVEDIGGER⌝ Mine, sir.
⌜*Sings.*⌝ ⟨O,⟩ a pit of clay for to be made
⟨For such a guest is meet.⟩

125. **out on 't:** outside of it

129. **quick:** living

131. **quick:** quickly moving

140. **absolute:** precise

140–41. **by the card:** i.e., with precision

143–45. **the age . . . kibe:** i.e., **the** present **age** has become so affected **that** peasants walk on the very heels of courtiers   **picked:** affected   **his kibe:** the courtier's sore **heel**

A courtier and a peasant. (5.1.143–44)
From Robert Greene, *A quip for an vpstart courtier . . .* [1592].

HAMLET I think it be thine indeed, for thou liest in 't.

⌜GRAVEDIGGER⌝ You lie out on 't, sir, and therefore 'tis   125
    not yours. For my part, I do not lie in 't, yet it is
    mine.

HAMLET Thou dost lie in 't, to be in 't and say it is thine.
    'Tis for the dead, not for the quick; therefore thou
    liest.   130

⌜GRAVEDIGGER⌝ 'Tis a quick lie, sir; 'twill away again
    from me to you.

HAMLET What man dost thou dig it for?

⌜GRAVEDIGGER⌝ For no man, sir.

HAMLET What woman then?   135

⌜GRAVEDIGGER⌝ For none, neither.

HAMLET Who is to be buried in 't?

⌜GRAVEDIGGER⌝ One that was a woman, sir, but, rest
    her soul, she's dead.

HAMLET How absolute the knave is! We must speak by   140
    the card, or equivocation will undo us. By the
    Lord, Horatio, this three years I have took note of
    it: the age is grown so picked that the toe of the
    peasant comes so near the heel of the courtier, he
    galls his kibe.—How long hast thou been grave-   145
    maker?

⌜GRAVEDIGGER⌝ Of ⟨all⟩ the days i' th' year, I came to 't
    that day that our last King Hamlet overcame
    Fortinbras.

HAMLET How long is that since?   150

⌜GRAVEDIGGER⌝ Cannot you tell that? Every fool can
    tell that. It was that very day that young Hamlet
    was born—he that is mad, and sent into England.

HAMLET Ay, marry, why was he sent into England?

⌜GRAVEDIGGER⌝ Why, because he was mad. He shall   155
    recover his wits there. Or if he do not, 'tis no great
    matter there.

HAMLET Why?

⌜GRAVEDIGGER⌝ 'Twill not be seen in him there. There
    the men are as mad as he.   160

165. **Upon what ground:** under what circumstances, for what reason

170. **pocky:** rotten, as if infected with syphilis

171. **scarce hold the laying in:** barely hold together long enough to be buried

177. **your water:** i.e., **water**

177–78. **your . . . body:** i.e., bodies **whoreson:** vile

178. **lien you:** lain

192. **fancy:** imagination

A jester. (5.1.186–87)
From George Wither, *A collection of emblemes . . .* (1635).

HAMLET How came he mad?

⌜GRAVEDIGGER⌝ Very strangely, they say.

HAMLET How "strangely"?

⌜GRAVEDIGGER⌝ Faith, e'en with losing his wits.

HAMLET Upon what ground? 165

⌜GRAVEDIGGER⌝ Why, here in Denmark. I have been
sexton here, man and boy, thirty years.

HAMLET How long will a man lie i' th' earth ere he rot?

⌜GRAVEDIGGER⌝ Faith, if he be not rotten before he die
(as we have many pocky corses ⟨nowadays⟩ that will 170
scarce hold the laying in), he will last you some
eight year or nine year. A tanner will last you nine
year.

HAMLET Why he more than another?

⌜GRAVEDIGGER⌝ Why, sir, his hide is so tanned with his 175
trade that he will keep out water a great while; and
your water is a sore decayer of your whoreson dead
body. Here's a skull now hath lien you i' th' earth
three-and-twenty years.

HAMLET Whose was it? 180

⌜GRAVEDIGGER⌝ A whoreson mad fellow's it was.
Whose do you think it was?

HAMLET Nay, I know not.

⌜GRAVEDIGGER⌝ A pestilence on him for a mad rogue!
He poured a flagon of Rhenish on my head once. 185
This same skull, sir, was, sir, Yorick's skull, the
King's jester.

HAMLET This?

⌜GRAVEDIGGER⌝ E'en that.

HAMLET, ⌜*taking the skull*⌝ (Let me see.) Alas, poor 190
Yorick! I knew him, Horatio—a fellow of infinite
jest, of most excellent fancy. He hath bore me on his
back a thousand times, and now how abhorred in
my imagination it is! My gorge rises at it. Here hung
those lips that I have kissed I know not how oft. 195
Where be your gibes now? your gambols? your

199. **chapfallen:** (1) dejected; (2) without the lower jaw (See picture, page 244.)

199–200. **my lady's chamber:** i.e., the room of the gentlewoman you would entertain

201. **favor:** appearance

204. **Alexander: Alexander** the Great, who died in 323 B.C.E. as ruler of the known world (See picture, below.)

212. **curiously:** elaborately

215. **modesty:** moderation, reserve

217. **returneth to dust:** See Genesis 3.19.

220. **Imperious:** imperial; majestic

222. **that earth:** the body of **Caesar** (line 220), made from **earth** (See Genesis 3.19.)

223. **expel:** keep out; **flaw:** gust of wind

226. **maimèd:** impaired, diminished

228. **Fordo:** destroy; **some estate:** high rank

229. **Couch we:** let us hide; **mark:** observe

Alexander. (5.1.204, 211, 216–17)
From Valentin Thilo, *Icones heroum . . .* (1589).

songs? your flashes of merriment that were wont to
set the table on a roar? Not one now to mock your
own grinning? Quite chapfallen? Now get you to my
lady's ⟨chamber,⟩ and tell her, let her paint an inch   200
thick, to this favor she must come. Make her laugh
at that.—Prithee, Horatio, tell me one thing.
HORATIO What's that, my lord?
HAMLET Dost thou think Alexander looked o' this
fashion i' th' earth?   205
HORATIO E'en so.
HAMLET And smelt so? Pah! ⌜*He puts the skull down.*⌝
HORATIO E'en so, my lord.
HAMLET To what base uses we may return, Horatio!
Why may not imagination trace the noble dust of   210
Alexander till he find it stopping a bunghole?
HORATIO 'Twere to consider too curiously to consider
so.
HAMLET No, faith, not a jot; but to follow him thither,
with modesty enough and likelihood to lead it, ⟨as   215
thus:⟩ Alexander died, Alexander was buried, Alex-
ander returneth to dust; the dust is earth; of earth
we make loam; and why of that loam whereto he
was converted might they not stop a beer barrel?
Imperious Caesar, dead and turned to clay,   220
Might stop a hole to keep the wind away.
O, that that earth which kept the world in awe
Should patch a wall t' expel the ⟨winter's⟩ flaw!

Enter King, Queen, Laertes, ⟨Lords attendant,⟩ and the
   corpse ⌜*of Ophelia, with a Doctor of Divinity.*⌝

But soft, but soft awhile! Here comes the King,
The Queen, the courtiers. Who is this they follow?   225
And with such maimèd rites? This doth betoken
The corse they follow did with desp'rate hand
Fordo its own life. 'Twas of some estate.
Couch we awhile and mark.   ⌜*They step aside.*⌝

234. **doubtful:** suspicious

235. **but that . . . order:** except for the fact **that** the king's **command** overrides the rule of the church

236–37. **in ground . . . trumpet: in** unhallowed **ground been** buried until the Judgment Day (See 1 Corinthians 15.52: "for **the trumpet** shall blow, and the dead shall be raised up incorruptible.") See picture, page 68, and note to 5.1.1.

237. **For:** instead of

238. **Shards:** bits of pottery

240. **crants:** garlands

241. **strewments:** flowers strewn on a grave

241–42. **bringing . . . burial:** being brought to the grave, her last **home,** to the sound of the **bell**

246. **such rest:** i.e., to pray for **such rest**

247. **peace-parted souls:** i.e., **souls** that depart in peace

252. **howling:** i.e., in hell

254. **Sweets to the sweet:** sweet flowers to the sweet maiden

256. **decked:** adorned, arrayed

260–61. **thy most . . . Deprived thee of:** i.e., **deprived** you **of** your mind

LAERTES   What ceremony else?   230
HAMLET   That is Laertes, a very noble youth. Mark.
LAERTES   What ceremony else?
DOCTOR
   Her obsequies have been as far enlarged
   As we have warranty. Her death was doubtful,
   And, but that great command o'ersways the order,
   She should in ground unsanctified been lodged
   Till the last trumpet. For charitable prayers   235
   ⟨Shards,⟩ flints, and pebbles should be thrown on
     her.
   Yet here she is allowed her virgin crants,
   Her maiden strewments, and the bringing home   240
   Of bell and burial.
LAERTES
   Must there no more be done?
DOCTOR   No more be done.
   We should profane the service of the dead   245
   To sing a requiem and such rest to her
   As to peace-parted souls.
LAERTES   Lay her i' th' earth,
   And from her fair and unpolluted flesh
   May violets spring! I tell thee, churlish priest,   250
   A minist'ring angel shall my sister be
   When thou liest howling.
HAMLET, ⌜to Horatio⌝   What, the fair Ophelia?
QUEEN   Sweets to the sweet, farewell!
                       ⌜*She scatters flowers.*⌝
   I hoped thou shouldst have been my Hamlet's wife;   255
   I thought thy bride-bed to have decked, sweet maid,
   And not have strewed thy grave.
LAERTES   O, treble woe
   Fall ten times ⟨treble⟩ on that cursèd head
   Whose wicked deed thy most ingenious sense   260
   Deprived thee of!—Hold off the earth awhile,
   Till I have caught her once more in mine arms.
                   (*Leaps in the grave.*)

265. **Pelion:** a high mountain on which, in Greek mythology, the giants placed Mount Ossa in their attempt to scale Mount **Olympus** (line 266) **sky-ish:** lofty

268. **an emphasis:** intensity, force of feeling

269. **wand'ring stars:** planets

275. **splenitive:** quick-tempered

289. **forbear him:** be patient with him

290. **'Swounds:** by Christ's wounds (a strong oath); **thou 't:** thou wilt

291. **Woo't:** wilt thou

293. **eisel:** vinegar

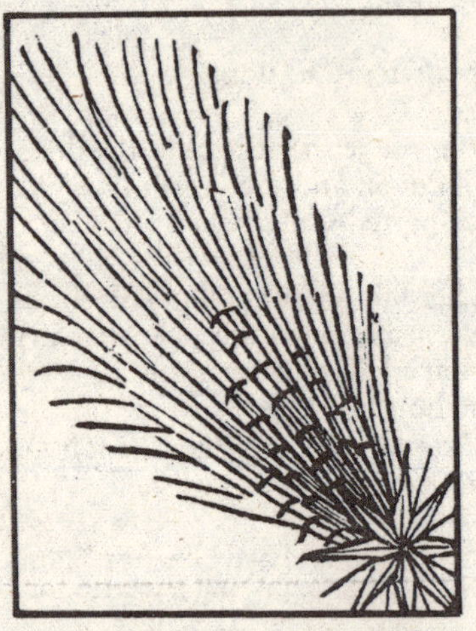

"As stars with trains of fire." (1.1.129)
From Hartmann Schedel, *Liber chronicorum* . . . [1493].

Now pile your dust upon the quick and dead, *really?*
Till of this flat a mountain you have made
T' o'ertop old Pelion or the skyish head   265
Of blue Olympus.

HAMLET, ⌐*advancing*¬
           What is he whose grief
Bears such an emphasis, whose phrase of sorrow
Conjures the wand'ring stars and makes them stand
Like wonder-wounded hearers? This is I,   270
Hamlet the Dane.

LAERTES, ⌐*coming out of the grave*¬
           The devil take thy soul!

HAMLET   Thou pray'st not well.   ⌐*They grapple.*¬
I prithee take thy fingers from my throat,
For though I am not splenitive ⟨and⟩ rash,   275
Yet have I in me something dangerous,
Which let thy wisdom fear. Hold off thy hand.

KING   Pluck them asunder.

QUEEN   Hamlet! Hamlet!

ALL   Gentlemen!   280

HORATIO   Good my lord, be quiet.
       ⌐*Hamlet and Laertes are separated.*¬

HAMLET
Why, I will fight with him upon this theme
Until my eyelids will no longer wag!

QUEEN   O my son, what theme?

HAMLET
blank verse, serious
I loved Ophelia. Forty thousand brothers   285
Could not with all their quantity of love
Make up my sum. What wilt thou do for her?

KING   O, he is mad, Laertes!

QUEEN   For love of God, forbear him. *← defending him*

HAMLET   'Swounds, show me what thou 't do.   290
Woo't weep, woo't fight, woo't fast, woo't tear
thyself,
Woo't drink up eisel, eat a crocodile?

how he crazy → prose

295. **outface me:** put me to shame

296. **quick:** alive

298. **our ground:** i.e., the mound of earth piled on us

299. **his pate:** its head; **the burning zone:** that **zone** in the celestial sphere in which the sun seems to circle the Earth

300. **Ossa:** See note to line 265. **mouth:** orate pompously

305. **golden couplets:** twin birds covered with yellow down; **disclosed:** hatched

308. **use me thus:** presumably referring to Laertes's curses on Hamlet at lines 258–61 and 272

310–11. **Let Hercules . . . day:** See longer note, page 294.

312. **wait upon him:** accompany him

315. **to the present push:** into immediate action

318. **thereby:** often replaced by F's "shortly"

Paíx.

Peace. (5.2.46)

From Gilles Corrozet, Hecatongraphie . . . (1543).

I'll do 't. Dost ⟨thou⟩ come here to whine?
To outface me with leaping in her grave?   295
Be buried quick with her, and so will I.
And if thou prate of mountains, let them throw
Millions of acres on us, till our ground,
Singeing his pate against the burning zone,
Make Ossa like a wart. Nay, an thou 'lt mouth,   300
I'll rant as well as thou.

QUEEN   This is mere madness;
And ⟨thus⟩ awhile the fit will work on him.
Anon, as patient as the female dove
When that her golden couplets are disclosed,   305
His silence will sit drooping.

HAMLET   Hear you, sir,
What is the reason that you use me thus?
I loved you ever. But it is no matter.
Let Hercules himself do what he may,   310
The cat will mew, and dog will have his day.

                         Hamlet exits.

KING
I pray thee, good Horatio, wait upon him.

                        Horatio exits.

⌜*To Laertes.*⌝ Strengthen your patience in our last
   night's speech.
We'll put the matter to the present push.—   315
Good Gertrude, set some watch over your son.—
This grave shall have a living monument.
An hour of quiet thereby shall we see.
Till then in patience our proceeding be.

                         They exit.

5.2 In the hall of the castle, Hamlet tells Horatio
how he discovered the king's plot against him and
how he turned the tables on Rosencrantz and Guild-
enstern. Osric enters to ask, on Claudius's behalf,
that Hamlet fence with Laertes. Hamlet agrees to
the contest, despite his misgivings.

Hamlet is winning the match when Gertrude
drinks from the poisoned cup that Claudius has
prepared for Hamlet. Laertes then wounds Hamlet
with the poisoned rapier. In the scuffle that follows,
Hamlet forces an exchange of rapiers, and Hamlet
wounds Laertes. As Gertrude dies, Laertes, him-
self dying, discloses his and Claudius's plot against
Hamlet. Hamlet kills Claudius. Before Hamlet dies,
he asks Horatio to tell the full story that has led to
these deaths and gives Fortinbras his support for the
kingship. After Hamlet's death, Fortinbras arrives,
claims the crown, and orders a military funeral for
Hamlet.

------

  6. **mutines:** mutineers; **bilboes:** shackles
  8. **indiscretion:** impulsive action
  9. **pall:** lose strength; **learn:** teach
11. **our ends:** outcome of our actions
12. **Rough-hew them how we will:** no matter
how roughly we ourselves shape them
18. **Fingered:** stole; **in fine:** finally
23. **Larded:** ornamented
25. **bugs and goblins in my life:** causes of alarm
if I were allowed to live   **bugs:** bugbears

(continued)

[⌜]Scene 2[⌝]

Enter Hamlet and Horatio.

HAMLET
  So much for this, sir. Now shall you see the other.
  You do remember all the circumstance?
HORATIO Remember it, my lord!
HAMLET
  Sir, in my heart there was a kind of fighting
  That would not let me sleep. ⟨Methought⟩ I lay   5
  Worse than the mutines in the ⟨bilboes.⟩ Rashly—
  And praised be rashness for it; let us know,
  Our indiscretion sometime serves us well
  When our deep plots do pall; and that should learn
    us   10
  There's a divinity that shapes our ends,
  Rough-hew them how we will—
HORATIO   That is most
    certain.
HAMLET Up from my cabin,   15
  My sea-gown scarfed about me, in the dark
  Groped I to find out them; had my desire,
  Fingered their packet, and in fine withdrew
  To mine own room again, making so bold
  (My fears forgetting manners) to unfold   20
  Their grand commission; where I found, Horatio,
  A royal knavery—an exact command,
  Larded with many several sorts of reasons
  Importing Denmark's health and England's too,
  With—ho!—such bugs and goblins in my life,   25
  That on the supervise, no leisure bated,
  No, not to stay the grinding of the ax,
  My head should be struck off.
HORATIO   Is 't possible?
HAMLET
  Here's the commission. Read it at more leisure.   30
                          [⌜]*Handing him a paper.*[⌝]

26–28. **on . . . struck off:** i.e., as soon as the document has been read, Hamlet is to be executed, the immediacy of the execution not being reduced (**bated**) by any delay (**leisure**) (See picture, page 196.)

34. **Or:** before

36. **fair:** in the clear hand of a clerk

37–38. **hold it . . . A baseness:** consider it, as **our** statesmen **do,** a lower-class skill

40. **yeoman's:** substantial; loyal

41. **effect:** substance

44. **tributary:** a nation that pays tribute to another nation (In this passage—lines 43–52—Hamlet parodies the formal language he used in writing the **new commission** [line 36].)

47. **stand . . . amities:** serve to link their friendship

48. **suchlike . . . charge:** similar "whereas" legal phrases **of great** import

51. **those bearers:** the men bearing the document

52. **shriving time:** time for confession

54. **ordinant:** working to control events

55. **signet:** small seal

56. **model:** replica

58. **Subscribed it, gave 't th' impression:** signed it, sealed it with the signet on wax

60. **changeling:** exchange (As the fairies substituted elves or imps for human babies, so Hamlet has replaced the king's document with his own forged one.)

61. **what to this was sequent:** what followed this

But wilt thou hear now how I did proceed?
HORATIO   I beseech you.
HAMLET
Being thus benetted round with ⌜villainies,⌝
Or I could make a prologue to my brains,
They had begun the play. I sat me down,   35
Devised a new commission, wrote it fair—
I once did hold it, as our statists do,
A baseness to write fair, and labored much
How to forget that learning; but, sir, now
It did me yeoman's service. Wilt thou know   40
Th' effect of what I wrote?
HORATIO   Ay, good my lord.
HAMLET
An earnest conjuration from the King,
As England was his faithful tributary,
As love between them like the palm might flourish,   45
As peace should still her wheaten garland wear
And stand a comma 'tween their amities,
And many suchlike ⌜ases⌝ of great charge,
That, on the view and knowing of these contents,
Without debatement further, more or less,   50
He should those bearers put to sudden death,
Not shriving time allowed.
HORATIO   How was this sealed?
HAMLET
Why, even in that was heaven ordinant.
I had my father's signet in my purse,   55
Which was the model of that Danish seal;
Folded the writ up in the form of th' other,
⟨Subscribed⟩ it, gave 't th' impression, placed it
    safely,
The changeling never known. Now, the next day   60
Was our sea-fight; and what to this was sequent
Thou knowest already.
HORATIO
So Guildenstern and Rosencrantz go to 't.

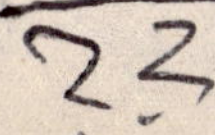

65. **defeat:** destruction

66. **insinuation:** winding themselves into the affair

67. **baser:** inferior

68. **pass:** thrust; **fell:** destructive; **points:** i.e., swords

71. **Does . . . upon—:** is it **not now** my duty—

73. **election:** See longer note, page 294. **hopes:** expectations

74. **angle:** fishhook; **proper:** very

77. **quit:** requite, pay back

79. **canker:** sore that eats and spreads; cancer

80. **In:** into

87–88. **by . . . his: I see the** portrait **of** Laertes's situation in that **of my** own

89. **bravery:** boastful showiness

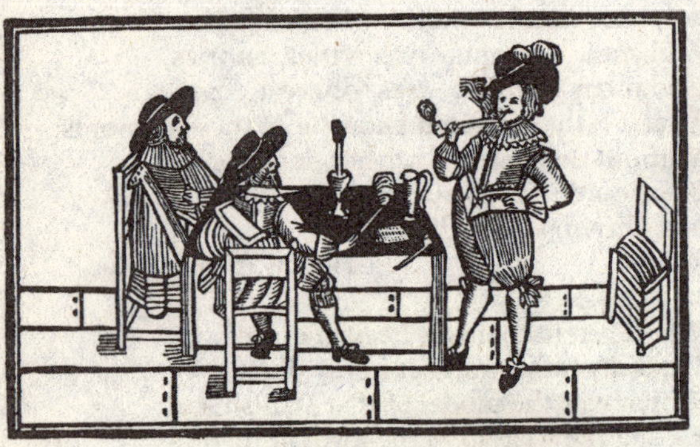

"Put your bonnet to his right use:
'tis for the head." (5.2.105–6)
From *Bagford Ballads* (printed in 1878).

HAMLET
⟨Why, man, they did make love to this employment.⟩
They are not near my conscience. Their defeat   65
Does by their own insinuation grow.
'Tis dangerous when the baser nature comes
Between the pass and fell incensèd points
Of mighty opposites.

HORATIO   Why, what a king is this!   70

HAMLET
Does it not, think thee, stand me now upon—
He that hath killed my king and whored my mother,
Popped in between th' election and my hopes,
Thrown out his angle for my proper life,
And with such cozenage—is 't not perfect   75
    conscience
⟨To quit him with this arm? And is 't not to be
    damned
To let this canker of our nature come
In further evil?   80

HORATIO
It must be shortly known to him from England
What is the issue of the business there.

HAMLET
It will be short. The interim's mine,
And a man's life's no more than to say "one."
But I am very sorry, good Horatio,   85
That to Laertes I forgot myself,
For by the image of my cause I see
The portraiture of his. I'll ⌜court⌝ his favors.
But, sure, the bravery of his grief did put me
Into a tow'ring passion.   90

HORATIO   Peace, who comes here?⟩

Enter ⟨Osric,⟩ a courtier.

OSRIC   Your Lordship is right welcome back to Den-
    mark.

95. **waterfly:** iridescent insect

99–100. **Let a beast ... king's mess:** if a man, no matter how bestial, has enough money he will be welcome at **the king's** table **crib:** stall of an ox **mess:** i.e., table (literally, regular eating companions)

100. **chough:** i.e., jackdaw (a chattering bird, and thus a chatterer)

105. **Put your bonnet ... use:** i.e., **put** on **your** hat (Hats were commonly worn by men, even indoors, but removed in the presence of superiors. Osric continues to hold his hat in his hand despite Hamlet's insistence; see 5.2.117.) See picture, page 262.

110. **indifferent:** somewhat

112. **complexion:** temperament

119–95. Throughout these exchanges, Osric's language is florid, affected, and imprecise; Hamlet answers him in a style even more exaggerated. Often we can only guess at what they may be saying.

121. **differences:** distinguishing characteristics

122–23. **the card or calendar of gentry:** perhaps, the model of courtly manners (See picture, page 242.)

124. **continent:** container, receptacle

125. **definement:** definition; **perdition:** loss

126–28. **to divide him ... quick sail:** perhaps, to inventory his qualities would stagger one's **memory,** but the inventory would fall short of his excellence

HAMLET I ⟨humbly⟩ thank you, sir. ⌜*Aside to Horatio.*⌝
    Dost know this waterfly?   95

HORATIO, ⌜*aside to Hamlet*⌝ No, my good lord.

HAMLET, ⌜*aside to Horatio*⌝ Thy state is the more gra-
    cious, for 'tis a vice to know him. He hath much
    land, and fertile. Let a beast be lord of beasts and his
    crib shall stand at the king's mess. 'Tis a chough,   100
    but, as I say, spacious in the possession of dirt.

OSRIC Sweet lord, if your Lordship were at leisure, I
    should impart a thing to you from his Majesty.

HAMLET I will receive it, sir, with all diligence of
    spirit. ⟨Put⟩ your bonnet to his right use: 'tis for the   105
    head.

OSRIC I thank your Lordship; it is very hot.

HAMLET No, believe me, 'tis very cold; the wind is
    northerly.

OSRIC It is indifferent cold, my lord, indeed.   110

HAMLET But yet methinks it is very ⟨sultry⟩ and hot ⟨for⟩
    my complexion.

OSRIC Exceedingly, my lord; it is very sultry, as
    'twere—I cannot tell how. My lord, his Majesty
    bade me signify to you that he has laid a great wager   115
    on your head. Sir, this is the matter—

HAMLET I beseech you, remember. ⌜*He motions to
    Osric to put on his hat.*⌝

OSRIC Nay, good my lord, for my ease, in good faith.
    [Sir, here is newly come to court Laertes—believe
    me, an absolute ⌜gentleman,⌝ full of most excellent   120
    differences, of very soft society and great showing.
    Indeed, to speak ⌜feelingly⌝ of him, he is the card
    or calendar of gentry, for you shall find in him the
    continent of what part a gentleman would see.

HAMLET Sir, his definement suffers no perdition in   125
    you, though I know to divide him inventorially
    would dozy th' arithmetic of memory, and yet but
    yaw neither, in respect of his quick sail. But, in the

129–33. a soul . . . nothing more: Hamlet's mockingly affected language says, in essence, that Laertes is a fine man, so special that he can be matched only by **his** image in a **mirror;** everyone else in comparison to him is only his **umbrage,** or shadow.

135–36. Why . . . breath? i.e., **why** are **we** talking about him?

138–39. Is 't . . . really: Editors are divided about whom these lines address and what they mean. Because Shakespeare does not use *really* elsewhere, some suggest substituting *rarely.*

140. nomination: naming

143. all 's: all his

147. would: wish

148. approve: commend

154–55. imputation: reputation

155. meed: merit

155–56. unfellowed: unmatched

158. Rapier and dagger: In rapier fencing, the **rapier,** carried in the right hand, led the attack; the **dagger,** in the left hand, parried the opponent's attack. (See picture, page 226.)

161. he has impawned: i.e., Laertes (or **the French** [line 176]) **has** pledged

162. poniards: daggers (See picture, page 272.)

163. assigns: accessories; **girdles, hangers, and so:** sword belts, attaching straps, **and so** forth

164. carriages: literally, wheeled supports on which cannons are mounted; **dear to fancy:** fancifully designed

verity of extolment, I take him to be a soul of great
article, and his infusion of such dearth and rareness 130
as, to make true diction of him, his semblable is his
mirror, and who else would trace him, his umbrage,
nothing more.

OSRIC Your Lordship speaks most infallibly of him.

HAMLET The concernancy, sir? Why do we wrap the 135
gentleman in our more rawer breath?

OSRIC Sir?

HORATIO Is 't not possible to understand in another
tongue? You will to 't, sir, really.

HAMLET, ⌜*to Osric*⌝ What imports the nomination of 140
this gentleman?

OSRIC Of Laertes?

HORATIO His purse is empty already; all 's golden words
are spent.

HAMLET Of him, sir. 145

OSRIC I know you are not ignorant—

HAMLET I would you did, sir. Yet, in faith, if you did, it
would not much approve me. Well, sir?]

OSRIC You are not ignorant of what excellence Laertes
is— 150

[HAMLET I dare not confess that, lest I should compare
with him in excellence. But to know a man well
were to know himself.

OSRIC I mean, sir, for ⌜his⌝ weapon. But in the imputa-
tion laid on him by them, in his meed he's unfel- 155
lowed.]

HAMLET What's his weapon?

OSRIC Rapier and dagger.

HAMLET That's two of his weapons. But, well—

OSRIC The King, sir, hath wagered with him six Barba- 160
ry horses, against the which he has impawned, as I
take it, six French rapiers and poniards, with their
assigns, as girdle, ⟨hangers,⟩ and so. Three of the
carriages, in faith, are very dear to fancy, very

165. **responsive:** well matched

166. **liberal conceit:** perhaps, imaginative design

167. **What call you the "carriages"?:** i.e., what are **you** calling **carriages**?

168–69. **edified by the margent:** aided through a note in the margin

173. **would . . . be: would** rather they **be** called

175. **liberal-conceited:** See note to line 166, above.

178. **laid:** bet

178–79. **a dozen passes between yourself and him: a dozen** exchanges **between** Hamlet and Laertes

180–81. **twelve for nine:** No one has satisfactorily explained this phrase so that it fits in with the terms of the wager.

182. **vouchsafe the answer:** condescend to present yourself at the match (Hamlet chooses to understand the words as meaning "give an **answer.**")

187. **breathing time of day:** the **time** I take my exercise

188. **foils:** weapons blunted for fencing

189. **an:** if

192. **deliver you e'en so:** relate your response in exactly these words

195. **commend:** offer (The word also means "praise," as Hamlet takes it at lines 196–97.)

197–98. **for 's turn:** for his purpose

199–200. **This lapwing . . . head:** i.e., this bird has just emerged from its **shell** (The baby **lapwing** reportedly ran around **with the shell on** its **head.**)

responsive to the hilts, most delicate carriages, and 165
of very liberal conceit.

HAMLET What call you the "carriages"?

[HORATIO I knew you must be edified by the margent
ere you had done.]

OSRIC The ⟨carriages,⟩ sir, are the hangers. 170

HAMLET The phrase would be more germane to the
matter if we could carry a cannon by our sides. I
would it ⟨might⟩ be "hangers" till then. But on. Six
Barbary horses against six French swords, their
assigns, and three liberal-conceited carriages— 175
that's the French bet against the Danish. Why is this
all ⌜"impawned,"⌝ ⟨as⟩ you call it?

OSRIC The King, sir, hath laid, sir, that in a dozen
passes between yourself and him, he shall not
exceed you three hits. He hath laid on twelve for 180
nine, and it would come to immediate trial if your
Lordship would vouchsafe the answer.

HAMLET How if I answer no?

OSRIC I mean, my lord, the opposition of your person
in trial. 185

HAMLET Sir, I will walk here in the hall. If it please his
Majesty, it is the breathing time of day with me. Let
the foils be brought, the gentleman willing, and the
King hold his purpose, I will win for him, an I can.
If not, I will gain nothing but my shame and the odd 190
hits.

OSRIC Shall I deliver you ⟨e'en⟩ so?

HAMLET To this effect, sir, after what flourish your
nature will.

OSRIC I commend my duty to your Lordship. 195

HAMLET Yours. ⌜*Osric exits.*⌝ ⟨He⟩ does well to com-
mend it himself. There are no tongues else for 's
turn.

HORATIO This lapwing runs away with the shell on his
head. 200

201. **comply . . . with his dug:** say polite things to the breast he was about to nurse from

203. **drossy:** worthless

204. **tune:** manner of speaking

204–7. **out . . . opinions:** perhaps, **out of** repeated social encounters, they have got a **collection** of frothy language that wins acceptance from refined persons

207–8. **blow . . . out:** In this image, Osric and his kind are themselves composed of froth; when one blows on **them** to see if there is anything to them, they collapse like **bubbles.**

209. **commended him: commended** himself

215–16. **If . . . now:** if the king is **ready,** so am I

219. **In happy time:** opportunely (a courteous phrase)

220–21. **use . . . Laertes:** receive **Laertes** in a friendly way

225–26. **at the odds:** with **the odds** (advantage) allowed me

230. **gaingiving:** misgiving

232. **repair:** coming

233–34. **a special providence . . . a sparrow:** See Matthew 10.29–31: "Are not two sparrows sold for a farthing, and one of them shall not fall on the ground without your Father? . . . Fear ye not, therefore, ye are of more value than many sparrows."

HAMLET He did ⟨comply,⟩ sir, with his dug before he
 sucked it. Thus has he (and many more of the same
 breed that I know the drossy age dotes on) only got
 the tune of the time, and, out of an habit of
 encounter, a kind of ⟨yeasty⟩ collection, which car- 205
 ries them through and through the most ⌜fanned⌝
 and ⟨winnowed⟩ opinions; and do but blow them to
 their trial, the bubbles are out.

    [*Enter a Lord.*

LORD My lord, his Majesty commended him to you by
 young Osric, who brings back to him that you 210
 attend him in the hall. He sends to know if your
 pleasure hold to play with Laertes, or that you will
 take longer time.

HAMLET I am constant to my purposes. They follow
 the King's pleasure. If his fitness speaks, mine is 215
 ready now or whensoever, provided I be so able as
 now.

LORD The King and Queen and all are coming down.

HAMLET In happy time.

LORD The Queen desires you to use some gentle 220
 entertainment to Laertes before you fall to play.

HAMLET She well instructs me. ⌜*Lord exits.*⌝

HORATIO You will lose, my lord.

HAMLET I do not think so. Since he went into France, I
 have been in continual practice. I shall win at the 225
 odds; ⟨but⟩ thou wouldst not think how ill all's here
 about my heart. But it is no matter.

HORATIO Nay, good my lord—

HAMLET It is but foolery, but it is such a kind of
 ⟨gaingiving⟩ as would perhaps trouble a woman. 230

HORATIO If your mind dislike anything, obey it. I will
 forestall their repair hither and say you are not fit.

HAMLET Not a whit. We defy augury. There is ⟨a⟩
 special providence in the fall of a sparrow. If it be
 ⟨now,⟩ 'tis not to come; if it be not to come, it will be 235

237–38. **of aught he leaves knows: knows** anything about what **he leaves** behind

238. **betimes:** early

238 SD. **Trumpets, Drums:** i.e., trumpeters, drummers; **state:** court

241. **This presence: this** royal audience

243. **needs:** necessarily

244. **sore:** severe, grave

245. **exception:** dislike, dissatisfaction

246. **Roughly awake:** harshly awaken

255. **disclaiming from:** proclaiming my innocence (disavowing all part in); **purposed:** intended

257. **That I have:** as if I had

259. **in nature:** in terms of my natural affection for my father and for my sister

261. **terms of honor:** offense to my **honor**

262–65. **will no reconcilement . . . ungored:
will** accept **no** reconciliation until experts in those questions give a decision that may serve as a **precedent** for making **peace,** thus freeing **my** reputation from a charge of dishonor   **voice:** authority   **name ungored:** reputation unwounded

Poniard. (5.2.162)
From Louis de Gaya, *A treatise of the arms . . .* (1678).

272

now; if it be not now, yet it ⟨will⟩ come. The
readiness is all. Since no man of aught he leaves
knows, what is 't to leave betimes? Let be.

*A table prepared. ⟨Enter⟩ Trumpets, Drums, and Officers
with cushions, King, Queen, ⌜Osric,⌝ and all the state,
foils, daggers, ⟨flagons of wine,⟩ and Laertes.*

KING
Come, Hamlet, come and take this hand from me.
⌜*He puts Laertes' hand into Hamlet's.*⌝
HAMLET, ⌜*to Laertes*⌝
Give me your pardon, sir. I have done you wrong;   240
But pardon 't as you are a gentleman. This presence
  knows,
And you must needs have heard, how I am punished
With a sore distraction. What I have done
That might your nature, honor, and exception   245
Roughly awake, I here proclaim was madness.
Was 't Hamlet wronged Laertes? Never Hamlet.
If Hamlet from himself be ta'en away,
And when he's not himself does wrong Laertes,
Then Hamlet does it not; Hamlet denies it.   250
Who does it, then? His madness. If 't be so,
Hamlet is of the faction that is wronged;
His madness is poor Hamlet's enemy.
⟨Sir, in this audience⟩
Let my disclaiming from a purposed evil   255
Free me so far in your most generous thoughts
That I have shot my arrow o'er the house
And hurt my brother.
LAERTES   I am satisfied in nature,
Whose motive in this case should stir me most   260
To my revenge; but in my terms of honor
I stand aloof and will no reconcilement
Till by some elder masters of known honor
I have a voice and precedent of peace
To ⟨keep⟩ my name ungored. But ⟨till⟩ that time   265

269. **frankly:** freely, willingly

272. **your foil:** i.e., the background against which you will shine (a courteous pun on the word **foils,** used at line 270 to request the blunted weapons)

274. **Stick fiery off:** stand out in brilliant contrast

280. **laid the odds . . . side:** i.e., the king's stake, much greater than Laertes's, is bet on Hamlet, who here again claims to be **weaker** than Laertes

282. **we have therefore odds: we have** been given **odds** (in that Laertes must make three more hits than Hamlet in order to win)

283. **Let me see another:** Here Laertes selects the sharpened, poisoned rapier.

284. **This likes me:** I like **this; have all a length:** are all the same **length**

285 SD. **play:** fence

288. **quit in answer of the third exchange:** requite (Laertes) for earlier hits by scoring **the third hit**

291. **union:** large pearl

I do receive your offered love like love
And will not wrong it.
HAMLET   I embrace it freely
And will this brothers' wager frankly play.—
Give us the foils. ⟨Come on.⟩   270
LAERTES   ·Come, one for me.
HAMLET
I'll be your foil, Laertes; in mine ignorance
Your skill shall, like a star i' th' darkest night,
Stick fiery off indeed.
LAERTES   You mock me, sir.   275
HAMLET   No, by this hand.
KING
Give them the foils, young Osric. Cousin Hamlet,
You know the wager?
HAMLET   Very well, my lord.
Your Grace has laid the odds o' th' weaker side.   280
KING
I do not fear it; I have seen you both.
But, since he is better, we have therefore odds.
LAERTES
This is too heavy. Let me see another.
HAMLET
This likes me well. These foils have all a length?
OSRIC   Ay, my good lord.   285
                              ⟨*Prepare to play.*⟩
KING
Set me the stoups of wine upon that table.—
If Hamlet give the first or second hit
Or quit in answer of the third exchange,
Let all the battlements their ordnance fire.
The King shall drink to Hamlet's better breath,   290
And in the cup an ⟨union⟩ shall he throw,
Richer than that which four successive kings
In Denmark's crown have worn. Give me the cups,

294. **kettle:** kettledrum
295. **without:** outside
314. **napkin:** handkerchief
315. **carouses:** drinks a toast

A duel. (4.7.113)
From Sebastian Heussler, *Künstliches Abprobirtes . . .* (1665).

And let the kettle to the trumpet speak,
The trumpet to the cannoneer without,   295
The cannons to the heavens, the heaven to earth,
"Now the King drinks to Hamlet." Come, begin.
And you, the judges, bear a wary eye.
                                        Trumpets the while.

HAMLET Come on, sir.
LAERTES Come, my lord.   ⟨*They play.*⟩ 300
HAMLET One.
LAERTES No.
HAMLET Judgment!
OSRIC A hit, a very palpable hit.
LAERTES Well, again.   305
KING
Stay, give me drink.—Hamlet, this pearl is thine.
Here's to thy health.
              ⌜*He drinks and then drops the pearl in the cup.*⌝
                              Drum, trumpets, and shot.
                    Give him the cup.
HAMLET
I'll play this bout first. Set it by awhile.
Come. ⌜*They play.*⌝ Another hit. What say you?   310
LAERTES
⟨A touch, a touch.⟩ I do confess 't.
KING
Our son shall win.
QUEEN   He's fat and scant of breath.—
Here, Hamlet, take my napkin; rub thy brows.
The Queen carouses to thy fortune, Hamlet.   315
                              ⌜*She lifts the cup.*⌝
HAMLET Good madam.
KING Gertrude, do not drink.
QUEEN
I will, my lord; I pray you pardon me.   ⌜*She drinks.*⌝
KING, ⌜*aside*⌝
It is the poisoned cup. It is too late.

326. **pass:** thrust

327. **make a wanton of me:** play with me as if I were a child

330 SD. **in scuffling they change rapiers:** This stage direction, in Q1, reads "they catch one anothers' rapiers," which suggests that Hamlet forces the exchange through a contemporary method of disarm called the "left-hand seizure." (See picture, below.)

336. **woodcock:** a proverbially stupid bird; **to mine own springe:** caught in my **own** trap (See picture, page 44.)

The left-hand seizure. (5.2.330 SD)
From Saint Didier, *Traicte contenant . . .* (1573).

HAMLET
  I dare not drink yet, madam—by and by.   320
QUEEN Come, let me wipe thy face.
LAERTES, ⌜*to Claudius*⌝
  My lord, I'll hit him now.
KING   I do not think 't.
LAERTES, ⌜*aside*⌝
  And yet it is almost against my conscience.
HAMLET
  Come, for the third, Laertes. You do but dally.   325
  I pray you pass with your best violence.
  I am ⟨afeard⟩ you make a wanton of me.
LAERTES Say you so? Come on.   ⟨*Play.*⟩
OSRIC Nothing neither way.
LAERTES Have at you now!   330
⌜*Laertes wounds Hamlet. Then* ⟨*in scuffling they change*
           rapiers,⟩ *and Hamlet wounds Laertes.*⌝
KING Part them. They are incensed.
HAMLET Nay, come again.
                     ⌜*The Queen falls.*⌝
OSRIC Look to the Queen there, ho!
HORATIO
  They bleed on both sides.—How is it, my lord?
OSRIC How is 't, Laertes?   335
LAERTES
  Why as a woodcock to mine own springe, Osric.
                    ⌜*He falls.*⌝
  I am justly killed with mine own treachery.
HAMLET
  How does the Queen?
KING   She swoons to see them bleed.
QUEEN
  No, no, the drink, the drink! O, my dear Hamlet!   340
  The drink, the drink! I am poisoned.   ⌜*She dies.*⌝
HAMLET
  O villainy! Ho! Let the door be locked. ⌜*Osric exits.*⌝
  Treachery! Seek it out.

348. **Unbated and envenomed:** sharp and poisoned; **foul practice:** disgraceful or shameful plot or conspiracy

351. **can no more: can** do or say nothing further

357. **union:** probable pun on **union** as "pearl" (See note to line 291.) and **union** in marriage and death

360. **tempered:** mixed, compounded

366. **this chance:** these events

367. **mutes:** actors without speaking parts

368. **fell sergeant:** cruel **sergeant** at arms (arresting officer) See picture, below.

"This fell sergeant, Death." (5.2.368)
From *Todten-Tantz . . .* (1696).

LAERTES
  It is here, Hamlet. ⟨Hamlet,⟩ thou art slain.
  No med'cine in the world can do thee good.   345
  In thee there is not half an hour's life.
  The treacherous instrument is in ⟨thy⟩ hand,
  Unbated and envenomed. The foul practice
  Hath turned itself on me. Lo, here I lie,
  Never to rise again. Thy mother's poisoned.   350
  I can no more. The King, the King's to blame.
HAMLET
  The point envenomed too! Then, venom, to thy
      work.   ⟨*Hurts the King.*⟩
ALL Treason, treason!
KING
  O, yet defend me, friends! I am but hurt.   355
HAMLET
  Here, thou incestuous, ⟨murd'rous,⟩ damnèd Dane,
  Drink off this potion. Is ⟨thy union⟩ here?
                      ⌈*Forces him to drink the poison.*⌉
  Follow my mother.   ⟨*King dies.*⟩
LAERTES   He is justly served.
  It is a poison tempered by himself.   360
  Exchange forgiveness with me, noble Hamlet.
  Mine and my father's death come not upon thee,
  Nor thine on me.   ⟨*Dies.*⟩
HAMLET
  Heaven make thee free of it. I follow thee.—
  I am dead, Horatio.—Wretched queen, adieu.—   365
  You that look pale and tremble at this chance,
  That are but mutes or audience to this act,
  Had I but time (as this fell sergeant, Death,
  Is strict in his arrest), O, I could tell you—
  But let it be.—Horatio, I am dead.   370
  Thou livest; report me and my cause aright
  To the unsatisfied.
HORATIO   Never believe it.

374. **antique Roman:** For ancient Romans, suicide was an honorable choice when faced with defeat or great loss.

382. **Absent thee from felicity awhile:** i.e., keep yourself from the happiness of death

384 SD. **A march . . . within:** i.e., the sounds of **a** distant **march and** shots offstage

386–88. **Young Fortinbras . . . volley:** i.e., **Fortinbras,** returning victoriously **from Poland,** has shot off a **volley** of gunfire to salute the **ambassadors** approaching from **England**

390. **o'ercrows:** triumphs over

392–93. **prophesy . . . Fortinbras:** predict that **Fortinbras** will be chosen as king (See longer note on **election** [5.2.73], page 294.)

393. **voice:** vote

394–95. **occurrents . . . solicited:** occurrences that have brought on

396. **O, O, O, O!:** This series of *Os*, usually omitted by editors, may simply be an indication for the actor to make the sounds appropriate to Hamlet's dying.

399 SD. **Colors:** those carrying the flags or standards of Fortinbras's army

I am more an antique Roman than a Dane.
Here's yet some liquor left.　　⌜*He picks up the cup.*⌝　375
HAMLET　　　　　　　　　　As thou 'rt a man,
Give me the cup. Let go! By heaven, I'll ha 't.
O God, Horatio, what a wounded name,
Things standing thus unknown, shall I leave behind
　　me!　　　　　　　　　　　　　　　　　　380
If thou didst ever hold me in thy heart,
Absent thee from felicity awhile
And in this harsh world draw thy breath in pain
To tell my story.
　　　　　　　A march afar off ⟨*and* ⌜*shot*⌝ *within.*⟩
　　　　　　What warlike noise is this?　　　　385

　　　　　　　　Enter Osric.

OSRIC
　Young Fortinbras, with conquest come from Poland,
　To th' ambassadors of England gives
　This warlike volley.
HAMLET　　　　　　　　O, I die, Horatio!
The potent poison quite o'ercrows my spirit.　　390
I cannot live to hear the news from England.
But I do prophesy th' election lights
On Fortinbras; he has my dying voice.
So tell him, with th' occurrents, more and less,
Which have solicited—the rest is silence.　　395
⟨O, O, O, O!⟩　　　　　　　　　　　　⟨*Dies.*⟩
HORATIO
Now cracks a noble heart. Good night, sweet prince,
And flights of angels sing thee to thy rest.
　　　　　　　　　　　⌜*March within.*⌝
Why does the drum come hither?

Enter Fortinbras with the ⌜*English*⌝ *Ambassadors* ⟨*with
　　Drum, Colors, and Attendants.*⟩

FORTINBRAS　Where is this sight?　　　　400

403. **This quarry ... havoc:** i.e., **this** heap of dead bodies proclaims that **havoc** (devastation, destruction) has been at work (The phrase "cry **havoc**" alludes to the military order "**Havoc!**" which signaled that massacre and pillage should begin.)

404. **toward:** in preparation

409. **senseless:** incapable of sensing

410. **him:** i.e., Claudius

417. **jump upon this bloody question:** so immediately after **this bloody** quarrel

420. **stage:** platform

424. **casual:** occurring by chance

425. **put on:** instigated

426. **this upshot: this** conclusion to it all

428. **deliver:** tell

432. **rights of memory: rights** remembered

433. **Which ... me: which my** presence here at this advantageous time invites **me to claim**

HORATIO What is it you would see?
  If aught of woe or wonder, cease your search.
FORTINBRAS
  This quarry cries on havoc. O proud Death,
  What feast is toward in thine eternal cell
  That thou so many princes at a shot   405
  So bloodily hast struck?
AMBASSADOR   The sight is dismal,
  And our affairs from England come too late.
  The ears are senseless that should give us hearing
  To tell him his commandment is fulfilled,   410
  That Rosencrantz and Guildenstern are dead.
  Where should we have our thanks?
HORATIO   Not from his
    mouth,
  Had it th' ability of life to thank you.   415
  He never gave commandment for their death.
  But since, so jump upon this bloody question,
  You from the Polack wars, and you from England,
  Are here arrived, give order that these bodies
  High on a stage be placed to the view,   420
  And let me speak to ⟨th'⟩ yet unknowing world
  How these things came about. So shall you hear
  Of carnal, bloody, and unnatural acts,
  Of accidental judgments, casual slaughters,
  Of deaths put on by cunning and ⟨forced⟩ cause,   425
  And, in this upshot, purposes mistook
  Fall'n on th' inventors' heads. All this can I
  Truly deliver.
FORTINBRAS Let us haste to hear it
  And call the noblest to the audience.   430
  For me, with sorrow I embrace my fortune.
  I have some rights of memory in this kingdom,
  Which now to claim my vantage doth invite me.
HORATIO
  Of that I shall have also cause to speak,

435–36. **And from his mouth . . . on more:** i.e., with words **from** Hamlet's **mouth, whose** vote **will** be seconded by others

437. **this same:** the process proposed in lines 419–22; **presently:** immediately

440. **On . . . happen:** i.e., **happen** as a result of **plots and errors**

443. **put on: put** to the test, allowed to rule as king

444. **passage:** passing, death

445. **rite of war:** perhaps, a special roll of drums; or, perhaps, a volley of gunfire

448. **field: field** of battle

Death's "eternal cell." (5.2.404)
From *Todten-Tantz . . .* (1696).

And from his mouth whose voice will draw ⟨on⟩ 435
  more.
But let this same be presently performed
Even while men's minds are wild, lest more
  mischance
On plots and errors happen. 440
FORTINBRAS   Let four captains
  Bear Hamlet like a soldier to the stage,
  For he was likely, had he been put on,
  To have proved most royal; and for his passage,
  The soldier's music and the rite of war 445
  Speak loudly for him.
  Take up the bodies. Such a sight as this
  Becomes the field but here shows much amiss.
  Go, bid the soldiers shoot.
            They exit, ⟨marching, after the which, a peal of
                        ordnance are shot off.⟩

Longer Notes

1.3.136–40. **brokers . . . beguile:** Polonius here characterizes Hamlet's "holy vows of heaven" (line 123) as, instead, mere sexual solicitations masquerading as sacred oaths. He anthropomorphizes the vows as brokers dressed in holy vestments but acting as panders to entice Ophelia into a sinful relationship. This reading of the lines depends upon an editorial decision to accept the word **bawds** at line 139, Lewis Theobald's emendation of Q2's *bonds*. Since bonds cannot breathe (or "speak," one meaning of *breathe*), and since **bawds** aligns with **brokers** and **implorators,** Theobald's change has been generally accepted. Editors who retain *bonds* define **breathing** as "acting" and note the alignment of *bonds* with **vows** and **suits.** With either editorial choice, the contrast of "holy vows" with "implorators of unholy suits" is clear.

1.5.105. **table:** This undoubtedly refers to the kind of tablet described by Peter Stallybrass and Roger Chartier as one or more pieces of coated vellum or paper, folded and stitched and sometimes elegantly bound, the coating allowing the vellum or paper to be written on with a stylus (which was attached to the tablet) and then erased with a moistened cloth or by scraping. Such writing tablets were common in Shakespeare's day.

2.2.121. **In her . . . these, etc.:** In letter-writing conventions of Shakespeare's day, this phrase, part of the letter's superscription, presents two unusual features. According to Alan Stewart and Heather Wolfe, the superscription is "the address or direction on the outer leaf of a letter" (*Letter Writing in Renaissance England*, Folger, 2004). The superscription on Hamlet's letter is unusual because, after the name of the letter's recipient ("To the celestial, and my soul's idol, the most beautified Ophelia") instead of Ophelia's "address"—i.e., where the letter should be delivered—we find instead "in her excellent white bosom, these, etc." Stewart, in his book *Shakespeare's Letters* (Oxford, 2009), suggests that this phrase has an inappropriate sexual tone in keeping with Hamlet's mad behavior; we would suggest alternatively that Shakespeare is perhaps playing with the letter-writing conventions of the day, substituting "in her excellent white bosom" for the expected standard address (such as "in his travels" or "at the North Gate Street in Chester"). Heather Wolfe, curator of manuscripts at the Folger, notes (personal correspondence) that the lack of an address generally indicates that the letter was to be delivered by a trusted agent or by the letter writer. The second unusual feature is the placement of "etc." While Wolfe was able to locate a letter in the State Papers that places "etc." after "these"—"To his excellent cousin, the Justice Aylmer, give these. With speed. From London, etc."—an "etc." at the end of a superscription was more likely to be found in a superscription that included a list of compliments to the recipient—e.g., "To her who is Day without Night, a Sun full of Shade, A Shade full of Light, Mistress, etc." (See *Letter Writing*, p. 109.)

2.2.604–5. **I am . . . bitter:** Continuing his attack on himself for inaction, Hamlet plays on the double meanings (physical and metaphorical) of the words **pigeon-livered, gall,** and **bitter.** On the physical level, pigeons were known to have no gallbladder (a small organ attached to the liver), which suggested to medieval physiologists that pigeons lacked gall (a bitter substance excreted by the liver), and that this explained their mild manner. Metaphorically, the term **pigeon-livered** meant "meek, mild"; **gall** meant "spirit to resent insult or injury"; **bitter** meant "feeling intense grief, misery, or affliction of spirit," and "causing pain, cruel, severe." The phrase "to make oppression bitter" perhaps means "to fill my distress with adequate affliction of spirit or intense grief."

3.1.64. **the question:** While it is generally assumed that Hamlet's **question** is whether or not to commit suicide, it can be argued that this soliloquy is instead (or is primarily) a posing of a philosophical question appropriate for a student from Wittenberg, followed by a scholarly analysis of that question. In this reading, Hamlet proposes as the question up for debate: "Which is the nobler action, suicide or acceptance of a painful life?" He first cites the attractions of suicide, then cites the most pressing argument against it, and, after describing the burdens of human life that make suicide so appealing, he concludes that fear and cowardice are the reasons humans do not take their own lives. Paradoxically, then, the answer to "the question" is that it is nobler, more courageous, to end one's life at one's own hands. (This reading of "To be or not to be" as a dispassionate mental exercise is in accord with current readings of John Donne's "suicide tract," *Biathanatos*.) Note that Hamlet's discourse is in effect set within a classical worldview (a view that Horatio will title "antique Roman"), a view in which God and heaven and hell and sin do not have a place, and in which the afterlife is simply "a bourn from which no traveler returns." This is a very different worldview from the one Hamlet revealed when he cried out his wish that God "had not fixed / His canon 'gainst self-slaughter" (1.2.135–36).

3.2.64. the candied ... pomp: This dense complex of metaphors has at its core the image of a fawning dog. The line begins with the metaphorically **candied** (honeyed, or sugared) **tongue** (i.e., the speech of the sweet-talking or dulcet-toned flatterer), which transforms into the physical tongue that licks (in Shakespeare, usually the tongue of a fawning dog, an animal licking sores, or a mother bear licking her cub into shape, but here probably echoing as well familiar phrases that indicate abject servility—to lick someone's shoe, as does Caliban in *The Tempest,* or to lick the ground before someone). The physical tongue becomes figurative again as the object of the licking is presented as the abstract **absurd pomp,** or ridiculous ostentatious display. The dog image is made a bit more concrete in line 66, where the word **fawning—** a word most commonly used in reference to dogs—is used to describe the flatterer. (See Caroline F. E. Spurgeon, *Shakespeare's Imagery and What It Tells Us* [1935; rpt., Cambridge: Cambridge University Press, 1958], pp. 195–99.)

3.2.116–31. Here's metal ... my lord: This passage of dialogue has been described as Hamlet's "teasing" or his "insulting" of Ophelia. Lewis Theobald, writing in 1726, called it "low and indecent Ribaldry . . . unbefitting the Dignity of [Shakespeare's] Characters as well as of his Audience" (*Shakespeare Restored,* p. 87). The words Hamlet uses seem innocent on the surface, but at the time the phrase **lie in your lap** could have a sexual meaning, there was frequent wordplay on the first syllable of **country,** and the word **nothing** could apply to both the male and female sexual parts.

3.2.176. Phoebus' cart: The apparent journey of the sun around the Earth, as described here, is often taken to be an annual circling, with lines 176–77 describing how the sun has circled the Earth 30 times in 30 years. After all, the journeys of the moon (described in lines 178–79) clearly take place over a 30-year period, and line 182 seems to equate the time spans symbolized by the sun's and the moon's journeys. Since in the astronomy dominant in Shakespeare's time the sun circles the Earth daily (and from an Earth-centered perspective continues to do so today), lines 176–77 must necessarily describe a 30-day period. In writing these lines, Shakespeare may have erred or been careless, or he may be deliberately mocking the pompous and sometimes empty or meaningless language of earlier dramatists, as he seems to be doing throughout "The Mousetrap," with its arcane words and twisted syntax.

3.4.215–18. Unpeg the basket . . . and break your own neck down: Hamlet seems to be saying to Gertrude "If you spread my secrets, you will be like the ape that freed the birds from a basket on a housetop, climbed into the basket, and, instead of being able to fly as the freed birds did, broke his neck when the basket fell from the roof." If Hamlet was alluding to a familiar story, that story is now lost.

4.5.91. In hugger-mugger: The eighteenth-century editor George Steevens noted that this description of hasty, secret burial occurs in Thomas North's 1579 translation of Plutarch's "Life of Julius Caesar," where Antony wants Caesar properly buried and "not in hugger-mugger." (See Arden3 *Hamlet,* p. 380.)

4.5.188–90. They . . . tear: These lines are thought to be from the song "Bonny Sweet Robin," almost all the lyrics of which have disappeared. Ophelia sings one of its extant lines (perhaps its refrain) at line 210, below. (Ross Duffin, *Shakespeare's Songbook*, Norton, 2000, p. 73.)

5.1.112. **pair of indentures:** Deeds were often written out twice on the same large piece of paper or parchment, which was then divided between the two copies by cutting on an irregular line. The two pieces (called a "pair of indentures") could later be matched to prove they came from the same document.

5.1.310–11. **Let Hercules . . . have his day:** Many editors have tried to explain these lines as if Hamlet is, for example, referring to Laertes as a Hercules and, in the second of the lines, uttering a veiled threat. In answer to such editorial attempts, George Lyman Kittredge, in his 1939 edition of *Hamlet*, writes that Hamlet suddenly remembers that he is supposed to be mad, and he here "reverts to his habitual style when counterfeiting insanity." Lines 310–11, "therefore, are not to be brought into logical connection with what precedes or with the situation at all. Certainly Hamlet does not mean 'Laertes must have his whine and his bark. If Hercules cannot silence dogs, much less I, who am little like that hero' (Dowden), or 'Bluster away, my young Hercules: but poor Hamlet's time will come' (Verity)."

5.2.73. **election:** Some earlier editors struggled with how to make sense of Hamlet's referring to the choice of a monarch as an "election." Willard Farnham, for instance, in his edition of the play for the Complete Pelican edition of 1969, glossed the word as follows: "**election:** i.e., to the kingship (the Danish kingship being elective)." Hamlet's use of this word is less problematic when we realize that in the twenty-two times Shakespeare uses the word *election* in his plays, in almost every case the word means simply "choice," "selection," or "preference." Even in plays where the word is used in dialogue about the selection of a ruler, the meaning is essentially "choice, selection" (as in *Titus Andronicus* 1.1.13 and *Coriolanus* 2.3.244). Earlier in *Hamlet,* the prince accuses Claudius of having stolen the crown (3.4.113–15); here, he accuses him of having suddenly and unexpectedly come between Hamlet's "hopes" (i.e., expectations) and "th' election." Given Shakespeare's usage in his other plays, the word here is probably shorthand for "choice or selection by the inner circle of the nobility," those whom Claudius thanks for having "freely gone . . . along" with his marriage to Gertrude—and presumably his related appointment as ruler of the kingdom (1.2.15–16). Hamlet's accusation here suggests that had not Claudius made this sudden and unexpected move, the crown would have naturally come to the prince of the realm.

Textual Notes

The reading of the present text appears to the left of the square bracket. The earliest sources of readings not in Q2, the Second Quarto text (upon which this edition is based), are indicated as follows: **Q1** is the First Quarto of 1603; **Q3** is the Third Quarto of 1611; **Q4** is the Fourth Quarto of ?1622; **Q5** is the Fifth Quarto of 1637; **F** is the First Folio of 1623; **F2** is the Second Folio of 1632; **F3** is the Third Folio of 1663–64; **F4** is the Fourth Folio of 1685; **Ed.** is an earlier editor of Shakespeare, beginning with Rowe in 1709. No sources are given for emendations of punctuation or for corrections of obvious typographical errors, like turned letters that produce no known word. **SD** means stage direction; **SP** means speech prefix; **uncorr.** means first or uncorrected state; **corr.** means second or corrected state; ~ stands in place of a word already quoted before the square bracket; ʌ indicates the omission of a punctuation mark.

1.1.   15. ho!] Q2; *omit* F   19. soldier] F; souldiers Q2   39. we have two nights seen] Q2; we two Nights haue seene F   46. SD *a half-line later in* F   47. off] Q2, F (of)   50. he] Q2; it F   51. harrows] F; horrowes Q2   53. Speak to] Q2; Question F   72. he] Q2; *omit* F   74. Polacks] Ed.; pollax Q2; Pollax F   76. jump] Q2; iust F   84. why . . . cast] F; with . . . cost Q2   100. those] F; these Q2   101. of] Q2; on F   103. returned] F; returne Q2   105. comart] Q2; Cou'nant F   106. designed] F2; desseigne Q2; designe F   110. lawless] Q2; Landlesse F   115. compulsatory] Q2; Compulsatiue F   120–37. Q2 *only*   133. feared] Ed.; feare Q2   137. SD *Ghost*] Q2; *Ghost againe.* F   139. SD *omit* F   150. you] F; your Q2   151. SD *omit* F   153. strike it] Q2; strike at it F   156.

SD *omit* Q2; *1 line later in* F   165. morn] Q2; day F
173. say] Q2; sayes F   175. This] Q2; The F   176. dare
stir] Q2; can walke F   178. takes] Q2; talkes F   179.
that] Q2; the F   182. eastward] Q2; Easterne F   190.
convenient] Q2; conueniently F

   1.2.   0. SD *the Council . . . Cornelius*] *Hamlet, Polo-*
nius, Laertes, and his Sister Ophelia, Lords Attendant F
1. SP KING] F; *Claud.* Q2   9. to] Q2; of F   11. an . . .
a] Q2; one . . . one F   21. this] Q2; the F   35. bearers]
Q2; bearing F   40. SP CORNELIUS/VOLTEMAND] Q2; *Volt.*
F   41. SD F; *omit* Q2   52. My dread lord] Q2; Dread
my Lord F   60. Hath] Q2; He hath F   60–62. wrung
. . . consent] Q2 *only*   69. so, my] F (~∧ ~); so much
my Q2   70. nighted] Q2; nightly F   80. good] F; coold
Q2   85. shapes] Q3; chapes Q2; shewes F   86. denote]
F; deuote Q2   100. a] F (~∧ ~); or Q2   116. you.] F;
~∧ Q2   123. pray thee] Q2; prythee F   131. heaven]
Q2; Heauens F   132. SD *Flourish . . . exit.*] Q2; *Exeunt*
| *Manet Hamlet.* F   133. sullied] Q2 (sallied); solid F
136. self-slaughter] F; seale slaughter Q2   136. God,
God] Q2; God, O God F   137. weary] F; wary Q2   138.
Seem] Q2; Seemes F   139. on 't, ah fie! 'Tis] Q2; on't?
Oh fie, fie, 'tis F   141. merely.] F; ~∧ Q2   141. to this]
F; thus Q2   145. beteem] Q2; beteene F   147. would]
F; should Q2   153. even she∧] Ed.; euen she. F; *omit*
Q2   154. God] Q2; Heauen F   160. in] Q2; of F   164.
SD *Barnardo*] Q2; *Barnard* F   177. hear] Q2; haue F
182. you to drink deep ere] F; you for to drinke ere Q2
185. see] F; *omit* Q2   190. Or ever I had seen] Q2; Ere
I had euer seene F   192. Where] Q2; Oh where F   205.
God's] Q2; Heauens F   210. at point exactly] Q2; at all
points exactly F   212. stately∧ . . . them.] Q2 (them;);
~: . . . ~∧ F   214. distilled] Q2; bestil'd F   219. Where,
as] Q1 (Where as); Whereas Q2, F   224. watch] Q2;
watcht F   237. Indeed, sirs] Q2; Indeed, indeed Sirs
F   239, 241, 243. SP ALL] Q2; *Both.* F   254. Very like.

Stayed] Q2; Very like, very like: staid F   257. SP BAR-
NARDO/MARCELLUS] Ed.; *Both.* Q2; *All.* F   259. grizzled]
Q2; grisly F   262. tonight] Q4; to nigh Q2; to Night F
263. walk] Q2; wake F   264. warrant it] Q2; warrant
you it F   269. tenable] Q2; treble F   270. whatsom-
ever] Q2; whatsoeuer F   276. loves] Q2; loue F   276.
SD *All . . . exit.*] Ed.; *Exeunt.* Q2, F *printing it 1 line ear-*
lier   279. Foul] F; fonde Q2

   1.3.   0. SD *his sister*] Q2; *omit* F   3. convey] Q2;
Conuoy F   3. is] F; in Q2   6. favor] Q2; fauours F   9.
Forward] Q2; Froward F   10. perfume and] Q2; *omit*
F   15. bulk] F; bulkes Q2   19. will] Q2; feare F   21.
F; *omit* Q2   24. safety] Q2; sanctity F   24. the health]
Ed.; health Q2, F   24. this whole] Q2; the weole F
30. particular act and place] Q2; peculiar Sect and
force F   38. you in] Q2; within F   44. their] Q2; the
F   50. watchman] Q2; watchmen F   53. like] F; *omit*
Q2   56. SD *1 line earlier in* Q2   62. for. There,] Q2 (~,
~∧); ~∧ ~: F   63. thee] Q2; you F   65. Look] Q2; See
F   68. Those] Q2; The F   69. unto] Q2; to F   71. new-
hatched] Q2; vnhatch't F   71. courage] Q2; Comrade
F   80. Are] F; Or Q2   81. be] F; boy Q2   82. loan] F;
loue Q2   83. dulls the] F; dulleth Q2   89. invests] Q2;
inuites F   89. you.]~∧ Q2   96. Lord] Q2; L. F   107.
you?] ~∧ Q2   115. these] Q2; his F   118. Running]
Ed.; Wrong Q2; Roaming F   123. With almost all the
holy vows] Q2; with all the vowes F   124. springes] F;
springs Q2   126. Lends] Q2; Giues F   129. From] Q2;
For F   129. time] Q2; time Daughter F   130. some-
thing] Q2; somewhat F   132. parle] Q2; parley F   134.
tether] F; tider Q2   137. that dye] Q2; the eye F   138.
implorators] F; imploratotors Q2   139. bawds] Ed.;
bonds Q2, F   140. beguile] F; beguide Q2

   1.4.   0. SD *and*] Q2; *omit* F   1. it is] Q2; is it F
2. a] F; *omit* Q2   6. It then] Q2; then it F   7. SD Q2;
omit F   10. wassail] Q2; wassels F   16. But] Q2; And

F   19–41. Q2 *only*   19. revel] Q5; reueale Q2   30. the]
Ed.; their Q2   39. evil] Ed.; eale Q2   47. intents] Q2;
euents F   50. O, answer] Q2; Oh, oh, answer F   54.
interred] Q2; enurn'd F   61. the reaches] Q2; thee;
reaches F   62. SD *Ghost beckons.*] Ed.; *Beckins.* Q2;
Ghost beckens Hamlet. F   67. waves] Q2; wafts F   70.
I will] Q2; will I F   78. summit] Ed.; somnet Q2; Son-
net F   80. assume] Q2; assumes F   82. madness?] ~,
Q2; ~∧ F   83–86. Q2 *only*   87. waves] Q2; wafts F   89.
hands] Q2; hand F   92. arture] Q2; Artire F   97. imag-
ination] F; imagion Q2

　　1.5.   1. Whither] Q2; Where F   24. knotted] Q2;
knotty F   26. fearful] Q2; fretfull F   28. List, list, O]
Q2; list *Hamlet,* oh F   30. God] Q2; Heauen F   35.
Haste me] Q2; Hast, hast me F   35. that I, with] Q2;
That with F   40. roots] Q2; rots F   50. with] Q2; hath
F   52. to his] Q2; to to this F   54. a] F; *omit* Q2   62.
lust] F; but Q2   63. sate] F; sort Q2   65. morning]
Q2; Mornings F   67. of] Q2; in F   69. hebona] Q2;
Hebenon F   71. leprous] Q2; leaperous F   75. posset]
F; possesse Q2   76. eager] Q2; Aygre F   78. barked]
Q2; bak'd F   82. of queen] Q2; and Queene F   84.
unaneled] F; vnnaneld Q2   86. With all] F; Withall Q2
91. howsomever] Q2; howsoeuer F   91. pursues] Q2;
pursuest F   98. adieu, adieu. Remember] Q2; adue,
Hamlet: remember F   98. SD F; *omit* Q2   100. Hold,
hold, my] Q2; hold my F   102. stiffly] F; swiftly Q2
111. Yes, by] Q2; yes, yes, by F   114. My tables—meet]
Q2; My Tables, my Tables; meet F   119. SD *1 line later
in* F, *which prefixes line 120 "Hor & Mar. within."*   122.
Heavens] Q2; Heauen F   123. SP HAMLET] Q2; *Mar.*
F   124. SP MARCELLUS] Q2; *Hor.* F   125. bird] F; and
Q2   136. SP HORATIO/MARCELLUS] Ed.; *Booth.* Q2; *Both.*
F   136. my lord] F; *omit* Q2 144. desire] Q2; desires
F   147. I will] Q2; Looke you, Ile F   148. whirling]
Q2; hurling F   152. Horatio] Q2; my Lord F   161. SP

HORATIO/MARCELLUS] Ed.; *Booth.* Q2; *Both.* F   168. SP GHOST. Q2, F   177. our] Q2; for F   180–81. *lines transposed in* F   182. by his sword] Q2; *omit* F   183. earth] Q2; ground F   188. your] Q2; our F   190. some'er] Q2; so ere F   193. times] Q2; time F   194. this] Q2; thus F   196. Well, well, we] Q2; well, we F   198. they] Q2; there F   201. this do swear] Q2; this not to doe F   202. you] Q2; you: | Sweare F   205. With all] F; Withall Q2

2.1.   0. SD *old . . . Reynaldo*] Ed.; *old Polonius, with his man or two* Q2; *Polonius, and Reynoldo* F   1. this] Q2; his F   3. marvelous] Q2; maruels F   4. to make inquire] Q2; you make inquiry F   16. As] Q2; And F   31. no] F; *omit* Q2   38. unreclaimèd] Q2; vnreclaim'd F   44. wit] Q2; warrant F   46. i' th'] F; with Q2   49. seen∧] Q2; ~. F   53. or] Q2; and F   59–60. at "friend . . . gentleman."] F; *omit* Q2   62. closes thus] Q2; closes with you thus F   64. such or such] Q2; such and such F   66. o'ertook] F; or tooke Q2   70. take . . . carp] Q2; takes . . . Cape F   83. SD *Reynaldo exits.*] Q2; *Exit.* F. *Both* Q2 *and* F *set* SD *1 line earlier.*   85. O, my lord] Q2; Alas F   86. i' th' . . . God] Q2; in the . . . Heauen F   87. closet] Q2; Chamber F   107. As] Q2; That F   109. shoulder] Q2; shoulders F   111. helps] Q2; helpe F   113. Come] Q2; *omit* F   117. passions] Q2; passion F   124. heed] Q2; speed F   125. feared] Q2; feare F   127. By heaven] Q2; It seemes F   134. Come] Q2; *omit* F

2.2.   0. SD *Flourish.*] Q2; *omit* F   0. SD *and Attendants*] *omit* Q2; *Cum alijs* F   5. so call] Q2; so I call F   6. Sith nor] Q2; Since not F   10. dream] Q2; deeme F   12. sith . . . havior] Q2; since . . . humour F   16. occasion] Q2; Occasions F   17. Q2; *omit* F   20. is] Q2; are F   31. But] Q2; *omit* F   33. service] Q2; Seruices F   39. these] Q2; the F   42. Ay] Q2; *omit* F   42. SD Q2; *Exit.* F, *set 1 line earlier*   46. I assure my] Q2; Assure you, my F   48. and] Q2; one F   51. it hath] Q2; I haue

F   53. do I] Q2; I do F   55. fruit] Q2; Newes F   57. dear Gertrude] Q2; sweet Queene F   60. o'erhasty] F; hastie Q2   61. SD *Enter . . . Polonius.*] *Enter Polonius, Voltumand, and Cornelius.* F, *set 1 line earlier in both Q2 and* F   62. my] Q2; *omit* F   77. three-score] Q2; three F   81. shown] Q2 (shone); F   83. this] Q2; his F   91. SD *Voltemand and Cornelius exit.*] Ed.; *Exeunt Embassadors.* Q2; *Exit Ambass.* F   92. is well] Q2; is very well F   97. since] F; *omit* Q2   106. 'tis 'tis] Q2; it is F   116. SD *He reads.*] Ed.; *The Letter.* F; *omit* Q2   120. Thus] Q2; these F   121. *etc.*] Q2; *omit* F   123. SD *He reads the letter.*] *Letter.* Q2; *omit* F   133. shown] Q2; shew'd F   134. above] F; about Q2   134. solicitings] Q2; soliciting F   146. winking] F; working Q2   149. bespeak:] Q2 (~,); ~∧ F   151. prescripts] Q2; Precepts F   152. his] F; her Q2   155. repelled] Q2; repulsed F   157. watch] F; wath Q2   158. a] F; *omit* Q2   159. wherein] Q2; whereon F   160. mourn] Q2; waile F   161. 'tis] F; *omit* Q2   162. like] Q2; likely F   175. does] Q2; ha's F   181. But] Q2; And F   186. SD Q2 *1 line earlier;* F *one-half line earlier*   190. Excellent well] Q2; Excellent, excellent well F   195. ten] Q2; two F   202. but, as] Q2; but not as F   206. far gone] Q2; farre gone, farre gone F   213. that you read] Q2; you meane F   214. rogue] Q2; slaue F   216. and] Q2; or F   217. lack] Q2; locke F   218. most] Q2; *omit* F   220–21. for yourself] Q2; for you your selfe F   221. shall grow] Q2; should be F   229. sanity] F; sanctity Q2   230–31. and . . . him] F; *omit* Q2   231. My lord] Q2; My Honourable Lord F   232. will take] Q2; I will most humbly | Take F   233. sir] F; *omit* Q2   234. will more] F; will not more Q2   234–35. except my life, except my life, except my life] Q2; except my life, my life F   237. SD *2 lines earlier in* Q2; *1 line later in* F   238. the] Q2; my F   242. excellent] F; extent Q2   246. overhappy.] F; euer happy∧ Q2   247. cap] F; lap Q2   254. What news] Q2; What's the newes F   255. that] F;

omit Q2   258–89. Let . . . attended.] F; *omit* Q2   286.
SP ROSENCRANTZ/GUILDENSTERN] Ed.; *Both* F   293. even]
F; euer Q2   300. Anything] Q2; Why any thing F   301.
of] Q2; *omit* F   310. can] Q2; could F   317. discov-
ery, and your] Q2; discouery of your F   318. Queen∧]
Q2; ~: F   320. exercises] Q2; exercise F   320. heav-
ily] Q2; heauenly F   324. firmament] Q2; *omit* F   325.
appeareth nothing] Q2; appeares no other thing F   326.
but] Q2; then F   327. a] F; *omit* Q2   328. faculties] Q2;
faculty F   328–30. moving∧ . . . admirable; . . . action∧
. . . angel, . . . apprehension∧] F (~∧ . . . ~? . . . ~, . . . ~?
. . . ~,); ~, . . . ~∧ . . . ~, . . . ~∧ . . . ~, Q2   333. no] F; *omit*
Q2   333. women] Q2; Woman F   337. then] Q2; *omit* F
344. on] Q2; of F   347–48. the clown . . . sear] F; *omit*
Q2   348. tickle] Ed.; tickled F   349. blank] F; black Q2
351. such] Q2; *omit* F   359. are they] Q2; they are F
360–85. F; *omit* Q2   365. berattle] F2; be-ratled F   372.
most like] Ed.; like most F   375. to-do] ~∧ ~ F   386.
very] Q2; *omit* F   387. mouths] Q2; mowes F   388.
fifty] Q2; *omit* F   390. 'Sblood] Q2; *omit* F   394. then]
Q2; *omit* F   396. this] Q2; the F   396. lest my] F; let
me Q2   407. swaddling] Q2; swathing F   408. Haply]
Q2, F (Happily)   410. prophesy∧] Q2 (~,); ~. F   411.
sir, a] Q2; Sir: for a F   412. then] Q2; so F   415. was]
Q2; *omit* F   419. came] Q2; can F   421–22. pastoral-
comical, historical-pastoral] Q2; ~-~-~-~ F   422–23.
tragical- . . . -pastoral] F; *omit* Q2   443. pious] Q2; *Pons*
F   444. abridgment comes] Q2; Abridgements come
F   444. SD *Enter the Players.*] Q2; *Enter foure or fiue*
Players. F   446. my] F; *omit* Q2   447. Why] Q2; *omit*
F   447. valanced] Q2; valiant F   449. By'r] F; by Q2
450. to] Q2; *omit* F   454. French falconers] F; friendly
Fankners Q2   457, 493, 527, 530. SP FIRST] F; *omit* Q2
457. good] Q2; *omit* F   462. judgments] Q2; Iudgement
F   466. were] Q2; was F   468. affection] Q2; affecta-
tion F   469–70. as wholesome . . . fine] Q2; *omit* F

470. One speech] Q2; One cheefe Speech F   471. tale]
F; talke Q2   472. when] Q2; where F   481. *dismal.*] F
(~:); ~∧ Q2   482. *total*] Q2; to take F   485. *a damnèd*]
Q2; damned F   486. *lord's murder*] Q2; vilde Murthers
F   490. Q2; *omit* F   496. *matched*] Q2; match F   499.
Then . . . Ilium] F; *omit* Q2   500. *this*] Q2; his F   506.
And] F; *omit* Q2   520. *fellies*] Ed.; follies Q2; Fallies F
527. *ah woe . . . moblèd*] Q2; O who . . . inobled F   528.
moblèd] Q2; inobled F   529. "Moblèd queen" is good]
Ed.; *omit* Q2; Inobled Queene is good F   530. *flames*]
Q2; flame F   531. *bisson rheum*] F; *Bison* rehume Q2
531. *upon*] Q2; about F   540. *husband's*] F; husband
Q2   546. Prithee] Q2; Pray you F   547–48. of this]
Q2; *omit* F   550. abstract] Q2; Abstracts F   552. live]
Q2; liued F   555. bodykins] F; bodkin Q2   555. much]
Q2; *omit* F   556. shall] Q2; should F   562. SD *As . . .*
Player.] This ed.; *Exeunt Pol. and Players.* Q2 *after line*
573; Exit Polon. F *after line 560*   566. ha 't] Q2 (hate), F
566. a] F; *omit* Q2   567. dozen or] F; dosen lines, or Q2
573. till] Q2 (tell); til F   575. good-bye to you] Q2 (God
buy to you); God buy'ye F   575. SD *Rosencrantz . . .*
exit.] *Exeunt.* Q2; *Exeunt. Manet Hamlet.* F, *both after*
line 574   580. own] Q2; whole F   581. his] F; the Q2
581. wanned] Q2; warm'd F   583. and] Q2 (an); and
F   586. to Hecuba] F; to her Q2   588. the cue] F; that
Q2   593. faculties] Q2; faculty F   603. 'Swounds] Q2;
Why F   606. have] F; a Q2   607. offal. Bloody, bawdy]
Q2 (~, ~, ~); Offall, bloudy: a Bawdy F   610. F; *omit*
Q2   611. Why] Q2; Who F   611. I! This] Q2; I? I sure,
this F   612. a] Q2; the F   612. father] Q3; *omit* Q2, F
616. stallion] Q2; Scullion F   617. brains!—Hum, I]
Q2; Braine. | I F   626. do] Q2; but F   628. a] Q2; the F
628. devil . . . devil] F; deale . . . deale Q2

3.1.   0. SD *and*] F; *omit* Q2   1. And] Q2 (An); And F
1. conference] Q2; circumstance F   18. o'erraught] Q2;
ore-wrought F   20. here] Q2; *omit* F   29. into] Q2; on

| To F   30. SD Q2; *Exeunt.* F   31. too] F; two Q2   33. here] Q2; there F   35. lawful espials] F; *omit* Q2   36. Will] F; Wee'le Q2   39. no∧] Q2; ~. F   52. loneliness] F; lowlines Q2   54. sugar] Q2; surge F   56. too] Q2; *omit* F   63. Let's] F; *omit* Q2   63. SD *Enter Hamlet.*] Q2 *1 line earlier;* F *Exeunt. Enter Hamlet*   68. die,] F; ~∧ Q2   68. sleep—] ~∧ Q2, F   72. wished.] F; ~∧ Q2   72. die,] ~∧ Q2, F   79. proud] Q2; poore F   80. despised] Q2; dispriz'd F   84. would fardels] Q2; would these Fardles F   91. of us all] F; *omit* Q2   93. sicklied] F; sickled Q2   94. pitch] Q2; pith F   95. awry] Q2; away F   101. well] Q2; well, well, well F   105. not I] Q2; no F   106. you know] Q2; I know F   108. the] F; these Q2   108–9. Their . . . lost] Q2; then . . . left F   117. your honesty] F; you Q2   120. with] Q2; your F   128. inoculate] F; euocutat Q2   131. to] F; *omit* Q2   137. in, imagination∧] Q2; ~∧ ~, F   139. earth and heaven] Q2; Heauen and Earth F   140. all] F; *omit* Q2   144. nowhere] Q2; no way F   149. nunnery, farewell] Q2; Nunnery. Go, Farewell F   153. Heavenly] Q2; O heauenly F   154. paintings] Q2; pratlings F   154. too] F; *omit* Q2   155–56. hath . . . face . . . yourselves] Q2; has . . . pace . . . your selfe F   156. jig and] Q2; gidge, you F   157. lisp] F; list Q2   157. you nickname] Q2; and nickname F   158. wantonness your] F; wantonness Q2   160. marriage] Q2; Marriages F   166. expectancy] F; expectation Q2   169. And] Q2; Haue F   170. musicked] Q2; Musicke F   171. that] F; what Q2   172. time] Q2; tune F   173. stature] Q2; Feature F   175. Q2 *uncorr. prints* "Exit."   176. SP KING, *advancing with Polonius*] Ed.; *Enter King and Polonius.* Q2, F   178. soul∧] Q2; ~? F   181. for] Q2; *omit* F   191. his] Q2; this F   197. grief] Q2; Greefes F   203. unwatched] F; vnmatcht Q2

3.2.   0. *three*] Q2; *two or three* F   1. pronounced] F; pronoun'd Q2   3. our] Q2; your F   4. town-crier spoke] Q2; Town-Cryer had spoke F   5. with] Q2; *omit*

F   6–7. say, whirlwind of your passion] Q2; say) the Whirle-winde of | Passion F   9. hear] Q2; see F   13. would] Q2; could F   20. o'erstep] Q2; ore-stop F   24. own] F; *omit* Q2   27. makes] Q2; make F   29. the] F; *omit* Q2   31. praise] F; praysd Q2   34. nor man] Q2; or Norman F   39. sir] F; *omit* Q2   47. SD *Players exit.*] F; *omit* Q2   47. SD *Enter . . . Rosencrantz.*] *placed as in* F; *2 lines later in* Q2   51. SD *Polonius exits.*] F; *omit* Q2   53. ROSENCRANTZ Ay] Q2; *Both.* We will F   53. SD *They exit.*] F; *Exeunt they two.* Q2   54. SD *1 line earlier in* F   59. SP HAMLET] F; *omit* Q2   64. lick] Q2; like F   66. fawning] Q2; faining F   67. her] Q2; my F   68. distinguish, her election] F; ~∧ ~ ~, Q2   69. Hath] F; S'hath Q2   72. Hast] Q2; Hath F   74. commeddled] Q2; comingled F   84. thy] Q2; my F   89. heedful] Q2; needfull F   92. In] Q2; To F   95. detecting] F; detected Q2   95. SD *omit* Q2; *following* 97 SD *in* F   97. SD *2 lines earlier in* Q2, F   97. SD *the King's*] Ed.; *his* F *torches*] *Torches. Danish March* F   104. mine now. My] ~ ~∧ ~ Q2; ~. ~ ~ F   106. did I] Q2; I did F   108. What] Q2; And what F   115. SP QUEEN] F; *Ger.* Q2   115. dear] Q2; good F   121–22. F; *omit* Q2   144. SD *The . . . follows.*] Q2; *Hoboyes play. The dumbe shew enters.* F   145. *a Queen*] Q2; *Queene* F   145. *very lovingly*] F; *omit* Q2   146. *and he her*] Q2; *omit* F   146–47. *She . . . him.*] F; *omit* Q2   148. *He lies*] Q2; *Layes* F   150. *comes*] F; *come* Q2   150. *another man*] Q2; *a Fellow* F   150. *it, pours*] Q2; *it, and powres* F   151. *sleeper's*] Q2; *Kings* F   151. *leaves him*] Q2; *Exits* F   152. *dead, makes*] Q2; *dead, and makes* F   153. *three or four*] Q2; *two or three Mutes* F   153–54. *come . . . seem to condole*] Q2; *comes . . . seeming to lament* F   155. *harsh*] Q2; *loath and vnwilling* F   156. *his*] F; *omit* Q2   156. SD *Players exit.*] Ed.; *Exeunt* F; *omit* Q2   158. is miching] F; munching Q2   158. It] Q2; that F   161. SD *one-half line later in* Q2; *after line 169 in* F   162. this fellow] Q2;

these Fellowes F   163. counsel] F; *omit* Q2   164. he]
Q2; they F   175. SD *and Queen*] Q2; *and his Queene*
F   176 *and hereafter to line 248.* SP PLAYER KING] Ed.;
King Q2, F   177. *orbèd*] F; orb'd the Q2   182 *and here-
after until line 251.* SP PLAYER QUEEN] *Quee.* Q2; *Bap.* F
185. *your*] F; our Q2   185. *former*] Q2; forme F   188.
Q2; *omit* F   189. *And*] Q2; For F   189. *hold*] Q2; holds
F   190. *In*] F; Eyther none, in Q2   191. *love*] F; Lord
Q2   193–94. Q2; *omit* F   196. *their*] Q2; my F   204.
That's] Q2; Wormwood F   205. SP *omit* Q2; *Bapt.* F
209. *you*∧] Q2; ~. F   213. *the fruit*] Q2; like Fruite F
219. *either*] Q2; other F   220. *enactures*] Q2; ennactors
F   222. *joys*] F; ioy Q2   227. *favorite*] Q2; fauourites
F   239. *me give*] Q2; giue me F   241–42. Q2; *omit* F
242. *An*] Ed.; And Q2   246. *once a . . . be wife*] F; once I
be a . . . be a wife Q2   247. *printed after line 245 in* Q2
250. SD F *only, 1 line later*   252. SD Ed.; *Exeunt.* Q2;
Exit F   254. doth protest] Q2; protests F   261. how?]
F; ~∧ Q2   267. SD *1 line later in* Q2   269. as good as a]
Q2; a good F   276. your] Q2; *omit* F   277. Pox] F; *omit*
Q2   282. *Confederate*] F; Considerat Q2   284. *infected*]
F; inuected Q2   286. *usurp*] F; vsurps Q2   286. SD
F; *omit* Q2   288. written] Q2; writ F   289. very] Q2;
omit F   292. F; *omit* Q2   296. SP POLONIUS] Q2; *All.*
F   300. *Thus*] Q2; So F   302. two] F; *omit* Q2   304.
players] Q2; Players, sir F   321. SD *placed as in* Q2;
after line 316 in F   330. lord, with] Q2; Lord, rather
with F   332. the] Q2; his F   333. into more] Q2; into
farre more F   336. start] F; stare Q2   346. my] F; *omit*
Q2   348. SP ROSENCRANTZ] Q2; *Guild.* F   350. answer]
Q2; answers F   351. as] Q2; *omit* F   358. Impart] Q2;
omit F   364. And do] Q2; And I do F   366. surely . . .
upon] Q2; freely . . . of F   372. sir] Q2; *omit* F   373.
SD *after line 371 in* Q2; *Enter one with a Recorder.* F
374. recorders] Q2; Recorder F   374. one] Q2; *omit*
F   387. It is . . . ventages] Q2; 'Tis . . . Ventiges F   388.

fingers] Q2; finger F   388. thumb] F; the vmber Q2
389. eloquent] Q2; excellent F   397. the top of] F; *omit*
Q2   399. speak. 'Sblood] Q2; Why F   400. think I] Q2;
thinke, that I F   401–2. you can fret] F; you fret Q2
402. me, you] F; me not, you Q2   402. SD *1 line later in*
Q2, F   406–7. yonder . . . of] Q2; that . . . like F   408.
Mass, and 'tis] Q2; Misse, and it's F   413. SP HAMLET] F;
omit Q2   413. I will] Q2; will I F   416. SP POLONIUS] F;
omit Q2   417. SP HAMLET] F; *omit* Q2   417–18. Leave
me, friends] *placed here in* F; *after line 415 in* Q2   418.
SD *omit* Q2; *Exit.* F *after line 416*   420. breathes] F;
breakes Q2   424. bitter business as the day] F; busines
as the bitter day Q2   429. daggers] F; dagger Q2   432.
SD Q2; *omit* F

3.3.   6. near 's] Q2; dangerous F   7. brows] Q2;
Lunacies F   15. weal] Q2; spirit F   16. cess] Q2;
cease F   18. or] Q2; *omit* F   19. summit] Ed.; som-
net Q2, F   20. huge] F; hough Q2   23. ruin] F; raine
Q2   24. with] F; *omit* Q2   26. about] Q2; vpon F   28.
SP ROSENCRANTZ] Q2; *Both.* F   28. SD *Rosencrantz . . .
exit.*] Ed.; *Exeunt Gent.* Q2, F   39. SD *Polonius exits.*]
Ed.; *Exit.* Q2 *after line 38; omit* F   54. pardoned] F;
pardon Q2   62. shove] F; showe Q2   77. pat] F; but
Q2   77. a-praying] Q2; praying F   80. revenged] F;
reuendge Q2   82. sole] Q2; foule F   84. Why] Q2; Oh
F   84. hire and salary] F; base and silly Q2   86. With
all] F; Withall Q2   86. flush] Q2; fresh F   96. game,
a-swearing] Q2; gaming, swearing F

3.4.   0. SD *Queen*] F; *Gertrard* Q2   7. with him] F;
omit Q2   8. F; *omit* Q2   9. SP *and hereafter in 3.4 and
4.1* QUEEN] F; *Ger.* Q2, *except line 61:* "Quee."   9. war-
rant] F; wait Q2   10. SD *Enter Hamlet.*] *placed as in* F;
Q2 *after line 7*   15. a wicked] Q2; an idle F   21. And
(would it . . . so)] And∧ would it . . . so, Q2; But∧ would
you . . . so. F   25. inmost] F; most Q2   27. Help] Q2;
Helpe, helpe F   28. Help] Q2; helpe, helpe, helpe F

29. SD *kills Polonius.*] F *1 line later; omit* Q2   39. better] Q2; Betters F   46. be] Q2; is F   51. off] Q2 (of); off F   53. sets] Q2; makes F   57–58. glow∧ | O'er] Q2; glow, | Yea F   59. heated] Q2; tristfull F   62. That] F; *Ham.* That Q2   63. SP HAMLET] F; *omit* Q2   65. this] Q2; his F   67. and] Q2; or F   69. heaven] F; heaue, a Q2   75. brother] Q2; breath F   81–86. Sense . . . difference.] Q2; *omit* F   88–91. Eyes . . . mope.] Q2; *omit* F   98. And] Q2; As F   98. panders] F; pardons Q2   100. eyes into my very soul] F; very eyes into my soule Q2   101. grainèd] F; greeued Q2   102. not leave their] F; leaue there their Q2   111. tithe] F; kyth Q2   117. SD *1 line earlier in* Q2, F   119. your] Q2; you F   134. do] Q2; *omit* F   135. th' incorporal] Q2; their corporall F   149. whom] Q2; who F   156. SD *Ghost exits.*] Q2; *Exit.* F   160. F; *omit* Q2   164. I] F; *omit* Q2   166. that] Q2; a F   172. on] Q2; or F   173. ranker] Q2; ranke F   174. these] Q2; this F   179. live] F; leaue Q2   181. Assume] F; Assune Q2   182–86. That . . . on] Q2; *omit* F   186. on.] ∼∧ Q2   186. Refrain tonight] F; to refraine night Q2   188–91. the . . . potency] Q2; *omit* F   200. This] Q2; Thus F   201. Q2; *omit* F   204. bloat] Q2; blunt F   208. ravel] F; rouell Q2   210. mad] Q2; made F   225–33. Q2; *omit* F   236. night∧ indeed] Q2; ∼. ∼ F   238. a foolish] F; a most foolish Q2   240. SD *They . . . Polonius.*] Ed.; *Exit.* Q2; *Exit Hamlet . . . Polonius.* F

4.1.   0. SD *Enter . . . Guildenstern.*] Q2; *Enter King.* F   1. matter] Q2; matters F   4. Q2; *omit* F   5. mine own] Q2; my good F   7. sea] Q2; Seas F   10. Whips out his rapier, cries] Q2; He whips his Rapier out, and cries F   11. this] Q2; his F   23. let] Q2; let's F   33. SD *Enter . . . Guildenstern.*] Q2 *1 line earlier;* F *one-half line earlier*   36. mother's closet] Q2; Mother Clossets F   36. dragged] F; dreg'd Q2   38. SD *Rosencrantz . . . exit.*] F (*Exit Gent.*); *omit* Q2   42–45. Whose . . . air.] Q2; *omit* F

4.2.   0. SD *Enter Hamlet.*] F; *Enter Hamlet, Rosencraus, and others.* Q2   2. F; *omit* Q2   3. SP HAMLET] F; *omit* Q2   3. But soft] Q2; *omit* F   4. SD *Enter . . . others.*] F (*Enter Ros. and Guildensterne.*)   6. Compounded] F; Compound Q2   17–18. an ape] F; *omit* Q2   18. an apple] Q2; *omit* F   30–31. Hide . . . after!] F; *omit* Q2

4.3.   0. SD *Enter . . . three.*] Q2; *Enter King.* F   7. never] Q2; neerer F   11. SD *Enter Rosencrantz.*] F; *Enter Rosencraus and all the rest.* Q2   18. Ho . . . lord] Q2; Hoa, *Guildensterne?* Bring in my Lord. F   18. SD *They . . . Hamlet.*] Ed.; *They enter.* Q2; *Enter Hamlet and Guildensterne.* F   23. politic] Q2; *omit* F   25. ourselves] Q2; our selfe F   27. service—two] Q2 (~, ~); seruice to F   29–32. Q2; *omit* F   33. SP KING] F; *King. King.* Q2   38. there] F; thrre Q2   39. if, indeed] Q2; indeed, if F   40. within] Q2; *omit* F   44. deed, for] Q2; deed of thine. for F   48. With fiery quickness] F; *omit* Q2   50. is] Q2; at F   56. them] Q2; him F   61. and so] F; so Q2   73. congruing] Q2; coniuring F   77. will ne'er begin] Q2; were ne'er begun F

4.4.   0. SD *Enter . . . stage.*] Q2; *Enter Fortinbras with an Armie.* F   3. Craves] Q2; Claimes F   9. softly] Q2; safely F   9. SD *All . . . others.*] Ed.; *Enter Hamlet, Rosencraus, &c.* Q2; *Exit.* F   10–69. Q2; *omit* F   20. name.] ~∧ Q2

4.5.   0. SD *Queen*] F; *Gertrard* Q2; *Enter Queene and Horatio.* F   2, 5. SP GENTLEMAN] Q2; *Hor.* F   11. aim] F; yawne Q2   15. might] Q2; would F   18. SP HORATIO] Q2; *Qu.* F   21. SP QUEEN] Ed.; *omit* Q2, F   22. SP To] F; *Quee.* Q2   25. SD *Enter . . . distracted.*] F; *Enter Ophelia.* Q2 *after line 21*   28. SD *sings*] Ed.; *shee sings.* Q2 *after line 27; omit* F   34. SD *Sings*] Ed.; *Song.* Q2 *after line 35; omit* F   38. Q2; *omit* F   41. SD *Enter King.*] Q2; *after line 37 in* F   43. SD *sings*] Ed.; *Song.* Q2 *after line 44; omit* F   43. all] Q2; *omit* F   44. ground] Q2;

graue F   47. God] F; good Q2   51. Pray let's] Q2; Pray you let's F   53. SD *Sings*] Ed.; *Song.* Q2 *after line 53; omit* F   62. Indeed, without] Q2; Indeed la? without F   69. Q2; *omit* F   70. '*a*] Q2; ha F   72. thus] Q2; this F   74. would] Q2; should F   77–78. Good . . . good . . . good . . . good] F; God . . . god . . . god . . . god Q2   78. SD F; *omit* Q2   81. and now behold] Q2; *omit* F   83. sorrows come] Q2; sorrowes comes F   84. battalions] Q2; Battaliaes F   87. their] F; *omit* Q2   96. Feeds] Q2; Keepes F   96. his] F; this Q2   100. person] Q2; persons F   104. F; *omit* Q2   105. Q2; *omit* F   106. is] Q2; are F   106. SD *after line 103* Q2, F   116. They] F; The Q2   118. SD *A noise within.*] Q2 *1 line later; Noise within.* F *2 lines later*   121. SD *Enter . . . others.*] Q2 *1 line earlier; Enter Laertes.* F *1 line earlier*   122. this king?—Sirs] Q2 (~ ~? ~); the King, sirs? F   130. that's calm] Q2; that calmes F   156. world] F; worlds Q2   161. father, is 't] Q2; Fathers death, if F   162. swoopstake] Ed.; soopstake Q2, F   168. pelican] Q2; Politician F   173. sensibly] Q2; sensible F   174. 'pear] Q2; pierce F   176. F; *Laer.* Let her come in. Q2, *printed after "Enter Ophelia."*   177. SP LAERTES] F; *omit* Q2   177. SD *Enter Ophelia.* F *1 line earlier;* Q2 *after line 175*   180. with] Q2; by F   181. turn] Q2; turnes F   184. an old] F; a poore Q2   185–87. F; *omit* Q2   188. SD *sings*] Ed.; *Song.* Q2 *after line 188; omit* F   189. F; *omit* Q2   190. *in . . . rained*] Q2; *on . . . raines* F   194. A-down a-down] Q2; downe a-downe F   200. you] Q2; *omit* F   200. pansies] Q2; Paconcies F   204. columbines] F; Colembines Q2   206. herb of grace] Q2; Herbe-Grace F   206. You] Q2; Oh you F   206. must] F; may Q2   211. afflictions] Q2; Affliction F   213. SD *sings*] Ed.; *Song.* Q2 *after line 213; omit* F   218. *was*] Q2; *omit* F   219. *All*] F; *omit* Q2   222. *God 'a mercy*] Q2; *Gramercy* F   223. Christians'] Q2; Christian F   223. I pray God] F; *omit* Q2   224. SD *She exits.*] F (*Exeunt*

Ophelia); *omit* Q2   225. see] F; *omit* Q2   225. O God]
Q2; you Gods F   226. commune] Q2; common F   238.
funeral] Q2; buriall F   242. call 't] Q2; call F

4.6.   0. SD *Enter . . . others.*] Q2; *Enter Horatio,
with an Attendant.* F   2. SP GENTLEMAN] Q2; *Ser.* F   2.
Seafaring men] Q2; Saylors F   6. greeted,] ~. Q2   6.
SD *Enter Sailors.*] Q2; *Enter Saylor.* F   9. an 't] F; and
Q2   10. came from th' ambassador] Q2; comes from
th'Ambassadours F   13. SP HORATIO] Q2; *omit* F   16.
warlike] Q2; *Warlicke* F   18. *and*] Q2; *omit* F   22.
good] F; *omit* Q2   23. *speed*] Q2; *hast* F   25. *thine*] Q2;
your F   26. *bore*] F; bord Q2   30. *He*] F; *So* Q2   32. SP
Come] F; *Hor.* Come Q2   32. give] F; *omit* Q2   34. SD
They exit.] Ed.; *Exeunt.* Q2; *Exit.* F

4.7.   7. proceeded] F; proceede Q2   8. criminal]
Q2; crimefull F   9. greatness] Q2; *omit* F   13. But] Q2;
And F   16. conjunctive] F; concliue Q2   22. Work] Q2;
Would F   24. loud a wind] F; loued Arm'd Q2   26. But
. . . have aimed] Q2; And . . . had arm'd F   29. Whose
worth] Q2; Who was F   37. SD *with letters*] Q2; *omit* F
38–40. F; *omit* Q2   41. SP These] Ed.; *Messen.* These
Q2; This F   45. Q2; *omit* F   48. SD F; *omit* Q2   51.
your] F; you Q2   52. *the occasion*] Q2; *th'Occasions*
F   53. *and more strange*] F; *omit* Q2   53. *Hamlet*] F;
omit Q2   54. SP What] F; *King.* What Q2   55. and]
Q2; Or F   59. advise] F; deuise Q2   62. shall] F; *omit*
Q2   67–68. Ay . . . will] Q2; If so you'l F   70. checking]
F; the King Q2   77–92. LAERTES . . . graveness.] Q2;
omit F   92. Two months since] Q2; Some two Monthes
hence F   95. can] Q2; ran F   96. unto] Q2; into F   99.
topped] Q2; past F   99. my] F; me Q2   104. Lamord]
Q2; *Lamound* F   107. the] Q2; our F   111. especial]
Q2; especially F   113–16. The . . . them.] Q2; *omit* F
119. you] Q2; him F   121. What] Q2; Why F   130–40.
Q2; *omit* F   139. spendthrift] Q5; spend thirfts Q2
142. yourself indeed your . . . son] Q2; your selfe your

... sonne indeed F   153. on] F; ore Q2   157. pass] F; pace Q2   160. that] F; *omit* Q2   162. that, but dip] Q2; I but dipt F   171. shape.] Ed.; ~∧ Q2; ~, F   176. did] Q2; should F   177. cunnings] Q2; commings F   180. that] Q2; the F   181. prepared] F; prefard Q2   185–86. But . . . noise] Q2; how sweet Queene F   188. they] Q2; they'l F   190. askant the] Q2; aslant a F   191. hoar] F; horry Q2   192. make] Q2; come F   195. our cold] F; our cull-cold Q2   199. her] Q2; the F   202. lauds] Q2; tunes F   206. their] Q2; her F   207. lay] Q2; buy F   209. she is] Q2; is she F   217. drowns] Q2; doubts F

5.1.   0.   SD   *Enter . . . Another.*] Ed.;   *Enter two Clownes.* Q2, F   1 *and throughout scene.* SP GRAVEDIG-GER] Ed.; *Clowne* Q2, F   2. when she] Q2; that F   3. is. Therefore] Q2; is, and therefore F   9. *se offendendo*] F; so offended Q2   12. to act] Q2; an Act F   12. do, to] Q2; doe, and to F   12. Argal] F; or all Q2   35–38. OTHER . . . arms?] F; *omit* Q2   44. frame] F; *omit* Q2   56. SD F; *omit* Q2   60. houses he] Q2; Houses that he F   61. in, and] Q2; to *Yaughan* F   62. stoup] F; soope Q2   62. SD This ed.; *Sings.* F; *Song.* Q2 *after line 63*   66. *a . . . a*] Q2; *omit* F   67. SP HAMLET] F; *Enter Hamlet and Horatio. Ham.* Q2   67. business? He] Q2 (busines? a); businesse, that he F   68. in] Q2; at F   72. daintier] F; dintier Q2   73. SD *sings*] F; *Song.* Q2 *after line 73*   74. *clawed*] Q2; *caught* F   75. *into*] Q2; *intill* F   80. This] Q2; It F   81. now] Q2; *omit* F   81. o'erreaches] Q2; o're Offices F   81. would] Q2; could F   85. thou, sweet] Q2; thou, good F   87. went] Q2; meant F   91. mazard] F; massene Q2   92. an] Q2 (and); if F   96. SD *sings*] F; *Song.* Q2   100. may] Q2; might F   101. of . . . quiddities] Q2; of of . . . Quiddits F   102. quillities] Q2 (quillites); Quillets F   103. mad] Q2; rude F   108–9. Is . . . recoveries] F; *omit* Q2   110. his] F; *omit* Q2   111. double ones too] F; doubles Q2   113. scarcely] Q2; hardly F   117. calves'] Q2; Calue F   118. which] Q2;

that F   120. sirrah] Q2; Sir F   122. *O*] F; or Q2   123.
F; *omit* Q2   126. in 't, yet] Q2; in't; and yet F   142. this
... took] Q2; these ... taken F   144. heel of the] Q2;
heeles of our F   145–46. been grave-maker] Q2; been
a Grauemaker F   147. all] F; *omit* Q2   152. that very]
Q2; the very F   153. is] Q2; was F   159. him there] Q2;
him F   167. sexton] Q2; sixeteene F   169. Faith] Q2;
Ifaith F   170. nowadays] F; *omit* Q2   178. now hath
lien you] Q2; now: this Scul, has laine F   186. sir, was,
sir, Yorick's] Q2; Sir, this same Scull sir, was *Yoricks* F
190. Let me see.] F; *omit* Q2   192. bore] Q2; borne F
193–94. and now how abhorred in my imagination it is]
Q2; And how abhorred my Imagination is F   198. Not]
Q2; No F   199. grinning] Q2; Ieering F   200. cham-
ber] F; table Q2   215–16. as thus] F; *omit* Q2   217.
to] Q2; into F   220. Imperious] Q2; Imperiall F   223.
winter's] F; waters Q2   223. SD *Enter ... Divinity.*]
Ed.; *Enter K. Q. Laertes and the corse.* Q2 *after line* 224;
*Enter King, Queene, Laertes, and a Coffin, with Lords
attendant.* F *after line* 224   224. awhile] Q2; aside F
225. this] Q2; that F   227. desp'rate] Q2; disperate F
228. of] Q2; *omit* F   233, 244. SP DOCTOR] Q2; *Priest.*
F   234. warranty] Q2; warrantis F   236. been] Q2;
haue F   237. prayers] Q2; praier F   238. Shards] F;
omit Q2   240. crants] Q2; Rites F   246. a] Q2; sage F
257. have] Q2; t'haue F   258. treble woe] Q2; terrible
woer F   259. treble] F; double Q2   262. SD F; *omit* Q2
267. grief] Q2; griefes F   269. Conjures] Q2; Coniure
F   275. For] Q2; Sir F   275. and] F; *omit* Q2   276.
in me something] Q2; something in me F   277. wis-
dom ... Hold off] Q2; wisenesse ... Away F   280. Q2;
omit F   281. SP HORATIO] Q2; *Gen.* F   290. 'Swounds]
Q2; Come F   291. woo't fast] Q2; *omit* F   294. thou]
F; *omit* Q2   302. SP QUEEN] Q2; *King.* F   303. thus] F;
this Q2   305. couplets] Q2; Cuplet F   311. SD *Ham-
let exits.*] Q2; *Exit.* F   312. thee] Q2; you F   312. SD

Horatio exits.] Q2 *here completes the* SD *begun in its margin 1 line above as "Exit Hamlet" with "and Horatio.";* omit F   313. your] Q2; you F   318. thereby] Q2 *corr.;* thirtie Q2 *uncorr.;* shortly F

5.2.   1. shall you] Q2; let me F   5. Methought] F; my thought Q2   6. bilboes] F; bilbo   Q2   7. praised] Q2; praise F   9. deep . . . learn] Q2; deare . . . teach F   9. pall] Q2 *uncorr.;* fall Q2 *corr.;* paule F   20. unfold] Q2; vnseale F   22. A] Q2; Oh F   23. reasons] Q2; reason F   31. now] Q2; me F   33. villainies] Ed.; villaines Q2, F   34. Or] Q2; Ere F   41. Th' effect] Q2; The effects F   45. like . . . might] Q2; as . . . should F   48. *as*es] Ed.; as sir Q2; Assis F   49. knowing] Q2; know F   51. those] Q2; the F   54. ordinant] Q2; ordinate F   57. the form] Q2; forme F   58. Subscribed] F; Subscribe Q2   61. sequent] Q2; sement F   64. F; *omit* Q2   65. defeat] Q2; debate F   71. think] Q2; thinkst F   77–91. F; *omit* Q2   88. court] Ed.; count F   91. SD *Enter . . . courtier.*] *Enter a Courtier.* Q2; *Enter young Osricke.* F   92 *and thereafter.* SP OSRIC] F; *Cour.* Q2   94. humbly] F; humble Q2   101. say] Q2; saw F   102. lordship] Q2; friendship F   104. sir] Q2; *omit* F   105. Put] F; *omit* Q2   111. But yet] Q2; *omit* F   111. sultry . . . for] F; sully . . . or Q2   114. how. My] Q2; how: but my F   118. good my lord] Q2; in good faith F   119–48. Q2; *omit* F   120. gentleman] Q3; gentlemen Q2   122. feelingly] Q3; sellingly Q2 *uncorr.;* fellingly Q2 *corr.*   127. dozy] Q2 *uncorr.;* dazzie Q2 *corr.*   128. yaw] Q2 *uncorr.;* raw Q2 *corr.*   139. to 't] Q2 *uncorr.;* doo't Q2 *corr.*   150. is] Q2; is at his weapon F   151–56. Q2; *omit* F   154. his] Q5; this Q2   160. King, sir, hath wagered] Q2; sir King ha's wag'd F   161. has impawned] Q2; impon'd F   163. hangers] F; hanger Q2   163. and] Q2; or F   168–69. Q2; *omit* F   170. carriages] F; carriage Q2   172. a] Q2; *omit* F   173. might be] F; be Q2 *uncorr.;* be might Q2 *corr.*   173. on. Six] Q2 (on, six); on sixe

F   176. bet] Q2; but F   176–77. this all "impawned,"
as you] Ed.; this all you Q2; this impon'd as F   178.
laid, sir, that] Q2; laid that F   179. yourself] Q2; you F
180–81. hath laid on . . . nine . . . it] Q2; hath one . . .
mine . . . that F   189. an] Q2 (and); if F   192. deliver]
Q2; redeliuer F   192. e'en] F; *omit* Q2   196. Yours . . .
He does] Ed.; Yours doo's Q2; Yours, yours; hee does F
198. turn] Q2; tongue F   201. did comply, sir] did sir
Q2 *uncorr.;* did so sir Q2 *corr.;* did Complie F   202–3.
has . . . many . . . breed] Q2; had . . . mine . . . Beauy F
204. out of an] Q2; outward F   205. yeasty] F; histy
Q2   206–7. fanned and winnowed] Ed.; prophane and
trennowed Q2; fond and winnowed F   208. trial] Q2;
tryalls F   208 SD–222. Q2; *omit* F   223. lose, my]
Q2; lose this wager, my F   226. but] F; *omit* Q2   226.
how ill all's here] Q2; how all heere F   230. gaingiv-
ing] F; gamgiuing Q2   231. it] Q2; *omit* F   233. a] F;
omit Q2   235. now] F; *omit* Q2   236. will] F; well Q2
237–38. of aught he leaves knows, what] Q2; ha's ought
of what he leaues. What F   238. SD Q2; *Enter King,
Queene, Laertes and Lords, with other Attendants with
Foyles, and Gauntlets, a Table and Flagons of Wine on it.*
F   244. a] Q2; *omit* F   254. F; *omit* Q2   258. brother]
Q2; Mother F   265. keep] F; *omit* Q2   265. ungored]
Q2; vngorg'd F   265. till] F; all Q2   268. I embrace]
Q2; I do embrace F   270. Come on] F; *omit* Q2   274.
off] Q2 (of)   282. better] Q2; better'd F   285. SD F *1
line earlier; omit* Q2   291. union] F; Vnice Q2 *uncorr.;*
Onixe Q2 *corr.*   294. trumpet] Q2; Trumpets F   298.
SD Q2; *omit* F   300. my lord] Q2; on sir F   300. SD F;
omit Q2   307. SD Q2 (*after line 304 and adding "Flor-
ish, a peece goes off."; Trumpets sound, and shot goes
off.* F *after line 308*   309. it] Q2; *omit* F   311. A touch,
a touch] F; *omit* Q2   311. confess 't] Q2; confesse F
314. Here . . . napkin] Q2; Heere's a Napkin F   325. do]
Q2; *omit* F   327. afeard] F; sure Q2   328. SD F; *omit*

Q2   330. SD F; *omit* Q2   336. own] Q2; *omit* F   344.
Hamlet. Hamlet] F; Hamlet Q2   346. an hour's] Q2;
houre of F   347. thy] F; my Q2   353. SD F; *omit* Q2
356. murd'rous] F; *omit* Q2   357. off] Q2 (of)   357.
thy union] F; the Onixe Q2   358. SD F; *omit* Q2   363.
SD F; *omit* Q2   371. cause aright] Q2; causes right F
378. God] Q2; good F   379. I leave] Q2; liue F   384.
SD *A march a farre off.* Q2; *March afarre off, and shout
within.* F   396. F; *omit* Q2   396. SD F; *omit* Q2   397.
cracks] Q2; cracke F   399. SD Q2; *Enter Fortinbras
and English Ambassador, with Drumme, Colours, and
Attendants.* F   403. This] Q2; His F   403. proud] F;
prou'd Q2   405. shot] Q2; shoote F   421. th'] F; *omit*
Q2   425. forced] F; for no Q2   433. now] Q2; are F
434. also] Q2; alwayes F   435. on] F; no Q2   444.
royal] Q2; royally F   445. rite] Q2; rites F   447. bod-
ies] Q2; body F   449. SD *Exeunt.* Q2; *Exeunt . . . off.* F

Hamlet:
A Modern Perspective

Michael Neill

The great Russian director Vsevolod Meyerhold used to maintain that "if all the plays ever written suddenly disappeared and only *Hamlet* miraculously survived, all the theaters in the world would be saved. They could all put on *Hamlet* and be successful."[1] Perhaps Meyerhold exaggerated because of his frustration—he was prevented from ever staging the tragedy by Soviet dictator Joseph Stalin, who apparently thought it too dangerous to be performed—but Meyerhold's sense of *Hamlet*'s extraordinary breadth of appeal is amply confirmed by its stage history. Praised by Shakespeare's contemporaries for its power to "please all" as well as "to please the wiser sort,"[2] it provided his company with an immediate and continuing success. It was equally admired by popular audiences at the Globe on the Bankside, by academic playgoers "in the two Universities of Cambridge and Oxford," and at court—where it was still in request in 1637, nearly forty years after its first performance.

In the four centuries since it was first staged, *Hamlet* has never lost its theatrical appeal, remaining today the most frequently performed of Shakespeare's trage-dies. At the same time, it has developed a reputation as the most intellectually puzzling of his plays, and it has already attracted more commentary than any other work in English except the Bible. Even today, when criticism stresses the importance of the reader's role in "constructing" the texts of the past, there is something astonishing about *Hamlet*'s capacity to accommodate the most bafflingly different readings.[3]

In the early nineteenth century, for instance, Romantic critics read it as the psychological study of a prince too delicate and sensitive for his public mission; to later nineteenth-century European intellectuals, the hero's anguish and self-reproach spoke so eloquently of the disillusionment of revolutionary failure that in czarist Russia "Hamletism" became the acknowledged term for political vacillation and disengagement. The twentieth century, not surprisingly, discovered a more violent and disturbing play: to the French poet Paul Valéry, the tragedy seemed to embody the European death wish revealed in the carnage and devastation of the First World War; in the mid-1960s the English director Peter Hall staged it as a work expressing the political despair of the nuclear age; for the Polish critic Jan Kott, as for the Russian filmmaker Gregori Kozintsev, the play became "a drama of a political crime" in a state not unlike Stalin's Soviet empire;[4] while the contemporary Irish poet Seamus Heaney found in it a metaphor for the murderous politics of revenge at that moment devouring his native Ulster:

> I am Hamlet the Dane,
> skull handler, parablist,
> smeller of rot
>
> in the state, infused
> with its poisons,
> pinioned by ghosts
> and affections
>
> murders and pieties[5]

Even the major "facts" of the play—the status of the Ghost, or the real nature of Hamlet's "madness"—are seen very differently at different times. Samuel Johnson, for example, writing in the 1760s, had no doubt that the hero's "madness," a source of "much mirth" to eighteenth-century audiences, was merely "pretended," but twentieth-century Hamlets onstage, even if they were not the full-fledged neurotics invented by Freud and his disciple Ernest Jones, were likely to show some signs of actual madness. Modern readings, too, while still fascinated by the hero's intellectual and emotional complexities, are likely to emphasize those characteristics that are least compatible with the idealized "sweet prince" of the Victorians—the diseased suspicion of women, revealed in his obsession with his mother's sexuality and his needless cruelty to Ophelia, his capacity for murderous violence (he dies with the blood of five people on his hands), and his callous indifference to the killing of such relative innocents as Polonius, Rosencrantz, and Guildenstern.

Hamlet's ability to adapt itself to the preconceptions of almost any audience, allowing the viewers, in the play's own sardonic phrase, to "botch the words up fit to their own thoughts" (4.5.12), results partly from the boldness of its design. Over the sensationalism and rough energy of a conventional revenge plot is placed a sophisticated psychological drama whose most intense action belongs to the interior world of soliloquy: Hamlet agrees to revenge his father's death at the urging of the Ghost, and thus steps into an old-fashioned revenge tragedy; but it is Hamlet's inner world, revealed to us in his soliloquies (speeches addressed not to other characters but to the audience, as if the character were thinking aloud), that equally excites our attention. It is as if two plays are occurring simultaneously.

Although *Hamlet* is often thought of as the most personal of Shakespeare's tragedies, Shakespeare did not invent the story of revenge that the play tells. The story was an ancient one, belonging originally to Norse saga. The barbaric narrative of murder and revenge—of a king killed by his brother, who then marries the dead king's widow, of the young prince who must pretend to be mad in order to save his own life, who eludes a series of traps laid for him by his wicked uncle, and who finally revenges his father's death by killing the uncle—had been elaborated in the twelfth-century *Historiae Danicae* of Saxo Grammaticus, and then polished up for sixteenth-century French readers in François de Belleforest's *Histoires Tragiques*. It was first adapted for the English theater in the late 1580s in the form of the so-called Ur-*Hamlet*, a play attributed to Thomas Kyd (unfortunately now lost) that continued to hold the stage until at least 1596; and it may well be that when Shakespeare began work on *Hamlet* about 1599, he had no more lofty intention than to polish up this slightly tarnished popular favorite. But Shakespeare's wholesale rewriting produced a *Hamlet* so utterly unlike Kyd's work that its originality was unmistakable even to playgoers familiar with Kyd's play.

The new tragedy preserved the outline of the old story, and took over Kyd's most celebrated contributions—a ghost crying for revenge, and a play-within-the-play that sinisterly mirrors the main plot; but by focusing upon the perplexed interior life of the hero, Shakespeare gave a striking twist to what had been a brutally straightforward narrative. On the levels of both revenge play and psychological drama, the play develops a preoccupation with the hidden, the secret, and the mysterious that does much to account for its air of mystery. In Maynard Mack's words, it is "a play in the interrogative mood" whose action deepens and complicates, rather than answers, the apparently casual question with which it begins, "Who's there?"[6]

"The Cheer and Comfort of Our Eye": *Hamlet* and Surveillance

The great subject of revenge drama, before *Hamlet*, was the moral problem raised by private, personal revenge: i.e., should the individual take revenge into his own hands or leave it to God? Kyd's *The Spanish Tragedy* (and, one assumes, his lost play about Hamlet as well) captured on the stage the violent contradictions of the Elizabethan attitudes toward this form of "wild justice." The surprising thing about Shakespeare's *Hamlet* is that it barely glances at the ethical argument raised by a hero's taking justice into his own hands—an argument central to *The Spanish Tragedy*. Of course, the controversy about the morality of private revenge must have provided an important context for the original performances of the play, giving an ominous force to Hamlet's fear that the spirit he has seen "may be a devil" luring him to damnation (2.2.628). But Shakespeare simply takes this context for granted, and goes on to discover a quite different kind of political interest in his plot—one that may help to explain the paranoiac anxieties it was apparently capable of arousing in a dictator like Stalin.

Turning away from the framework of ethical debate, Shakespeare used Saxo's story of Hamlet's pretended madness and delayed revenge to explore the brutal facts about survival in an authoritarian state. Here too the play could speak to Elizabethan experience, for we should not forget that the glorified monarchy of Queen Elizabeth I was sustained by a vigorous network of spies and informers. Indeed, one portrait of Elizabeth shows her dressed in a costume allegorically embroidered with eyes and ears, partly to advertise that her watchers and listeners were everywhere. Shakespeare's Elsinore, too—the castle governed by Claudius and home to Hamlet—is full of eyes and ears; and behind the public charade of warmth, magnanimity, and open government that King Claudius so carefully constructs, the lives of the King's subjects are exposed to merciless inquisition.

It is symbolically appropriate that the play should begin with a group of anxious watchers on the battlemented walls of the castle, for nothing and no one in Claudius's Denmark is allowed to go "unwatched": every appearance must be "sifted" or "sounded," and every secret "opened." The King himself does not hesitate to eavesdrop on the heir apparent; and his chief minister, Polonius, will meet his death lurking behind a curtain in the same squalid occupation. But they are not alone in this: the wholesale corruption of social relationships, even the most intimate, is an essential part of Shakespeare's chilling exposure of authoritarian politics. Denmark, Hamlet informs Rosencrantz and Guildenstern accurately enough, is "a prison" (2.2.262); and the treachery of these former school friends of Hamlet illustrates how much, behind the mask of uncle Claudius's concern, his court is ruled by the prison-house customs of the stool pigeon and the informer. How readily first Ophelia and then Gertrude allow themselves to become passive instruments of Polonius's and Claudius's spying upon the Prince; how easily Rosencrantz and Guildenstern are persuaded to put their friendship with Hamlet at the disposal of the state. Even Laertes's affectionate relationship with his sister is tainted by a desire to install himself as a kind of censor, a "watchman" to the fortress of her heart (1.3.50). In this he is all too like his father, Polonius, who makes himself an interiorized Big Brother, engraving his cautious precepts on Laertes's memory (1.3.65 ff.) and telling Ophelia precisely what she is permitted to think and feel:

OPHELIA
I do not know, my lord, what I should think.
POLONIUS
Marry, I will teach you. Think yourself a baby. . . .
(1.3.113–14)

Polonius is the perfect inhabitant of this court: busily policing his children's sexuality, he has no scruple about prostituting his daughter in the interests of state security, for beneath his air of senile wordiness and fatherly anxiousness lies an ingrained cynicism that allows him both to spy on his son's imagined "drabbing" in Paris and to "loose" his daughter as a sexual decoy to entrap the Prince.

Hamlet's role as hero at once sets him apart from this prison-house world and yet leads him to become increasingly entangled in its web of surveillance. To the admiring Ophelia, Hamlet remains "Th' observed of all observers" (3.1.168), but his obvious alienation has resulted in his being "observed" in a much more sinister sense. He is introduced in Act 1, scene 2, as a mysteriously taciturn watcher and listener whose glowering silence calls into question the pomp and bustle of the King's wordy show, just as his mourning blacks cast suspicion on the showy costumes of the court. Yet he himself, we are quickly made to realize, is the object of a dangerously inquisitive stare—what the King smoothly calls "the cheer and comfort of our eye" (1.2.120).

The full meaning of that silky phrase will be disclosed on Claudius's next appearance, when, after Hamlet has met the Ghost and has begun to appear mad, Claudius engages Rosencrantz and Guildenstern to probe his nephew's threatening transformation (2.2.1–18). "Madness in great ones," the King insists, "must not unwatched go" (3.1.203):

> There's something in his soul
> O'er which his melancholy sits on brood,
> And I do doubt the hatch and the disclose
> Will be some danger.   (3.1.178–81)

But of course Hamlet's madness is as much disguise as it is revelation; and while the Prince is the most ruthlessly observed character in the play, he is also its most unremitting observer. Forced to master his opponent's craft of smiling villainy, he becomes not merely an actor but also a dramatist, ingeniously using a troupe of traveling players, with their "murder in jest," to unmask the King's own hypocritical "show."

The scene in which the Players present *The Murder of Gonzago*, the play that Hamlet calls "The Mousetrap," brings the drama of surveillance to its climax. We in the audience become participants in the drama's claustrophobic economy of watching and listening, as our attention moves to and fro among the various groups on the stage, gauging the significance of every word, action, and reaction, sharing the obsessional gaze that Hamlet describes to Horatio:

> Observe my uncle. . . . Give him heedful note,
> For I mine eyes will rivet to his face,
> And, after, we will both our judgments join
> In censure of his seeming.   (3.2.85–92)

"The Mousetrap" twice reenacts Claudius's murder of his brother—first in the dumb show and then in the play proper—drawing out the effect so exquisitely that the King's enraged interruption produces an extraordinary discharge of tension. An audience caught up in Hamlet's wild excitement is easily blinded to the fact that this seeming climax is, in terms of the revenge plot, at least, a violent anticlimax. Kyd's *Spanish Tragedy* had developed the play-within-the-play as a perfect vehicle for the ironies of revenge, allowing the hero to take his actual revenge in the very act of staging the villain's original crime. Hamlet's play, however, does not even make public Claudius's forbidden story. Indeed, while it serves to confirm the truth of what the Ghost has said, the only practical effect of the Prince's theatrical triumph is to hand the initiative decisively to Claudius. In the scenes that follow, Hamlet shows himself capable of both instinctive violence and of cold-blooded calculation, but his behavior is purely reactive. Otherwise he seems oddly paralyzed by his success—a condition displayed in the prayer scene (3.3.77–101) where he stands behind the kneeling Claudius with drawn sword, "neutral to his will and matter," uncannily resembling the frozen revenger described in the First Player's speech about Pyrrhus standing over old Priam (2.2.493 ff.). All Hamlet can do is attempt to duplicate the triumph of "The Mousetrap" in his confrontation with Gertrude by holding up to her yet another verbal mirror, in which she is forced to gaze in horror on her "inmost part" (3.4.25).

Hamlet's sudden loss of direction after the "Mousetrap" scene lasts through the fourth act of the play until he returns from his sea voyage in that mysteriously altered mood on which most commentators remark—a kind of fatalism that makes him the largely passive servant of a plot that he now does little to advance or impede. It is as if the springing of the "Mousetrap" leaves Hamlet with nowhere to go—primarily because it leaves him with nothing to say. But from the very beginning, his struggle with Claudius has been conceived as a struggle for the control of language—a battle to determine what can and cannot be uttered.

Speaking the Unspeakable:
Hamlet and Memory

If surveillance is one prop of the authoritarian state, the other is its militant regulation of speech. As Claudius flatters the court into mute complicity with his theft of both the throne and his dead brother's wife, he genially insists "You cannot speak of reason to the Dane / And lose your voice" (1.2.44–45); but an iron wall of silence encloses the inhabitants of his courtly prison. While the flow of royal eloquence muffles inconvenient truths, ears here are "fortified" against dangerous stories (1.1.38) and lips sealed against careless confession: "Give thy thoughts no tongue," Polonius advises Laertes, "... Give every man thy ear, but few thy voice ... reserve thy judgment" (1.3.65–75). Hamlet's insistent warnings to his fellow watchers on the battlements "Never to speak of this that you have seen" (1.5.174) urge the same caution: "Let it be tenable in your silence still ... Give it an understanding but no tongue" (1.2.269–71). What for them is merely common prudence, however, is for the hero an absolute prohibition and an intolerable burden: "... break, my heart, for I must hold my tongue" (1.2.164).

Hamlet has only two ways of rupturing this enforced silence. The "pregnant" wordplay of his "mad" satire, as Polonius uneasily recognizes (2.2.226–27), is one way, but it amounts to no more than inconclusive verbal fencing. Soliloquy is a more powerful resource because, since it is heard by no one (except the audience), its impenetrable privacy defines Hamlet's independence from the corrupt public world. From his first big speech in the play, he has made such hiddenness the badge of his resistance to the King and Queen: "I have that within which passes show" (1.2.88), he announces. What is at issue here is not simply a contrast between hypocrisy and true grief over the loss of his king and father: rather, Hamlet grounds his very claim to integrity upon a notion that true feeling can never be expressed: it is only "that . . . which *passes show*" that can escape the taint of hypocrisy, of "acting." It is as if, in this world of remorseless observation, the self can survive only as a ferociously defended secret, something treasured for the very fact of its hiddenness and impenetrability. Unlike Gertrude, unlike Ophelia, unlike those absorbent "sponges" Rosencrantz and Guildenstern, Hamlet must insist he is not made of "penetrable stuff."

If Hamlet's "antic disposition" is the guardian of his rebellious inwardness, soliloquy is where this inwardness lives, a domain which (if we except Claudius's occasional flickers of conscience) no other character is allowed to inhabit. Hamlet's soliloquies bulk so large in our response to the play because they not only guarantee the existence of the hero's secret inner life; they also, by their relentless self-questioning, imply the presence of still more profoundly secret truths "hid . . . within the center" (2.2.170–71): "I *do not know* / Why yet I live to say 'This thing's to do,' / Sith I have cause, and will, and strength, and means / To do 't" (4.4.46–49). The soliloquies are the focus of the play's preoccupation with speaking and silence. Hamlet is set apart from those around him by his access to this region of private utterance: in it he can, as it were, "be bounded in a nutshell and count [himself] a king of infinite space" (2.2.273–74).

Yet there is a paradox here: the isolation of soliloquy is at once his special strength and the source of peculiar anguish. It saves him from the fate of Ophelia, who becomes "Divided from herself and her fair judgment" (4.5.92) by her grief at Polonius's death and hasty burial; accustomed to speak only in the voice that others allow her, dutifully resolved to "think nothing, my lord" (3.2.124), she is left with no language other than the disconnected fragments of her madness to express outrage at a murder which authority seems determined to conceal. Hamlet, by contrast, finds in soliloquy an arena where the unspeakable can be uttered. But the very fact that these are words that others do not hear also makes soliloquy a realm of noncommunication, of frustrating silence—a prison as well as a fortress in which the speaker beats his head unavailingly against the walls of his own cell. Thus the soliloquy that ends Act 2 reproaches itself for a kind of speechlessness—the mute ineffectuality of a "John-a-dreams," who, unlike the Player, "can *say* nothing"—and at the same time mocks itself as a torrent of empty language, a mere unpacking of the heart with words (2.2.593–616). For all their eloquence, the soliloquies serve in the end only to increase the tension generated by the pressure of forbidden utterance.

It is from this pressure that the first three acts of the play derive most of their extraordinary energy; and the energy is given a concrete dramatic presence in the form of the Ghost. The appearance of a ghost demanding vengeance was a stock device borrowed from the Roman playwright Seneca; and the Ur-*Hamlet* had been notorious for its ghost, shrieking like an oysterwife, "Hamlet, revenge!" But the strikingly unconventional thing about Shakespeare's Ghost is its melancholy preoccupation with the silenced past and its plangent cry of "Remember me" (1.5.98), which makes remembrance seem more important than revenge. "The struggle of humanity against power," the Czech novelist Milan Kundera has written, "is the struggle of memory against forgetfulness"; and this Ghost, which stands for all that has been erased by the bland narratives of King Claudius, is consumed by the longing to speak that which power has rendered unspeakable. The effect of the Ghost's narrative upon Hamlet is to infuse him with the same desire; indeed, once he has formally inscribed its watchword—"Remember me"— on the tables of his memory, he is as if possessed by the Ghost, seeming to mime its speechless torment when he appears to Ophelia, looking "As if he had been loosèd out of hell / To speak of horrors" (2.1.93–94).

For all its pathos of silenced longing, the Ghost remains profoundly ambivalent, and not just because Elizabethans held such contradictory beliefs about ghosts.[7] The ambivalence is dramatized in a particularly disturbing detail: as the Ghost pours his story into Hamlet's ear (the gesture highlighted by the Ghost's incantatory repetition of "hear" and "ear"), we become aware of an uncanny parallel between the Ghost's act of narration and the murder the Ghost tells about:

> 'Tis given out that, sleeping in my orchard,
> A serpent stung me. So the whole ear of Denmark
> Is by a forgèd process of my death
> Rankly abused. . . .
> Upon my secure hour thy uncle stole
> With juice of cursèd hebona in a vial
> And in the porches of my ears did pour
> The leprous distilment. . . .   (1.5.42–71)

If Claudius's propaganda has abused "the whole ear of Denmark" like a second poisoning, the Ghost's own story enters Hamlet's "ears of flesh and blood" (line 28) like yet another corrosive. The fact that it is a story that demands telling, and that its narrator is "an honest ghost," cannot alter the fact that it will work away in Hamlet's being like secret venom until he in turn can vent it in revenge.

The "Mousetrap" play is at once a fulfillment and an escape from that compulsion. It gives, in a sense, a public voice to the Ghost's silenced story. But it is only a metaphoric revenge. Speaking daggers and poison but using none, Hamlet turns out only to have written his own inability to bring matters to an end. It is no coincidence, then, that he should foresee the conclusion of his own tragedy as being the product of someone else's script: "There's a divinity that shapes our ends, / Rough-hew them how we will" (5.2.11–12).

"To Tell My Story": Unfinished *Hamlet*

In the last scene of the play, the sense that Hamlet's story has been shaped by Providence—or by a playwright other than Hamlet—is very strong: the swordplay with Laertes is a theatrical imitation of dueling that becomes the real thing, sweetly knitting up the paralyzing disjunction between action and acting; at the same time, revenge is symmetrically perfected in the spectacle of Claudius choking on "a poison tempered by himself," Laertes "justly killed with his own treachery," and the Queen destroyed in the vicious pun that has her poisoned by Claudius's "union." Yet Hamlet's consoling fatalism does not survive the final slaughter. Instead, he faces his end tormented by a sense of incompleteness, of a story still remaining to be told:

> You that look pale and tremble at this chance,
> That are but mutes or audience to this act,
> Had I but time (as this fell sergeant, Death,
> Is strict in his arrest), O, I could tell you—
> But let it be.   (5.2.366–70)

Within a few lines Hamlet's distinctive voice, which has dominated his own tragedy like that of no other Shakespearean hero, will be cut off in midsentence by the arrest of death—and "the rest is silence" (5.2.395).

The play is full of such unfinished, untold, or perhaps even untellable tales, from Barnardo's interrupted story of the Ghost's first appearance to the Player's unfinished rendition of "Aeneas' tale to Dido" and the violently curtailed performance of *The Murder of Gonzago*. In the opening scene the Ghost itself is cut off, before it can speak, by the crowing of a cock; and when it returns and speaks to Hamlet, it speaks first about a story it cannot tell:

> But that I am forbid
> To tell the secrets of my prison house,
> I could a tale unfold whose lightest word
> Would harrow up thy soul, freeze thy
>   young blood . . .   (1.5.18–21)

Even the tale it *is* permitted to unfold is, ironically, one of murderous interruption and terrible incompleteness:

> *Cut off*, even in the blossoms of my sin,
> Unhouseled, disappointed, unaneled,
> No reck'ning made, but sent to my account
> With all my *imperfections* on my head.
>   (1.5.83–86)

Act 5 at last produces the formal reckoning of this imperfect account, yet it leaves Hamlet once again echoing the Ghost's agony of frustrated utterance.

But what, we might ask, can there be left to tell, beyond what we have already seen and heard? It seems to be part of the point, a last reminder of Hamlet's elusive "mystery," that we shall never know. The Prince has, of course, insisted that Horatio remain behind "to tell my story"; but the inadequacy of Horatio's response only intensifies the sense of incompleteness. All that his stolid imagination can offer is that bald plot summary of "accidental judgments [and] casual slaughters," which, as Anne Barton protests, leaves out "everything that seems important" about the play and its protagonist.[8] Nor is Fortinbras's attempt to make "The soldier's music and the rite of war / Speak loudly for [Hamlet]" (5.2.445–46) any more satisfactory, for the military strongman's cannon are no better tuned to speak for Hamlet than the player's pipe.

It would be a mistake, of course, to underestimate the dramatic significance of Horatio's story or of the "music and the rite of war"—these last gestures of ritual consolation—especially in a play where, beginning with the obscene confusion of Claudius's "mirth in funeral" and including Polonius's "hugger-mugger" interment and Ophelia's "maimed rites," we have seen the dead repeatedly degraded by the slighting of their funeral pomps. In this context it matters profoundly that Hamlet alone is accorded the full dignity of obsequies suited to his rank, for it signals his triumph over the oblivion to which Claudius is fittingly consigned, and, in its gesture back toward Hamlet's story as Shakespeare has told it (so much better than Horatio does), it brings Hamlet's story to a heroic end.

"The Undiscovered Country":
Hamlet and the Secrets of Death

How we respond to the ending of *Hamlet*—both as revenge drama and as psychological study—depends in part on how we respond to yet a third level of the play—that is, to *Hamlet* as a prolonged meditation on death. The play is virtually framed by two encounters with the dead: at one end is the Ghost, at the other a pile of freshly excavated skulls. The skulls (all but one) are nameless and silent; the Ghost has an identity (though a "questionable" one) and a voice; yet they are more alike than might at first seem. For this ghost, though invulnerable "as the air," is described as a "dead corse," a "ghost . . . come from the grave," its appearance suggesting a grotesque disinterment of the buried king (1.4.52–57; 1.5.139). The skulls for their part may be silent, but Hamlet plays upon each to draw out its own "excellent voice" ("That skull had a tongue in it and could sing once"; 5.1.77–78), just as he engineered that "miraculous organ" of the Ghost's utterance, the "Mousetrap."

There is a difference, however: Hamlet's dressing up the skulls with shreds of narrative ("as if 'twere Cain's jawbone . . . This might be the pate of a politician . . . or of a courtier . . . Why may not that be the skull of a lawyer"; 5.1.78–101) only serves to emphasize their mocking anonymity, until the Gravedigger offers to endow one with a precise historical identity: "This same skull . . . was . . . Yorick's skull, the King's jester" (5.1.186–87). Hamlet is delighted: now memory can begin its work of loving resurrection. But how does the Gravedigger *know?* The answer is that of course he cannot; and try as Hamlet may to cover this bare bone with the flesh of nostalgic recollection, he cannot escape the wickedly punning reminder of "this *same* skull" that all skulls indeed look frightfully the same. Ironically, even Yorick's distinctive trademark, his grin, has become indistinguishable from the mocking leer of that grand jester of the *Danse Macabre*, Death the Antic: "Where be your gibes now? . . . Not one now to mock your own grinning?"; so that even as he holds it, the skull's identity appears to drain away into the anonymous *memento mori* sent to adorn "my lady's" dressing table. It might as well be Alexander the Great's; or Caesar's; or anyone's. It might as well be what it will one day become—a handful of clay, fit to stop a beer barrel.

It is significant that (with the trivial exception of 4.4) the graveyard scene is the only one to take place outside the confines of Claudius's castle-prison. As the "common" place to which all stories lead, the graveyard both *invites* narrative and *silences* it. Each blank skull at once poses and confounds the question with which the tragedy itself began, "Who's there?," subsuming all human differences in awful likeness: "As you are now," goes the tombstone verse, "so once was I / As I am now, so shall you be." In the graveyard all stories collapse into one reductive history ("Alexander died, Alexander was buried, Alexander returneth to dust"; 5.1.216–17). In this sense the Gravedigger is the mocking counterpart of the Player: and the houses of oblivion that gravediggers make challenge the players' memorial art by lasting "till doomsday" (5.1.61). Hamlet shares with the Gravedigger the same easy good-fellowship he extends to the play's other great outsider, the First Player; but the Gravedigger asserts a more sinister kind of intimacy with his claim to have begun his work "that very day that young Hamlet was born" (5.1.152–53). In this moment he identifies himself as the Prince's mortal double, the Sexton Death from the *Danse Macabre* who has been preparing him a grave from the moment of birth.

If there is a final secret to be revealed, then, about that "undiscovered country" on which Hamlet's imagination broods, it is perhaps only the Gravedigger's spade that can uncover it. For his digging lays bare the one thing we can say for certain lies hidden "within" the mortal show of the flesh—the emblems of Death himself, that *Doppelgänger* who shadows each of us as the mysterious Lamord (*La Mort*) shadows Laertes. If there is a better story, one that would confer on the rough matter of life the consolations of form and significance, it is, the play tells us, one that cannot finally be told; for it exists on the other side of language, to be tantalizingly glimpsed only at the point when Hamlet is about to enter the domain of the inexpressible. The great and frustrating achievement of this play, its most ingenious and tormenting trick, the source of its endlessly belabored mystery, is to persuade us that such a story might exist, while demonstrating its irreducible hiddenness. The only story Hamlet is given is that of a hoary old revenge tragedy, which he persuades himself (and us) can never denote him truly; but it is a narrative frame that nothing (not even inaction) will allow him to escape. The story of our lives, the play wryly acknowledges, is always the wrong story; but the rest, after all, is silence.

———

1. Dmitri Shostakovich, *Testimony: The Memoirs of Dmitri Shostakovich*, as related to and edited by Solomon Volkow, trans. Antonina W. Bouis (London: Faber, 1981), p. 84.

2. See F. E. Halliday, *A Shakespeare Companion, 1564–1964* (Harmondsworth: Penguin, 1964), pp. 435, 209; see also pp. 262 and 403.

3. The most lucid guide to this critical labyrinth, though he deals with no work later than 1960, is probably still Morris Weitz, *Hamlet and the Philosophy of Literary Criticism* (London: Faber, 1964).

4. Jan Kott, *Shakespeare Our Contemporary* (London: Methuen, 1964).

5. Excerpt from "Viking Dublin: Trial Pieces" from *Poems, 1965–1975* by Seamus Heaney. Copyright © 1975, 1980 by Seamus Heaney. Reprinted by permission of Farrar, Straus and Giroux, Inc. Permission for use of these lines from *North* by Seamus Heaney, published by Faber and Faber Limited, is also acknowledged.

6. See Mack's classic essay, "The World of *Hamlet*," *Yale Review* 41 (1952): 502–23; Mack's approach is significantly extended in Harry Levin's *The Question of Hamlet* (New York: Oxford University Press, 1959).

7. The most balanced treatment of this and other contentious historical issues in the play is in Roland M. Frye, *The Renaissance Hamlet* (Princeton: Princeton University Press, 1984).

8. Introduction to T. J. B. Spencer, ed., *Hamlet* (Harmondsworth: Penguin, 1980), p. 52. See also James L. Calderwood's *To Be and Not To Be: Negation and Metadrama in "Hamlet"* (New York: Columbia University Press, 1983).

Further Reading

Hamlet

Belsey, Catherine. "Shakespeare's Sad Tale for Winter: *Hamlet* and the Tradition of Fireside Ghost Stories." *Shakespeare Quarterly* 61 (2010): 1–27.

At the heart of Belsey's essay is the question of "textual strategies": "[N]ot what the Elizabethans made of ghosts, so much as the matter out of which they made their ghost *stories*." Looking closely at the suspenseful manner in which Shakespeare opens *Hamlet*—particularly his depiction of a ghost so different from the specters who were "conventionally bloodcurdling but not eerie"—Belsey asks whether this emphasis on "deepening mystery" and mounting unease, "hovering between disbelief and fear," was Shakespeare's invention or an example of his indebtedness to other influences that "relished the uncanny." Whereas critics interested in exploring the antecedents of *Hamlet*'s Ghost have focused on either the influence of Senecan spirits or the ghost lore informing purgatorial narratives, Belsey investigates the popular narrative tradition of fireside ghost stories, old wives' tales, and winter's tales. Her close attention to the medieval legend called "The Three Living and the Three Dead"—the story of an unnerving encounter between three extravagantly attired, pleasure-seeking kings and the emaciated, terrifying corpses of three dead kings—and to its visual/narrative afterlife in the fourteenth, fifteenth, and sixteenth centuries reveals several similarities between the Ghost in *Hamlet* and the walking dead of the variously rendered legend: the revenant's corporeality, capacity to provoke fear, desire to be addressed, demands on the living, and questionable identity (possibly demoniacal in nature). Tales of wandering corpses of popular imagination "testify to a tradition of winter's tales that foreground the uncanny, the component that is so conspicuously missing from the early modern stage convention derived from Seneca," but so palpable in Act 1 of *Hamlet*. "With an intensity unique among Shakespeare's tragedies," the play engages mortality in various forms ("bereavement, murder, military heroics, disintegration in the grave, [and] the fear of damnation") and ends with an acknowledgment of the inevitability of death. But it begins by raising such issues "in the most theatrical of modes: a winter's tale of an unquiet spirit walking the earth with a deadly mission for the living hero."

Calderwood, James L. *To Be and Not to Be: Negation and Metadrama in "Hamlet."* New York: Columbia University Press, 1983.

Calderwood begins his highly original approach to *Hamlet*, as do many critics, by setting Hamlet between Fortinbras and Laertes. Fortinbras, who, like Hamlet, shares a name with his father, initially defines himself as the son of his father in seeking revenge through a projected attack on Denmark, but then is persuaded to set aside revenge and instead achieve his own identity through a military conquest in Poland, quite unrelated to his father. In contrast, Laertes never escapes the role of son, accepting, after the loss of his father, the paternal domination of Claudius. Hamlet, were he to adopt his father's cause, as Laertes does, would have to betray himself, like Laertes; to remain true to himself, undefiled by taking action in a corrupt world, he would have to betray his father, as Fortinbras might be said to have done, although Fortinbras does indeed take action. In the middle of the play, when Hamlet seems arrested between these two undesirable alternatives, his "identity grows complex not by multiplying relationships but by multiplying disrelationships," self-determination by negation, as "his roaming and irresolute *self* takes priority over the revenge-minded *son*" (italics added). Shakespeare metadramatically calls such attention to the hiatus between Hamlet's vow of revenge (Act 1) and fulfillment of it (Act 5) as a way of differentiating his play from conventional revenge tragedy "with its built-in hiatus [see *The Spanish Tragedy,* below] . . . usually obscured." It is only with "the return to Elsinore after the sea-voyage . . . [that] Hamlet begins to acquiesce to the dramatic context [of revenge tragedy] rather than trying to dominate and transcend it." Finally, though, "Hamlet kills Claudius . . . not for his father, but for himself, . . . in direct retaliation for the attack on his own life." After proposing this interpretation, Calderwood goes on to "suggest some of the ways in which the play resists positive interpretation, especially by its employment of the negative mode." After also detailing the role of mediation in the play, he returns at the end to champion interpretation in the face of the threat to it posed by deconstruction.

Charnes, Linda. "The Hamlet Formerly Known as Prince." In *Shakespeare and Modernity: Early Modern to Millennium,* edited by Hugh Grady, pp. 189–219. Accents on Shakespeare. London: Routledge, 2000. (The essay also appears as Chapter 5 in Charnes's *Hamlet's Heirs: Shakespeare and the Politics of a New Millennium* [London: Routledge, 2006].)

Seeking an explanation for the "unmatched boom" in American mass media *Hamlet*s of the last decade of the twentieth century, Charnes uses the "prerogatives of patriarchy and monarchy" to shed light on the titular figure's "startling" link with contemporary America, where the political and ideological touchstones of Shakespeare's England have become "increasingly subsumed into and even transmogrified by the operations of an ideologically democratic nation." She contends that Hamlet's failure to inherit and refusal to seek his royal patrimony, the throne of Denmark, hold the key to his becoming the "unofficial legislator of late-twentieth-century democratic man—the man who would and would not be king." Central to her argument are the plot's "invoked and then forgotten" initial paternal crime (the "whisper" recounted by Horatio of Old Hamlet's and Old Norway's refusals to will entailed property to their respective sons [1.1.92–107]) and the command of the Ghost that Hamlet revenge and remember but not replace him as king (1.5.31, 98). Called to enact his father's will "without succeeding him," Prince Hamlet is robbed of substance: "An only son and first-born royal heir cannot be a once and future Prince." While Hamlet speaks cogently to post-modern America's "general dissatisfaction, nervous boredom," and penchant for "rationalized delay," the deeper connection may, surprisingly, lie in something he does not share with us: a strong sense of entitlement. "Even as we [who are not heirs apparent] demand our riches, we refuse to be held responsible for how the political system is actually run. To this extent Hamlet can certainly be regarded as a postmodern Everyman; or at least as a model of what the new American cyber-dream tells us we can all be—a virtual Prince."

Dawson, Anthony. *Hamlet: Shakespeare in Performance.* Manchester: Manchester University Press, 1995.

After considering the theatrical record spanning the years 1600–1900 (commenting specifically on the *Hamlet*s of David Garrick, Edmund Kean, Edwin Booth, and Henry Irving), Dawson provides chapter-length studies of major revivals in the twentieth century. The discussion of "old ways meet[ing] the new stagecraft" in the 1920s focuses on productions starring John Barrymore (New York [1922] and London [1925]) and the "landmark" revival by Barry Jackson and H. K. Ayliff for the Birmingham Repertory Theatre (1925), its modern-dress, "anti-Romantic" presentation becoming a staple of *Hamlet* production. The chapter on *Hamlet* in the 1930s considers John Gielgud's several portrayals of Hamlet (1930, 1934, 1936, 1939, and 1944) alongside Laurence Olivier's single stage rendering (1937); for all their differences, the two rival actors are best seen "as complementary rather than opposed." Subsequent chapters deal with postwar *Hamlet*s at Stratford-upon-Avon (Michael Benthall's 1948 version with Robert Helpmann and Paul Scofield alternating as Hamlet and Peter Hall's 1965 "anti-establishment" staging with David Warner in the title role); London revivals at the Royal Shakespeare and Royal Court in 1980 (John Barton's starring Michael Pennington and Richard Eyre's featuring Jonathan Pryce, respectively); and the afterlife of *Hamlet* on film and television (the versions of Laurence Olivier [1948], Grigori Kozintsev [1964], Franco Zeffirelli [1990, with Mel Gibson], and Rodney Bennett [BBC, 1980, with Derek Jacobi]). Recognizing that Shakespeare is "one part of an elaborate system of global interchange," Dawson devotes the final chapter to productions in Germany (Bochum, 1977; Deutsches Theater, Berlin, 1990) and the former Soviet Union (Taganka Theatre, Moscow, 1971). Commentary on Adrian Noble's 1992 revival at London's Barbican, starring Kenneth Branagh, frames this study of the reciprocity "between how the theatre gives *Hamlet* meaning and produces Hamlet's subjectivity and how the culture generally approaches problems of meaning, value, and selfhood."

Frye, Roland Mushat. *The Renaissance Hamlet: Issues and Responses in 1600*. Princeton: Princeton University Press, 1984.

Frye's object is to reconstruct "the audience responses upon which Shakespeare played" in *Hamlet* by documenting "Elizabethan frames of reference" for the issues raised in the play. Among the events and documents Frye invokes are the following: "Homily against Disobedience and Willful Rebellion," ordered read in all Anglican churches; the Wars of Religion in France that began in 1562 between Huguenots and Catholics (including *Hamlet*-like assassinations of rulers); Protestant beliefs that ghosts were demons, beliefs shared by Catholics, who also believed ghosts might be souls from purgatory; scripture, sermons, and conduct books forbidding private revenge; the obligation to revenge his father's death laid on the infant King James I by his paternal grandparents, which James tried but failed to discharge; debates over the legitimacy of tyrannicide; the unseating of Lady Jane Grey from the throne of England in 1553 by Queen Mary, recognized as the legitimate heir by virtue of being (like Hamlet) the offspring of a former king; the considerable length of the mourning observed by Henry VIII after the death of his consort Jane Seymour; the marriage in 1567 of Mary Queen of Scots to the Earl of Bothwell, widely reputed to have assassinated her former husband, Lord Darnley, only three months earlier; the depiction of Fortune and Prudence in Renaissance visual art; emblems of Mars-Mercury; the opinion of the theologian William Perkins that "the excellency, goodness, and dignity of conscience, stands not in accusing, but in excusing"; the Babington Plot of 1586 designed to replace Elizabeth I on the throne of England with Mary Queen of Scots; the popularity of skulls, including skull-shaped watches, among the fashionable in sixteenth-century

England; the fashion of *transi* as tomb effigies: beginning with "*caro vilis*, the merely lifeless corpse, . . . next came the *vermis*, with the flesh now rotting away and worms crawling in and out; . . . finally, there was the *pulvis*, either a shrunken, mummified cadaver or a skeleton"; the *danse macabre*, or Dance of Death; and biblical texts on the readiness for death.

Greenblatt, Stephen. *Hamlet in Purgatory*. Princeton: Princeton University Press, 2001.

Greenblatt examines the afterlife of purgatory—specifically, the traces of purgatory in *Hamlet*—in order to better understand how the Ghost achieves its "weird, . . . amazingly disturbing and vivid" effect. His concern is not with the "theology behind the ghost" or its provenance as either "Catholic" or "Protestant," but rather with the play's "magical intensity." In the first three chapters, the author draws on a variety of materials—religious tracts, devotional works, narrative accounts of spectral hauntings, rites of memory (i.e., prayers and masses for the dead, chantries, and indulgences), and artwork (funerary inscriptions and sculptures, paintings, and manuscript illuminations)—to investigate the rise and fall of purgatory, as both a doctrine and a profitable institution by which Christians sought to ease the passage to heaven for both themselves and their deceased loved ones. In their staging of an "ontological argument about spectrality and remembrance," early sixteenth-century texts (such as Simon Fish's *A Supplication for the Beggars* and Thomas More's *Supplication of Souls*) "unsettled the institutional moorings of a crucial body of imaginative materials and therefore made them available for theatrical appropriation." Greenblatt follows his study of the "cult" and "poetics" of purgatory with a chapter on the staging of ghosts in the Elizabethan and Jacobean theaters; the focus is on the Shakespeare canon because, of all the major Renaissance English dramatists, only Shakespeare "fully participates in the popular vogue for presenting ghosts onstage." In the chapter titled "Remember Me" (pp. 205–57), the author brings the historical and theatrical findings of the first four chapters to bear on an analysis of *Hamlet* and "literature's most famous ghost." He states that questions relating to Shakespeare's motivation for shifting the dramatic emphasis of *Hamlet* from vengeance to remembrance and for placing the command "to remember" in the mouth of a ghost are best answered "by recognizing that the psychological in Shakespeare's tragedy is constructed almost entirely out of the theological, and specifically out of the issue of remembrance that . . . lay at the heart of the crucial early-sixteenth-century debate about Purgatory," which English Protestants attacked as being not only a fraud but also a "poet's fable." This turning of "negotiations with the dead from an institutional process governed by the church to a poetic process governed by guilt, projection, and imagination," Greenblatt argues, "facilitated Shakespeare's crucial appropriation of Purgatory in *Hamlet*": a tragedy of "uncanny power," resonant with the complexity of memory and the tangle of emotions felt by the living as they engage their dead.

Kinney, Arthur, ed. *Hamlet: New Critical Essays.* Shakespeare Criticism 23. New York: Routledge, 2002.

Kinney's anthology consists of an introductory overview of the play's critical and theatrical reception and ten new essays ranging in focus from editorial and production issues to studies of race and gender dynamics. The essays are grouped under three headings: (1) "Tudor-Stuart *Hamlet*" (E. Pearlman, "Shakespeare at Work: The Invention of the Ghost"; R. A. Foakes,

"Hamlet's Neglect of Revenge"; and Philip Edwards, "The Dyer's Infected Hand: The Sonnets and the Text of *Hamlet*"); (2) "Subsequent *Hamlets*" (Paul Werstine, " 'The cause of this defect': *Hamlet*'s Editors," and Catherine Belsey, "Was Hamlet a man or a woman? The Prince in the Graveyard, 1800–1920"); and (3) "*Hamlet* after Theory" (Jerry Brotton, "Ways of Seeing *Hamlet*"; Terence Hawkes, "The Old Bill"; Ann Thompson, "*Hamlet* and the Canon"; Peter Erickson, "Can We Talk about Race in *Hamlet*?"; and Richard Levin, "Hamlet, Laertes, and the Dramatic Functions of Foils"). Kinney's introduction identifies major critical issues and problems raised in *Hamlet* scholarship: Hamlet's age, inconsistencies in the depiction of Horatio and Fortinbras, the Ghost as either purgatorial or demonic, and the play's refraction of cultural conditions and beliefs relating to melancholy, suicide, and revenge. The essay also charts critical trends from the seventeenth and eighteenth centuries through the Romantic and Victorian periods of the nineteenth century to the modern and postmodern phases of the twentieth, assesses the critical discourse that has linked the play to various ideological concerns (namely, the strands of deconstructivist readings that can be distinguished as feminist criticism, neo-Marxist criticism, New Historicism, and Cultural Materialism), and provides an overview of stage productions (from a performance said to have taken place on a voyage to the East Indies in 1607 to Mark Rylance's revival at the new Globe Theatre in London in 2000) and cinematic transformations (with particular attention to the filmed *Hamlet*s of Laurence Olivier [1948], Grigori Kozintsev [1964], Franco Zeffirelli [1990], and Kenneth Branagh [1995]). The volume underscores Kinney's claim that "there is no end to meanings in *Hamlet*, since in 'hold[ing] . . . the mirror up to nature' [3.2.23–24], to changing human nature, it is ever capable of transference and transformation. . . . Discrepant readings and discrepant productions have, since the sixteenth century, been the result."

Kott, Jan. "*Hamlet* of the Mid-Century." In *Shakespeare Our Contemporary*, pp. 57–73. London: Methuen, 1964.

For Kott, "an ideal [stage production of] *Hamlet* would be one most true to Shakespeare and most modern at the same time." The production he foregrounds took place in Cracow, Poland, shortly after the twentieth Congress of the Soviet Communist Party and made *Hamlet* "a political drama par excellence," with everyone under constant surveillance by the state—Polonius eying even his own son in Paris through his agent Reynaldo, and then watching from behind the arras the Queen with her son; the King watching Hamlet through his spies Rosencrantz and Guildenstern. Shifting to a more general level, Kott divides the roles in the *Hamlet* of the midcentury into those clearly defined by their situations and those not so defined. Among the first are Claudius and Polonius: "Claudius does not play the part of a murderer and a king. He *is* the murderer and the King. Polonius does not play the part of a despotic father and a king's councillor. He *is* the despotic father and the King's councillor." Among the second are Hamlet and Ophelia: "The situation does not define Hamlet. . . . The situation has been imposed on him. . . . He accepts the part, but is beyond and above it"; Ophelia is "an ordinary girl, who loved her boy, but has been given by the scenario of history a tragic part." At the end, Fortinbras ("the man of the strong arm"), "a vigorous young lad[,] comes, and says with a charming smile: 'Take away these corpses. Now I shall be your king.' "

Kyd, Thomas. *The Spanish Tragedy.* London, 1594.

Shakespeare may have drawn on *The Spanish Tragedy* (c. 1589) in writing *Hamlet*, for Kyd's drama includes many elements also found in Shakespeare's play: the ghost, the difficulty in verifying that the party accused of murder is indeed guilty, the resulting need for delay, the apparent madness of the avenger (however feigned or real), the play-within-the-play, and the moral perplexities facing a sensitive man called to revenge. These shared elements are handled rather differently in the two plays. Kyd's ghost is the Spaniard Don Andrea, killed in battle by the Portuguese Don Balthazar; however, Don Andrea does not visit his friend Don Horatio and impose on him an obligation to avenge his death, but enters at the beginning with the allegorical character Revenge, and the two watch the entire play, remaining aloof from the other characters. It is not, then, the death of Don Andrea that is avenged, but the murder of Don Horatio, whose avenger is his father, the Knight Marshall Hieronimo. The accusation of murder directed against Don Lorenzo and Don Balthazar by Bel-Imperia, the beloved of Don Andrea and then of Don Horatio, literally falls from the sky into Hieronimo's hands in the form of a letter written in blood. Suspecting that the letter is part of a plot to ensnare his own life, Hieronimo delays. The play-within-the-play, arranged by Hieronimo once he has verified Bel-Imperia's accusation, is the tragedy of Soliman the Turkish emperor, performed by Don Balthazar and the members of the Spanish court. In the course of it, Hieronimo, aided by Bel-Imperia, accomplishes his revenge. In spite of these differences, *The Spanish Tragedy* provides a remarkable counterpoint to *Hamlet*.

Levin, Harry. *The Question of Hamlet*. New York: Oxford University Press, 1959.

For Levin, "Hamlet is, above all, a man in a plight, a mind resisting its body's destiny, a fighter against cosmic odds." Without forgetting that *Hamlet* is an "Elizabethan dramatic production" and that it is a "vehicle for ideas," Levin takes his critical method of a close reading of the play's style and structure from the trivium—rhetoric, logic, and grammar—taught in the schools of Shakespeare's day. His first chapter, called "Interrogation" after the rhetorical trope *interrogatio*, contemplates the play as "a mystery in the . . . highly speculative sense, a rite of initiation to painful experience, an exploration of stages of consciousness which dazzle and elude the spectator 'With thoughts beyond the reaches of our souls.'" His second chapter, called "Doubt" after the *dubitatio*, in which the orator deliberates between rival options, focuses on the oppositions between Claudius and Hamlet Senior (which Hamlet in 1.2 presents in terms of the rhetorical figure *icon*, or verbal portraiture), between Ophelia and Gertrude, and between "to be" and "not to be." He concludes with the observation that *Hamlet* "never regains its lost certitudes; nor does it ever relax its movement of vacillation; but it derives new meaning out of its clash of values; and its overclouded patterns merge into a grander design." Levin's third chapter, called "Irony" after the rhetorical trope *ironia*, considers a number of different kinds of irony: "'the drye mock,'" which is a statement that "means the contrary of what it purports to say" (as when Polonius asks to take his leave of Hamlet and Hamlet replies "You cannot, sir, take from me anything that I will more willingly part withal," Hamlet's politeness barely disguising his eagerness to be free of Polonius); dramatic irony (as when the audience is aware of Hamlet's knowledge regarding Claudius's plot on his life in sending him to England, while Claudius is unaware); irony of situation (as when Hamlet, "a cunning hero," is "forced to wear the mask of stupidity," his "antic disposition"); and, finally, "cosmic irony," which "cannot resolve the incalculable contradictions between personal life and the nature of things, yet . . . can teach us to live with them."

Mack, Maynard. "The World of *Hamlet*." *Yale Review* 41 (1952): 502–23.

By "the world of *Hamlet*" Mack means "the imaginative environment that the play asks us to enter when we read it or go to see it." This world is "like our own" in some respects, "but [also] unlike our own in being perfectly, or almost perfectly, significant and coherent." Mack finds the first attribute of *Hamlet*'s world to be mysteriousness, which "is not simply a matter of missing motivations, to be expunged if only we could find the perfect clue." Among its mysteries are Hamlet's "delay, his madness, his ghost, his treatment of Polonius, or Ophelia, or his mother," and whether the play is a success or failure, whether Hamlet is "a man of exquisite moral sensibility . . . or an egomaniac." A second attribute of *Hamlet*'s world is its interrogative mood ("To be or not to be—that is the question"; "What should such fellows as I do crawling between earth and heaven?") and its riddles, as, for example, Hamlet's madness: "How much is real? How much is feigned? What does it mean?" In connection with this interrogative mood, Mack also contemplates "the problematic nature of reality and the relation of reality to appearance." Behind the "glittering surface of Claudius's court" may lie murder, adultery, and incest, at least according to an apparition, the Ghost. Or, in 3.3, Hamlet comes upon Claudius, who appears to be praying; but after Hamlet accepts this appearance for reality, we learn that Claudius was unable to pray. The third attribute of *Hamlet*'s world is a "powerful sense of mortality . . . conveyed . . . in three ways": "the failure in man [as] time qualifies everything . . . including love, including purpose," "the emphasis on infection" and poison, and "a profound consciousness of loss." It is in this world that Hamlet is required to take revenge, an act, "though retributive justice, . . . that necessarily involves the doer in the general guilt."

McCoy, Richard C. "A Wedding and Four Funerals: Conjunction and Commemoration in *Hamlet*." *Shakespeare Survey* 54 (2001): 122–39

McCoy examines the play's four funerals (King Hamlet's expedited obsequies, Polonius's "huggermugger" burial [4.5.91], Ophelia's "maimèd rites" [5.1.226], and the "somewhat incongruous" soldier's funeral for Prince Hamlet) in the context of the ambiguity ("liturgical double-bookkeeping") that marked the Elizabethan compromise over Catholic-Protestant funerary practices and intercessory rituals for the deceased. Informing the discussion is the doctrine known as "the King's Two Bodies" (i.e., the Body natural and the Body politic), specifically the efforts of the "cult of Elizabeth" to continue what has been called "the migration of the holy" begun by Henry VIII's reforms in which " 'the socially integrative powers of the host' were transferred 'to the rituals of monarchy and secular community,' " a shifting from the eucharistic real presence to the royal presence. McCoy focuses on the closet scene (3.4) and the final episode (5.2) to argue that in the first, Hamlet desires a "regal apotheosis," a supernatural conjoining of the king's two bodies ("form and cause" [3.4.143]) that would recover sacramentally the royal presence. In the second, and more powerful, conjunction, Hamlet "supplants the ghost[,] acquir[ing] some of its uncanny powers." In asking Horatio to tell his story, Hamlet not only reprises the paternal imperative "Remember me" but also appears to want the conjoining of his own "form and cause"; the final act thus "sustains the kind of conjunction described by [the theologian] Richard Hooker, making Hamlet 'a *presence of force and efficacie* throughout all generations of men.' " Fortinbras may assert his own "rights of memory in this kingdom" (5.2.432) and order "rite[s] of war" (445) in honor of the dead prince, but Hamlet's "rights of memory" are "powerfully vindicated" by the play's conclusion. He, not Fortinbras, dominates modern memory. Like the venerated tomb of Elizabeth (circulating pictures of which, along with other memorial objects, invested commemoration with a degree of intercessory power), the conjunctions in *Hamlet* "permit contact with things absent even if they do not make them a real presence," thereby demonstrating how "relationships with the living and the dead, with the actual and the imaginary, are . . . inescapable—and the source of much that matters in literature and in life." Reformation rites and "rights of memory," McCoy argues, enjoyed a greater resilience and efficacy than is generally thought.

Mowat, Barbara. "The Form of *Hamlet*'s Fortunes." *Renaissance Drama* 19 (1988): 97–126.

Mowat engages the view of 1980s editors of *Hamlet* who represent the tradition of editing the play as monolithic. According to such editors, their predecessors uniformly conflated (combined into a composite) the texts of the Second Quarto (Q2 1604–5) and the Folio (F 1623). These 1980s editors react against this imagined tradition by omitting from their editions a great many of the passages unique to Q2. Mowat notes that the *Hamlet* editorial tradition can be characterized as monolithic only in the period 1866–1980, during which the Cambridge edition (1866), produced by W. Aldis Wright and W. G. Clark, exercised, for reasons we cannot now entirely recover, enormous influence on succeeding editors and thereby fixed in place a text of the play. Reviewing the earlier editorial tradition, Mowat finds no uniform practice of conflation of Q2 and F. The play's first editor, Nicholas Rowe, evidently compared in detail the 1676 quarto (Q1676, based on Q2) with the Fourth Folio (F4, based on F); he included in his edition all passages peculiar to F4, but was highly selective in admitting passages unique to Q1676. Alexander Pope, Rowe's immediate successor, based his edition on Rowe's but consulted Q2; Pope not only included yet more Q2-only passages but also cut some F-only passages. The play's next editor, Lewis Theobald, basing his edition on Pope's, left out still more F-only lines and added still more Q2-only ones. Edward Capell's edition of 1768, Mowat notes, was reputed by some twentieth-century experts to have initiated a reliance on Q2 (although only as conflated with F, as in the 1866 Cambridge edition) that would later characterize twentieth-century editing of *Hamlet*, beginning with J. Dover Wilson's 1934 New Shakespeare edition. However, Mowat finds Capell by no means stable in his preference for Q2. Capell's successors (up to the 1866 Cambridge editors) provide their readers with an ever-changing text of *Hamlet* in their inclusion and exclusion of Q2- and F-only passages and in their preference for the readings of individual words in Q2 and F. Thus the 1980s editors in their reaction against the 1866 Cambridge text of *Hamlet* return the editorial tradition to its customary state—instability.

Neely, Carol Thomas. " 'Documents in Madness': Reading Madness and Gender in Shakespeare's Tragedies and Early Modern Culture." *Shakespeare Quarterly* 42 (1991): 315–38.

Making reference to Hamlet's feigned and Ophelia's real madness, as well as madness in *Macbeth* and *King Lear*, Neely sets out "to begin to examine why, how, and with what consequences madness was read and represented in England in the early modern period by focusing on how representations of madness in Shakespeare's tragedies function within cultural contexts." To establish such contexts, Neely consults a number of contemporary texts: Edward Jorden's treatise on hysteria, *The Suffocation of the Mother*; Timothy Bright's *Treatise of Melancholy*; Reginald Scot's *Discouerie of Witchcraft*; Samuel Harsnett's *Declaration of Egregious Popish Impostures;* and the records of the physician Richard Napier from 1598 to 1624 as presented by Michael MacDonald in his *Mystical Bedlam: Madness, Anxiety, and Healing in Seventeenth-Century England.* All these works witness the English Renaissance's distinguishing of human madness from the supernatural (demonic or divine possession), the spiritual (sin, guilt, doubt), and witchcraft and bewitchment, and understand madness instead in secular and medical terms. The representation of madness in the secular context of the stage in such plays as *Hamlet* participates in this larger cultural shift. In *Hamlet* itself, Neely observes how madness is gendered, with only Ophelia's madness somatized and eroticized, while Hamlet's feigned madness is "fashionably introspective and melancholy," its implications read as political. Neely notes that the language of what we are to take for actual madness on the stage is marked by fragmentation, obsession, and repetition, which, although prominent in Ophelia's lines in the fourth act, are to be found in Hamlet's speeches only directly after his first encounter with the Ghost in 1.5.

Schleiner, Louise. "Latinized Greek Drama in Shakespeare's Writing of *Hamlet.*" *Shakespeare Quarterly* 41 (1990): 29–48.

Schleiner proposes that Aeschylus's *Oresteia* and Euripides' *Orestes* possibly influenced Shakespeare's *Hamlet.* Though scholars have generally thought that Shakespeare read relatively little Greek, Schleiner claims he may have had access to the two Greek plays through Latin translations and a pair of now-lost

English plays of 1599 titled *Agamemnon* and *Orestes' Furies*. In particular, Schleiner detects the possible influence of the graveyard and matricide scenes of the *Choephori* (*Libation Bearers*) in Aeschylus' *Oresteia* on *Hamlet*'s churchyard scene (5.1), for which there is no precedent in the play's known sources and analogues. She also notes similarities in the roles of Horatio and Pylades (in both Aeschylus and Euripides). Even if Shakespeare did not read the Latin translations of these Greek plays himself, he could have learned of them from such fellow playwrights as Ben Jonson, John Marston, George Chapman, or Thomas Dekker, all of whom adapted Latin texts. Among the details shared by *Hamlet* and the Latinized Greek texts are the emergence from concealment of a pair of young men (Hamlet and Horatio in 5.1, Orestes and Pylades) to confront mourners, and the validation provided by a male friend (Horatio for Hamlet in 5.1, Pylades for Orestes) for the killing of a relative (Claudius by Hamlet, Clytemnestra—his mother—by Orestes). Schleiner concludes her discussion by invoking Julia Kristeva's theory of intertextuality or "transposition" to analyze the relations of the Greek plays to *Hamlet*.

Shakespeare Quarterly 62.2 (Summer 2011).

This issue of *Shakespeare Quarterly* consists of nine entries on *Hamlet* under the headings "Positions," "Articles," and "Horatio Cluster." In the first section, Lee Edelman ("Against Survival: Queerness in a Time That's Out of Joint"), Carla Freccero ("Forget *Hamlet*"), and Kathryn Schwarz ("*Hamlet* without Us") examine the play in light of the work of Jacques Derrida, specifically his notions of spectral haunting, "archive," and "fratriarchy." Bernice W. Kliman's article "All at Sea about *Hamlet* at Sea" claims that the frequently cited record of performances of *Hamlet* off the coast of Africa in 1607 is most likely a forgery by John Payne Collier and should no longer be included in accounts of the play's performance history. Elizabeth Hanson's "Fellow Students: Hamlet, Horatio, and the Early Modern University" examines Prince Hamlet's friendship with the poor scholar Horatio, both students at the University of Wittenberg, finding it "emblematic of the uneasy interpenetration of nobility and the clerical culture of the universities in sixteenth-century England." In " 'Caviare to the general'? Taste, Hearing, and Genre in *Hamlet*," Allison Kay Deutermann attends to an overlooked "crucial aspect of the play's interest in audition—its intervention in a turn-of-the-century contest over how plays should sound, and how audiences should hear them." Hamlet's investigation of "formally specific modes of hearing" recuperates "revenge tragedy from charges of creaking irrelevance." The "Horatio Cluster" provides three readings of the lines "Horatio, thou art e'en as just a man / As e'er my conversation coped withal" (3.2.56–57). Lars Engle ("How Is Horatio Just? How Just Is Horatio?") claims that for Hamlet, being just and being conscientious derive from an ability "to take a disinterested, nonstakeholder's attitude toward what one is thinking about," a relative rather than absolute mode of moral thinking that Hamlet admires in Horatio but that he does not claim to have "with any consistency himself." In "Reading Horatio," Jonathan Crewe examines the passage as it appears in the First Quarto and the Folio; while almost identical in both versions, the lines reveal "significant variations" in their respective textual settings to yield different readings of the "same" lines. Karen Newman's "Two Lines, Three Readers: *Hamlet* TLN 1904–05" addresses the "question of male friendship and the intimacies implied in Hamlet's 'my conversation.' " After reviewing the multiple meanings of "conversation" and "coped," she contextualizes the passage by noting how Hamlet's critique of theater and his call for its reform in the lines immediately preceding explain his choice of Horatio as a co-critic in the play-within-the-play scene.

Stallybrass, Peter, Roger Chartier, J. Franklin Mowery, and Heather Wolfe. "Hamlet's Tables and the Technologies of Writing in Renaissance England." *Shakespeare Quarterly* 55 (2004): 379–419.

Beginning with the observation that "books play a prominent role in *Hamlet*," the authors suggest that the most important book in the play, "both figuratively and literally," is the book of memory, a book which Hamlet imagines as an inscribed "table" that can be wiped clean (1.5.102–11)—a "virtual table," however, requiring "the supplement of actual tables" (1.5.114–15). Philip Melanchthon's *Rhetoric* (1525) suggests that the indiscriminate collection of maxims and adages in writing tables and commonplace books could produce what is now called "information overload," something that could be prevented by the use of erasable tables. With its ten blank leaves of specially treated paper and cleaning instructions, the 1604 almanac *Writing Tables with a Kalender for xxiiii. yeeres, with sundry necessarie rules* attests to the existence of such notebooks in England by the early seventeenth century. The essay deals with characteristics of Renaissance erasable notebooks and how one wrote in them without ink under the following headings: "wax tablets," "erasable paper and asses' skin," "marketing writing tables," "purchasing, giving, and using writing tables," and "writing implements." In the final two sections of the essay, "Tables, Memory, and Erasure" and "The Tables of the Mind," the authors relate the table as an erasable technology to the erasure of memory in both

Hamlet and Sonnet 122 and argue that the opposition between "technologies of permanence and technologies of erasure" runs throughout the play. To the extent that memory itself works like a table-book—an enduring record and a surface that can be wiped clean—it implies forgetfulness as much as remembrance. "The 'Booke and Volume' in which Hamlet imagines memorializing his father's command fails to work, while the erasable tables, filled with commonplaces and jests, perform an ever-greater role within the play." As the memory of his father's ghost is attenuated after Act 3, the "trivial, fond records" of Yorick, the jester, "increasingly haunt, inhabit, and shape Hamlet." Ultimately, the ghost of Old Hamlet "suffers an even more ignominious fate than does his murderous brother: he simply fades away, erased from the tables of memory."

Weitz, Morris. *Hamlet and the Philosophy of Literary Criticism.* London: Faber, 1964.

Weitz believes that the history of criticism on *Hamlet* is so extensive and varied that an exploration of it can provide the opportunity to address "the traditional question, What is Criticism?" The first part of his book consists of a systematic exposition of the views of some major critics of *Hamlet.* These include from the twentieth century (1) A. C. Bradley, who in his *Shakespearean Tragedy* (1904) concentrates on the character Hamlet, whom he identifies as suffering from melancholy; (2) Ernest Jones, with his Freudian psychoanalytical approach in *Hamlet and Oedipus* (1949); (3) G. Wilson Knight, who in *The Wheel of Fire* (1930) offers to interpret "the inner core or essence" of *Hamlet* as "the triumph of mortality over life"; (4) T. S. Eliot, charging, in his essay "Hamlet" (1919), that the play is an artistic failure because its action is allegedly in excess of its essential emotion; (5) "Historical Critics," includ-

ing J. M. Robertson (*The Problem of "Hamlet"* [1919]),
E. E. Stoll (*Hamlet: An Historical and Comparative
Study* [1919]; *Art and Artifice in Shakespeare: A Study in
Dramatic Contrast and Illusion* [1933]; *Hamlet the Man*
[1935]), L. L. Shücking (*Character Problems in Shake-
speare's Plays* [1922]; *The Meaning of "Hamlet"* [1937];
The Baroque Character of the Elizabethan Tragic Hero
[1938]; *Shakespeare und der Tragödienstil seiner Zeit*
[1947]), Theodore Spencer (*Shakespeare and the Nature
of Man* [1942]), and Lily Bess Campbell (*Shakespeare's
Tragic Heroes: Slaves of Passion* [1930]), all of whom are
committed to the view that *Hamlet* "can be correctly
understood only in Elizabethan terms, where by 'terms'
they mean Elizabethan theatrical conditions, stage and
dramatic conventions, or philosophical, psychological,
and political ideas and ideals"; (6) Francis Fergusson,
who in *The Idea of a Theater* (1940) links *Hamlet* with
Greek tragedy and ancient ritual; (7) J. Dover Wilson
(*The Manuscript of Shakespeare's "Hamlet"* [1934]; a
1934 edition of the play in the New Shakespeare series;
What Happens in "Hamlet" [1935]), whose twin goals
are the establishment of the play's text and the eluci-
dation of its plot; (8) Caroline Spurgeon (*Shakespeare's
Imagery* [1935]) and W. H. Clemen (*The Development of
Shakespeare's Imagery* [1951]), who seek to understand
plays including *Hamlet* in terms of their dominant
imagery, that is, their similes and metaphors. Weitz
also surveys the writing of earlier critics, beginning as
early as the seventeenth century with John Dryden and
going forward with Alexander Pope, Samuel Johnson,
Samuel Taylor Coleridge, and Leo Tolstoy. In the sec-
ond part Weitz outlines what he sees as the main issues
in *Hamlet* criticism, including "Is Hamlet mad?," "Does
Hamlet vacillate?," "Is Ophelia honest, weak, in love
with Hamlet?," "Is Gertrude an adultress?," and "Why
is Hamlet tragic?," among many more.

Werstine, Paul. "The Textual Mystery of *Hamlet*." *Shakespeare Quarterly* 39 (1988): 1–26.

Werstine contemplates the differences among three of the *Hamlet* texts: the Second Quarto (Q2) of 1604–5, the Folio (F) of 1623, and the combination of the two (Q2/F) by the recent editorial tradition (see Mowat, above). He abstracts from the early printed texts (Q2 and F) a number of contrasting patterns regarding, especially, Laertes and Fortinbras, Hamlet's relations to them, and his relation to Claudius. Because of a number of cuts from 1.2 (60–62), 4.7 (77–92, 130–40), and 5.2 (119–48, 151–56), as well as a small addition to 4.5 (185–87), F provides the play a Laertes who is more attractive than his counterpart in Q2. It may therefore be appropriate, argues Werstine, that the F Hamlet explicitly identify himself with Laertes in 5.2 in a passage that is not printed in Q2. The editorial combination Q2/F obscures this pattern, for it presents a Laertes who is mocked at length by both Claudius (in 4.7) and Hamlet (in 5.2) but is nonetheless also recognized by a sympathetic Hamlet in 5.2 as pursuing a cause similar to his own. A second patterned difference between Q2 and F arises for Werstine from Q2 Hamlet's ability to maintain an advantage over Claudius until very near the end of the play by inexplicably anticipating the King's plots against him. Only the Q2 Hamlet, because of a substantial cut in that text in 2.2 (258–89), is able immediately to detect that Rosencrantz and Guildenstern are Claudius's spies without their betraying themselves to him with their speeches, as they do in F. And only the Q2 Hamlet knows of Claudius's plot to kill him in sending him to England before he boards his ship, as is revealed in a Q2-only speech by Hamlet near the end of 3.4 (225–33). In contrast the F Hamlet seems far more limited in his ability to contend with Claudius. In the combined Q2/F text it is the limited F Hamlet who appears in 2.2 and the powerfully knowledgeable one in 3.4. However, Werstine does not argue that Shakespeare must be the one who created the patterns of contrast thus abstracted from Q2 and F. Instead Werstine recognizes that his patterns fail to embrace a great many other differences between Q2 and F that can be distributed into no patterned relations at all; hence his patterns fall short of accounting for texts of Q2 and F as wholes. He therefore observes that other agents, such as theatrical adapters making cuts (as they are known to have done), could have created, perhaps accidentally, the patterns he identifies, if these patterns are not simply the products of his own critical method.

Shakespeare's Language

Abbott, E. A. *A Shakespearian Grammar.* New York: Haskell House, 1972.

This compact reference book, first published in 1870, helps with many difficulties in Shakespeare's language. It systematically accounts for a host of differences between Shakespeare's usage and sentence structure and our own.

Blake, Norman. *Shakespeare's Language: An Introduction.* New York: St. Martin's Press, 1983.

This general introduction to Elizabethan English discusses various aspects of the language of Shakespeare and his contemporaries, offering possible meanings for hundreds of ambiguous constructions.

Dobson, E. J. *English Pronunciation, 1500–1700.* 2 vols. Oxford: Clarendon Press, 1968.

This long and technical work includes chapters on

spelling (and its reformation), phonetics, stressed vowels, and consonants in early modern English.

Hope, Jonathan. *Shakespeare's Grammar.* London: Arden Shakespeare, 2003.

Commissioned as a replacement for Abbott's *Shakespearian Grammar,* Hope's book is organized in terms of the two basic parts of speech, the noun and the verb. After extensive analysis of the noun phrase and the verb phrase come briefer discussions of subjects and agents, objects, complements, and adverbials.

Houston, John. *Shakespearean Sentences: A Study in Style and Syntax.* Baton Rouge: Louisiana State University Press, 1988.

Houston studies Shakespeare's stylistic choices, considering matters such as sentence length and the relative positions of subject, verb, and direct object. Examining plays throughout the canon in a roughly chronological, developmental order, he analyzes how sentence structure is used in setting tone, in characterization, and for other dramatic purposes.

Onions, C. T. *A Shakespeare Glossary.* Oxford: Clarendon Press, 1986.

This revised edition updates Onions's standard, selective glossary of words and phrases in Shakespeare's plays that are now obsolete, archaic, or obscure.

Robinson, Randal. *Unlocking Shakespeare's Language: Help for the Teacher and Student.* Urbana, Ill.: National Council of Teachers of English and the ERIC Clearinghouse on Reading and Communication Skills, 1989.

Specifically designed for the high-school and undergraduate college teacher and student, Robinson's book addresses the problems that most often hinder present-day readers of Shakespeare. Through work with his own students, Robinson found that many readers today are particularly puzzled by such stylistic characteristics as subject-verb inversion, interrupted structures, and compression. He shows how our own colloquial language contains comparable structures, and thus helps students recognize such structures when they find them in Shakespeare's plays. This book supplies worksheets—with examples from major plays—to illuminate and remedy such problems as unusual sequences of words and the separation of related parts of sentences.

Williams, Gordon. *A Dictionary of Sexual Language and Imagery in Shakespearean and Stuart Literature.* 3 vols. London: Athlone Press, 1994.

Williams provides a comprehensive list of words to which Shakespeare, his contemporaries, and later Stuart writers gave sexual meanings. He supports his identification of these meanings by extensive quotations.

Shakespeare's Life

Baldwin, T. W. *William Shakspere's Petty School.* Urbana: University of Illinois Press, 1943.

Baldwin here investigates the theory and practice of the petty school, the first level of education in Elizabethan England. He focuses on that educational system primarily as it is reflected in Shakespeare's art.

Baldwin, T. W. *William Shakspere's Small Latine and Lesse Greeke.* 2 vols. Urbana: University of Illinois Press, 1944.

Baldwin attacks the view that Shakespeare was an uneducated genius—a view that had been dominant among Shakespeareans since the eighteenth century. Instead, Baldwin shows, the educational system of Shakespeare's time would have given the playwright a strong background in the classics, and there is much in the plays that shows how Shakespeare benefited from such an education.

Beier, A. L., and Roger Finlay, eds. *London 1500–1700: The Making of the Metropolis.* New York: Longman, 1986.

Focusing on the economic and social history of early modern London, these collected essays probe aspects of metropolitan life, including "Population and Disease," "Commerce and Manufacture," and "Society and Change."

Bentley, G. E. *Shakespeare's Life: A Biographical Handbook.* New Haven: Yale University Press, 1961.

This "just-the-facts" account presents the surviving documents of Shakespeare's life against an Elizabethan background.

Chambers, E. K. *William Shakespeare: A Study of Facts and Problems.* 2 vols. Oxford: Clarendon Press, 1930.

Analyzing in great detail the scant historical data, Chambers's complex, scholarly study considers the nature of the texts in which Shakespeare's work is preserved.

Cressy, David. *Education in Tudor and Stuart England.* London: Edward Arnold, 1975.

This volume collects sixteenth-, seventeenth-, and early-eighteenth-century documents detailing aspects of formal education in England, such as the curriculum, the control and organization of education, and the education of women.

Dutton, Richard. *William Shakespeare: A Literary Life.* New York: St. Martin's Press, 1989.

Not a biography in the traditional sense, Dutton's very readable work nevertheless "follows the contours of Shakespeare's life" as he examines Shakespeare's career as playwright and poet, with consideration of his patrons, theatrical associations, and audience.

Honan, Park. *Shakespeare: A Life.* New York: Oxford University Press, 1998.

Honan's accessible biography focuses on the various contexts of Shakespeare's life—physical, social, political, and cultural—to place the dramatist within a lucidly described world. The biography includes detailed examinations of, for example, Stratford schooling, theatrical politics of 1590s London, and the careers of Shakespeare's associates. The author draws on a wealth of established knowledge and on interesting new research into local records and documents; he also engages in speculation about, for example, the possibilities that Shakespeare was a tutor in a Catholic household in the north of England in the 1580s and that he played particular roles in his own plays, areas that reflect new, but unproven and debatable, data—though Honan is usually careful to note where a particular narrative "has not been capable of proof or disproof."

Schoenbaum, S. *William Shakespeare: A Compact Documentary Life.* New York: Oxford University Press, 1977.

This standard biography economically presents the essential documents from Shakespeare's time in an accessible narrative account of the playwright's life.

Shakespeare's Theater

Bentley, G. E. *The Profession of Player in Shakespeare's Time, 1590–1642*. Princeton: Princeton University Press, 1984.

Bentley readably sets forth a wealth of evidence about performance in Shakespeare's time, with special attention to the relations between player and company, and the business of casting, managing, and touring.

Berry, Herbert. *Shakespeare's Playhouses*. New York: AMS Press, 1987.

Berry's six essays collected here discuss (with illustrations) varying aspects of the four playhouses in which Shakespeare had a financial stake: the Theatre in Shoreditch, the Blackfriars, and the first and second Globe.

Berry, Herbert, William Ingram, and Glynne Wickham, eds. *English Professional Theatre, 1530–1660*. Cambridge: Cambridge University Press, 2000.

Wickham presents the government documents designed to control professional players, their plays, and playing places. Ingram handles the professional actors, giving as representative a life of the actor Augustine Phillips, and discussing, among other topics, patrons, acting companies, costumes, props, playbooks, provincial playing, and child actors. Berry treats the twenty-three different London playhouses from 1560 to 1660 for which there are records, including four inns.

Cook, Ann Jennalie. *The Privileged Playgoers of Shakespeare's London*. Princeton: Princeton University Press, 1981.

Cook's work argues, on the basis of sociological, economic, and documentary evidence, that Shakespeare's audience—and the audience for English Renaissance drama generally—consisted mainly of the "privileged."

Greg, W. W. *Dramatic Documents from the Elizabethan Playhouses.* 2 vols. Oxford: Clarendon Press, 1931.
Greg itemizes and briefly describes almost all the play manuscripts that survive from the period 1590 to around 1660, including, among other things, players' parts. His second volume offers facsimiles of selected manuscripts.

Gurr, Andrew. *Playgoing in Shakespeare's London.* Cambridge: Cambridge University Press, 1987.
Gurr charts how the theatrical enterprise developed from its modest beginnings in the late 1560s to become a thriving institution in the 1600s. He argues that there were important changes over the period 1567–1644 in the playhouses, the audience, and the plays.

Harbage, Alfred. *Shakespeare's Audience.* New York: Columbia University Press, 1941.
Harbage investigates the fragmentary surviving evidence to interpret the size, composition, and behavior of Shakespeare's audience.

Hattaway, Michael. *Elizabethan Popular Theatre: Plays in Performance.* London: Routledge & Kegan Paul, 1982.
Beginning with a study of the popular drama of the late Elizabethan age—a description of the stages, performance conditions, and acting of the period—this volume concludes with an analysis of five well-known plays of the 1590s, one of them (*Titus Andronicus*) by Shakespeare.

Shapiro, Michael. *Children of the Revels: The Boy Companies of Shakespeare's Time and Their Plays*. New York: Columbia University Press, 1977.

Shapiro chronicles the history of the amateur and quasi-professional child companies that flourished in London at the end of Elizabeth's reign and the beginning of James's.

The Publication of Shakespeare's Plays

Blayney, Peter. *The First Folio of Shakespeare*. Hanover, Md.: Folger, 1991.

Blayney's accessible account of the printing and later life of the First Folio—an amply illustrated catalogue to a 1991 Folger Shakespeare Library exhibition—analyzes the mechanical production of the First Folio, describing how the Folio was made, by whom and for whom, how much it cost, and its ups and downs (or, rather, downs and ups) since its printing in 1623.

Hinman, Charlton. *The Printing and Proof-Reading of the First Folio of Shakespeare*. 2 vols. Oxford: Clarendon Press, 1963.

In the most arduous study of a single book ever undertaken, Hinman attempts to reconstruct how the Shakespeare First Folio of 1623 was set into type and run off the press, sheet by sheet. He also provides almost all the known variations in readings from copy to copy.

Hinman, Charlton. *The Norton Facsimile: The First Folio of Shakespeare*. New York: W. W. Norton, 1968.

This facsimile presents a photographic reproduction of an "ideal" copy of the First Folio of Shakespeare; Hinman attempts to represent each page in its most fully corrected state.

Key to
Famous Lines and Phrases

For this relief much thanks.   [*Francisco*—1.1.8]

. . . prologue to the omen coming on . . .
        [*Horatio*—1.1.135]

. . . the morn in russet mantle clad . . .
        [*Horatio*—1.1.181]

A little more than kin and less than kind.
        [*Hamlet*—1.2.67]

O, that this too, too sullied flesh would melt . . .
        [*Hamlet*—1.2.133]

. . . frailty, thy name is woman!   [*Hamlet*—1.2.150]

In my mind's eye[.]   [*Hamlet*—1.2.193]

A countenance more in sorrow than in anger.
        [*Horatio*—1.2.247]

. . . the primrose path of dalliance . . . [*Ophelia*—1.3.54]

This above all: to thine own self be true[.]
        [*Polonius*—1.3.84]

Something is rotten in the state of Denmark.
        [*Marcellus*—1.4.100]

Murder most foul, as in the best it is[.] [*Ghost*—1.5.33]

Leave her to heaven[.] [*Ghost*—1.5.93]

. . . one may smile and smile and be a villain.
[*Hamlet*—1.5.115]

There are more things in heaven and earth, Horatio,
Than are dreamt of in your philosophy.
[*Hamlet*—1.5.187–88]

The time is out of joint. [*Hamlet*—1.5.210]

. . . brevity is the soul of wit[.] [*Polonius*—2.2.97]

More matter with less art. [*Queen*—2.2.103]

Though this be madness, yet there is method in 't.
[*Polonius*—2.2.223–24]

. . . there is nothing either good or bad but thinking
makes it so. [*Hamlet*—2.2.268–70]

What a piece of work is a man . . . [*Hamlet*—2.2.327]

I am but mad north-north-west. . . . I know a hawk
from a handsaw. [*Hamlet*—2.2.402–3]

. . . caviary to the general. [*Hamlet*—2.2.461]

Use every man after his desert and who shall 'scape
whipping? [*Hamlet*—2.2.555–57]

O, what a rogue and peasant slave am I!
[*Hamlet*—2.2.577]

What's Hecuba to him, or he to Hecuba[.]
[*Hamlet*—2.2.586]

. . . the devil hath power
T' assume a pleasing shape[.]   [*Hamlet*—2.2.628–29]

The play's the thing[.]   [*Hamlet*—2.2.633]

To be or not to be—that is the question[.]
                                      [*Hamlet*—3.1.64]

The glass of fashion and the mold of form,
Th' observed of all observers[.]   [*Ophelia*—3.1.167–68]

It out-Herods Herod.   [*Hamlet*—3.2.14–15]

Suit the action to the word, the word to the action[.]
                                   [*Hamlet*—3.2.18–19]

The lady doth protest too much, methinks.
                                      [*Queen*—3.2.254]

A king of shreds and patches[.]   [*Hamlet*—3.4.117]

. . . 'tis the sport to have the enginer
Hoist with his own petard[.]   [*Hamlet*—3.4.229–30]

How all occasions do inform against me[.]
                                       [*Hamlet*—4.4.34]

There's such divinity doth hedge a king . . .
                                        [*King*—4.5.138]

Alas, poor Yorick! I knew him, Horatio[.]
                                   [*Hamlet*—5.1.190–91]

Imperious Cæsar, dead and turned to clay . . .
                                      [*Hamlet*—5.1.220]

Sweets to the sweet[.]   [*Gertrude*—5.1.254]

There's a divinity that shapes our ends[.]
                              [*Hamlet*—5.2.11]

There is a special providence in the fall of a sparrow.
                              [*Hamlet*—5.2.233–34]

THE FOLGER SHAKESPEARE LIBRARY

The world's leading center for Shakespeare studies presents
acclaimed editions of Shakespeare's plays and poems.

All's Well That Ends Well

Antony and Cleopatra

As You Like It

The Comedy of Errors

Coriolanus

Cymbeline

Hamlet

Henry IV, Part 1

Henry IV, Part 2

Henry V

Henry VI, Part 1

Henry VI, Part 2

Henry VI, Part 3

Henry VIII

Julius Caesar

King John

King Lear

Love's Labor's Lost

Macbeth

Measure for Measure

The Merchant of Venice

The Merry Wives of Windsor

A Midsummer Night's Dream

Much Ado About Nothing

Othello

Pericles

Richard II

Richard III

Romeo and Juliet

Shakespeare's Sonnets

Shakespeare's Sonnets and Poems

The Taming of the Shrew

The Tempest

Timon of Athens

Titus Andronicus

Troilus and Cressida

Twelfth Night

The Two Gentlemen of Verona

The Two Noble Kinsmen

The Winter's Tale

Three Comedies: The Taming of the Shrew/A Midsummer Night's Dream/Twelfth Night

Three Tragedies: Hamlet/Macbeth/Romeo and Juliet

For more information on Folger Shakespeare Library Editions, including
Shakespeare Set Free teaching guides, visit www.simonandschuster.com.